KEYS TO A
POWERFUL
VOCABULARY
Level 2

KEYS TO A POWERFUL VOCABULARY

Level 2

THIRD EDITION

Minnette Lenier
Los Angeles Pierce College

Janet Maker
Los Angeles Trade-Technical College

Prentice Hall
Englewood Cliffs, New Jersey 07632

Library of Congress Cataloging-in-Publication Data

Lenier, Minnette.
    Keys to a powerful vocabulary : level II / Minnette Lenier, Janet
Maker.—3rd ed.
      p. cm.
    Includes bibliographical references and index.
    ISBN 0–13–668955–8
    1. Vocabulary. I. Maker, Janet. II. Title.
PE1449.L38   1994
428.1—dc20

93–10923
CIP

Dictionary excerpts, pronunciation guide, and art on pages 53, 61, 182, 232, 233–234, 238–239, and 249 reprinted with permission from *Webster's New World Dictionary,* Third College Edition. Copyright © 1988 by Simon & Schuster, Inc.

Dictionary excerpts on pages 45–53, 61–62, and 231 reprinted with permission from *Webster's New World Dictionary,* Popular Library Paperback Edition. Copyright © 1990 by William Collins Publishers, Inc.

Thesaurus excerpts on pages 203–206, 230, and 231 reprinted with permission from *The New American Roget's College Thesaurus in Dictionary Form* by Albert H. Morehead. Revised edition prepared by Philip D. Morehead. Copyright © 1958, 1962 by Albert H. Morehead, Copyright © 1978 by Andrew T. Morehead and Philip D. Morehead. Reprinted by arrangement with The New American Library, Inc., New York, N.Y.

Specified excerpts on pages 208 and 209 from *Roget's Pocket Thesaurus.* Based on *Roget's International Thesaurus* (Thomas Y. Crowell Company) edited by C. O. Sylvester Mawson—assisted by Katherine Aldrich Whiting. Copyright 1922, 1942 by Thomas Y. Crowell Company. Copyright 1946 by Simon & Schuster, a division of Gulf & Western Corporation. Reprinted by permission of Harper & Row, Publishers, Inc.

Acquisitions editor: Carol Wada
Editorial assistant: Joan Polk
Editorial/production supervision and
   interior design: Mary McDonald
Copy editor: Durrae Johanek
Cover design: Wendy Alling Judy
Prepress buyer: Herb Klein
Manufacturing buyer: Bob Anderson

 © 1994, 1991, 1983 by Prentice-Hall, Inc.
A Paramount Communications Company
Englewood Cliffs, New Jersey 07632

Printed in the United States of America
10 9 8 7 6 5 4 3 2 1

ISBN 0-13-668955-8

Prentice-Hall International (UK) Limited, *London*
Prentice-Hall of Australia Pty. Limited, *Sydney*
Prentice-Hall Canada Inc., *Toronto*
Prentice-Hall Hispanoamericana, S.A., *Mexico*
Prentice-Hall of India Private Limited, *New Delhi*
Prentice-Hall of Japan, Inc., *Tokyo*
Simon & Schuster Asia Pte. Ltd., *Singapore*
Editora Prentice-Hall do Brasil, Ltda., *Rio de Janeiro*

CONTENTS

PREFACE

Keys to a Powerful Vocabulary was written with three major purposes in mind. First, we wanted to teach the words most essential for college students. The words in this book were chosen because they appear very frequently in college textbooks. Essential words were also suggested by our students and by other instructors.

Secondly, we wanted the book to teach the skills necessary for students to improve their vocabularies on their own—use of context, word memory techniques, dictionary, word parts, etymology, thesaurus, and usage.

Our third purpose was to make students excited about words. We know that vocabulary has often been presented in school in painful ways: long, boring lists of words. We tried to make this book fun, to communicate to students the enjoyment of words that we feel. The exercises involve interesting information, stories, and a variety of activities—sentences using words in context; matching words with synonyms, antonyms, definitions, and etymologies; filling in word parts; analogies; crossword puzzles; and completing open-ended sentences.

The book is designed so that students can progress at their own rates. We begin with a pretest and end with a posttest so students can evaluate their progress. The exercises are self-checking, with the answers in the back of the book. Chapters 3 through 12 contain reviews of words in previous chapters, as an aid to memory. Halfway through the book we review all the words in Chapters 1 through 6, and there is a final review of words in Chapters 1 through 12 in the back of the book, immediately before the posttest. These reviews are included to assist those students who are using the book as a text to prepare for midterm and final exams. The new edition expands the Review Words section in each chapter to include definitions and context sentences. A new Progress Chart appears in the back of the book.

ACKNOWLEDGMENTS

For their creative and/or editorial assistance we wish to thank Sallie Brown, Bill Broderick, Jules Lenier, Anne-Kristin Noer, Claudia Gumbiner, and Carolyn Taffel, and also Carol Wada, and Phil Miller at Prentice Hall.

For assistance with field testing and/or research, thanks to Barbara Scheibel, the hundreds of instructors and students who responded to our endless surveys on words, and the Prentice Hall representatives who convinced the instructors to respond.

A special thanks to Bill Proctor, who created some of the drawings in this book.

Thank you to the reviewers: Dr. Javier Ayala, University of Texas at Brownsville; Paulette Diamond, Queensborough Community College; Diane B. Tingle, Delaware Technical and Community College; and Jo Devine, University of Alaska at Juneau.

Pronunciations of words are from *Webster's New World Dictionary of the American Language,* Pocket-size Edition (Simon & Schuster, 1990). Synonym entries in Chapter 12 are based on *Webster's New World Dictionary of the American Language,* Third College Edition (Simon & Schuster, 1988). Many of the obscure facts in the book are from the *Guinness Book of World Records* and *Ripley's Believe It or Not.*

KEYS TO A POWERFUL VOCABULARY

Level 2

chapter 1

INTRODUCTION

Drabble

© 1980 "Drabble" is reprinted by permission of UFS, Inc.

Did you know that *apple* comes from a word in a language spoken 4,000 years ago? This language gave birth not only to our own, but also to more than a dozen other modern languages as well. On the other hand, the word *hello* came into being only about 100 years ago after the invention of the telephone created a need for a shortened expression for "How do you do?" When people found they needed a shorter greeting that could be heard over the noise on early telephone wires, the shout used by farmers and hunters to call long distances, *hollo*, was adopted.

Words are created whenever they are needed. Those that are no longer commonly used are labeled *archaic*. New words are being invented all the time. Only about 250,000 of the estimated 450,000 words now in general use in English would have been understood by Shakespeare. About 200,000 of the words that have been added since Shakespeare's time have come into use during the past 50 years. In 1988 the words *glasnost* and *cellular phone system* were added to the *Webster's New World Dictionary* (Third College Edition) because they had begun to be used in everyday conversations. Words such as *yclept, zounds,* and *sennight* are no longer used and are now listed as archaic in dictionaries if they are listed at all.

A good vocabulary enables you to speak and write efficiently. New words allow us to think about new ideas or modify old ones. Therefore, it is important to constantly learn new words. Just as "a picture is worth a thousand words," the right word can substitute for 24 words: If we didn't have the word *cousin* we would have to say "a collateral relative more distant than a brother or sister, descended from a common ancestor," or "the son or daughter of one's uncle or aunt."[1]

Learning vocabulary is essential to your success in life. As Funk of the famous *Funk and Wagnall's Dictionary* said over 35 years ago, "Success and vocabulary go hand in hand. This has been proven so often that it no longer admits to argument."[2] Study after study confirms that intelligence tests, job advancement, salaries, and grades correlate with vocabulary ability. It stands to reason that knowing the words used in college textbooks and lectures increases your chances of success in reading textbooks, writing papers, and passing examinations.

The question then is not *why* you should expand your vocabulary, but *how* to expand it as quickly as needed to meet the special demands of college classes. In this book you will learn 440 words frequently found in college classes. In addition, you will learn methods for learning and remembering other words you will need to know.

Methods of Learning Vocabulary

This book is organized to help you learn vocabulary as quickly and efficiently as possible. As an example of making hard words easier to learn, we will trace how the word *pusillanimous* would be learned in different chapters.

Pusillanimous: timid, cowardly

---

[1]With permission from *Webster's New World Dictionary*, Third College Edition. Copyright © 1988 by Simon & Schuster, Inc.
[2]Wilfred Funk, *Six Weeks to Words of Power* (New York: Simon & Schuster, Inc., 1953), p. 1.

Word Memory (Chapter 2)

To help yourself associate the word *pusillanimous* with its meaning, you might picture a scared pussycat. The sound of *pussycat* will help you remember the word. You could try to remember the words *scaredy cat* or *pussyfoot* to help you, too.

Using the Context (Chapter 3)

"He was so pusillanimous that he would not enter a dark room."

The sentence gives you a good clue to the meaning of the word.

Getting the Most from Your Dictionary (Chapter 4)[3]

Main entry   *Pronunciation*   *Part of speech*

pu·sil·lan·i·mous (pyo͞o′si lan′ə məs) *adj.* [< L. *pusillus,* — *Etymology*
tiny + *animus,* the mind] timid; cowardly —**pu′sil·la·
nim′i·ty** (-si lə nim′ə tē) *n.*

Definition   *origin or development of a word.*

Suffixes, Prefixes, and Roots (Chapters 5–9)

pusillus = petty or tiny   *animus* = mind or spirit   *ous* = full of

These three word parts, taken together, refer to someone filled with a petty or tiny spirit.

Word Histories (Chapter 10)

The word *pusillanimous* comes from Latin. *Pusillus* comes from *pusus,* meaning a little boy. So a pusillanimous person has the fear-filled mind of a little boy.

Thesaurus (Chapter 11)

synonyms (similar words) for *pusillanimous:* cowardly, chicken, cowhearted, timid, craven, gutless, lily-livered, spunkless, unmanly, yellow, dastardly, frightened

antonyms (opposite words) for *pusillanimous:* brave, courageous, fearless, intrepid, valiant, daring, reckless

Using Words Correctly (Chapter 12)[4]

Shades of meaning: When would you use *pusillanimous* rather than *cowardly, craven, dastardly, timid,* or *frightened?*

> SYN—**cowardly,** the general term, suggests a shameful lack of courage in the face of danger or pain [a *cowardly* deserter]; **craven** implies an extremely cowardly or faint-hearted fear [a *craven* fear for one's life]; **pusillanimous** implies a dishonorable, contemptible lack of courage or endurance [*pusillanimous* submission]; **dastardly** suggests a sneaking, intentionally harmful cowardice that is shown in a despicable act [a *dastardly* informer]; **timid** implies a lack of courage or self-confidence and suggests overcautiousness, shyness, etc. [he is *timid* about investing money]; **frightened** implies a sudden, usually temporary seizure of fear [the child was *frightened* by the dog].

Getting Started

Because students differ in their vocabulary needs, each chapter contains three lists of words: Review Words, New Words, and Advanced Words. The Review Words are 10 words you should already know. We include them in case some are unfamiliar. The New Words are the 20 main words you will be studying in each chapter. Advanced Words are 10 more difficult words. We include them for those students ready for more advanced work. The following pretest is a self-checking quiz to help you measure your present vocabulary. Circle the best definition for each word, and then check your answers in the back of the book.

---

[4]Based on samples from *Webster's New World Dictionary,* Third College Edition. Copyright © 1988 by Simon & Schuster, Inc.

PRETEST

1. lament   a. mourn   b. take out   c. expand   d. put in

2. furor   a. sound   b. disturbance   c. favor   d. insanity

3. refute   a. accept   b. give up   c. disprove   d. repair

4. satiate   a. satisfy   b. overpower   c. eat   d. starve

5. wary   a. strong   b. cautious   c. tired   d. rested

6. flaunt   a. show off   b. argue against   c. tell   d. capture

7. ire   a. happiness   b. sadness   c. sympathy   d. anger

8. prudent   a. simple   b. careful   c. loud   d. quick

9. stealthy   a. wise   b. steady   c. sneaky   d. suspicious

10. taciturn   a. wild   b. quiet   c. sensible   d. painful

11. buoyant   a. wet   b. tense   c. cheerful   d. active

12. façade   a. front   b. door   c. building   d. costume

13. oblique   a. visible   b. indirect   c. large   d. sharp

14. prone   a. flexible   b. timely   c. likely   d. stiff

15. staunch   a. stuffy   b. unstable   c. loyal   d. new

16. compliant   a. obedient   b. valuable   c. useful   d. complex

17. enormity   a. normality   b. difference   c. selection   d. vastness

18. hindrance   a. link   b. reminder   c. obstacle   d. response

19. lineage   a. following   b. friends   c. accuracy   d. ancestry

20. transitory   a. complete   b. brief   c. dangerous   d. steady

21. cohesion   a. improvement   b. helpfulness   c. separateness   d. unity

22. digress   a. wander   b. explain   c. divide   d. confuse

23. extrinsic   a. outgoing   b. external   c. extreme   d. necessary

24. predecessor   a. follower   b. forerunner   c. teacher   d. offspring

25. altercation   a. alliance   b. substitution   c. mixture   d. fight

26. complacent   a. happy   b. lazy   c. self-satisfied   d. ambitious

27. congenial   a. defective   b. agreeable   c. sick   d. confident

28. gratis   a. free   b. carefully   c. thankfully   d. solemnly

29. overt   a. concealed   b. illegal   c. open   d. twisted

30. artifice   a. painting   b. trickery   c. creativity   d. odor

31. constituent   a. component   b. opponent   c. amendment   d. descendant

32. innate   a. ancient   b. important   c. inborn   d. easy

33. lucid   a. clever   b. fast   c. clear   d. lucky

34. supplication   a. invention   b. supplement   c. plea   d. prediction

35. expedite   a. change   b. sample   c. help   d. slow

36. inception   a. idea   b. start   c. blocking   d. alteration

37. pensive   a. thoughtful   b. harmful   c. fearless   d. ready

38. tenable   a. defensible   b. far-fetched   c. dangerous   d. stubborn

39. candid   a. cautious   b. surprised   c. open   d. hidden

40. dispel   a. mistake   b. gather in   c. release   d. drive away

41. furtive   a. partial   b. undercover   c. intelligent   d. attractive

42. innuendo   a. suggestion   b. statement   c. insight   d. accusation

43. augment   a. fight   b. anger   c. expand   d. explain

44. blatant   a. truthful   b. obvious   c. mad   d. colorless

45. deter   a. remove   b. attract   c. discourage   d. attempt

46. insipid   a. dull   b. tasteful   c. horrible   d. awkward

47. assent   a. agree   b. climb   c. take   d. comfort

48. cryptic   a. written   b. mysterious   c. deadly   d. long

49. discern   a. concern   b. detect   c. compose   d. build

50. reticent   a. eager   b. reserved   c. harsh   d. honest

After checking your answers in the back of the book, fill in your score here:

_____

The Meaning of Your Score

If you scored:

Below 20:   You may want to concentrate on the Review Words as well as on the New Words or you may wish to work on *Keys to a Powerful Vocabulary,* Level I.

20–29:   You should concentrate on the New Words in the book.

30–50:   You may want to concentrate on the Advanced Words as well as on the New Words.

chapter 2

WORD MEMORY

Drabble

© 1981 "Drabble" is reprinted by permission of UFS, Inc.

Several studies have shown that the average ten-year-old has a vocabulary of about 20,000 words. That means he or she has learned and remembered an average of 2,000 new words per year. By comparison, most adults learn only about 25 to 50 new words a year, and have an average vocabulary of about 40,000 words. The reason children learn so many new words so quickly is not that they are smarter than adults (they aren't) but rather that they are constantly coming across new ideas (to a baby, *everything* is new). New facts and ideas require new words that can describe them. Many adults, on the other hand, go every day to a routine job, talk to the same people, and don't read very much. You, as a college student, are different from those adults. The classes you are taking introduce you to new ideas all the time. Exploring these ideas will require you to learn and remember hundreds of new words each year; this chapter will teach you techniques for remembering them.

Four Memory Techniques

- Pronounce the word aloud.
- Give the word meaning.
- Use mnemonic devices.
- Review often.

1. *Pronounce the word aloud.* Unfortunately, this is sometimes more easily said than done. English spelling often fails to indicate the pronunciation of a word, as described in the following poem:

Hints on Pronunciation for Foreigners[1]

I take it you already know
Of tough and bough and cough and dough?
Others may stumble but not you,
On hiccough, thorough, laugh and through.
Well done! And now you wish, perhaps
To learn of less familiar traps?

Beware of heard, a dreadful word
That looks like bread and sounds like bird,
And dead: it's said like bed, not bead—
For goodness' sake don't call it "deed"!
Watch out for meat and great and threat
(They rhyme with suite and straight and debt.)

A moth is not a moth in mother
Nor both in bother, broth in brother,
And here is not a match for there
Nor dear and fear for bear and pear,
And there's dose and rose and lose—
Just look them up—and goose and choose,

---

[1]Quoted in Carol Chomsky, "Reading, Writing and Phonology," in M. Wolf, M. K. McQuillen, and E. Radwin (eds.), "Thought and Language/Language and Reading," *Harvard Educational Review,* (1980).

And cork and work and card and ward,
And font and front and word and sword,
And do and go and thwart and cart—
Come, come, I've hardly made a start!
A dreadful language? Man alive.
I'd mastered it when I was five.

T.S.W.
(only the initials of the writer are known)

The peculiarities of English spelling require that you understand the use of the dictionary pronunciation guide. The New Word lists presented in this book have the following pronunciation guide at the bottom of the same page:

fat, āpe, cär; ten, ēven; is, bīte; gō, hôrn, tōol, look; oil, out; up, fur; get; joy; yet; chin; she; thin, *th*en; zh, leisure; ŋ, ring; ə for *a* in *ago*, *e* in *agent*, *i* in *sanity*, *o* in *comply*, *u* in *focus*; ' as in *able* (ā'b'l)

As an example, let's look at the word *satiate*. If you were to look in the dictionary, you would see that it is pronounced **sā′shē āt′**. Using the guide as a key, we see that

s is not in the guide. This is because there is only one possible way to pronounce it.

ā is pronounced as in *a*pe.

sh is pronounced as in *sh*e.

ē is pronounced as in *e*ven.

ā is pronounced as in *a*pe.

t is not in the guide, because there is only one way to pronounce it.

Putting the sounds together, we see that the first syllable (*sā*) sounds like *say*. The second syllable (*shē*) sounds like *she*, and the last syllable (*āt*) sounds like *ate*. The heavy accent mark after the first syllable (*sā′*) means that the first syllable receives the most stress. The lighter mark after the third syllable (*āt′*) means that the third syllable receives the lightest stress.

One symbol that often gives students problems is the *schwa*, which is written ə. It occurs only in unaccented syllables, and is always pronounced the same way: a sort of "uh" sound. There are 25 ways the schwa can be spelled. Following are some examples, with the letter representing the schwa sound in italics.

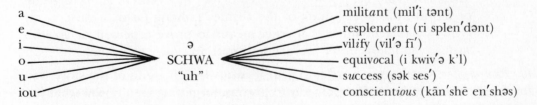

As you can see, it doesn't matter whether the schwa is spelled with an *a, e, i, o, u, iou,* or other spelling; it's still pronounced "uh."

For practice with the pronunciation guide, use it to translate the following three proverbs into English spelling:

a. bʉrdz uv ə feth′ər fläk tə geth′ər.

Translation _____

b. tōō men′ē kooks spoil thə brôth.

Translation _____

c. ə stich in tīm sāvz nīn.

Translation _____

Check your answers in the back of the book.

2. *Give the word meaning.* You will thoroughly understand a word only if you can define it in your own words and then use it as part of your vocabulary. Just reading the dictionary definition is not enough. Therefore, after you have pronounced the word, read the definition and restate it in your own words. Then use the word in a meaningful sentence. For example, to remember that *depict* means *picture,* you might write, "Early cave paintings *depicted* hunting scenes."

3. *Use mnemonic devices.* Mnemonic (pronounced nē män′ ik) devices are tricks that aid memory. The word *mnemonic* comes from the name of the Greek goddess of memory, Mnemosyne. The following three mnemonic devices can help you to memorize vocabulary; you can also make up your own mnemonic devices.

a. *Word Association:* Sometimes you can associate a new word with a word you already know that gives a clue to the meaning. For example, you could associate *resplendent,* which means dazzling or shining brightly, with the word *splendid.* To remember that *militant* means ready to fight for a cause, you could think of the word *military.*

b. *Visual Association:* It's always easier to remember things that make vivid pictures in our minds. For example, to remember that *conform* means to be or make similar, you might picture a group of *con*victs all dressed alike in striped uni*forms.* To remember that the word *wary* means cautious, you might picture a sign in front of a house saying "Be *wary* of the dog."

c. *Rhyming:* Some people find it easier to remember sounds than pictures. For example, if you want to remember that *lament* means to grieve or mourn, you might think of the rhyme "I always *lament* a raise in my rent." Or to remember that *refute* means to prove a person or an idea wrong, you might think "To win a dispute you have to *refute.*"

4. *Review often.* Getting the word into your memory isn't the end of the story. You also have to keep it there. The only way to prevent forgetting is to review what you have learned. One way of reviewing is to use the new information. In the case of vocabulary, use the new words, both in your reading and in your speaking. Another method is to use flash cards (blank file cards).

Each chapter in this book gives you practice exercises for reviewing the words you have learned. If, after you have completed the exercises, you still aren't sure you will remember a certain word, put it on a flash card. Write the word and the pronunciation on the front. On the back, write the definition and perhaps a sentence that gives the meaning of the word:

Front

renown

ri noun´

Back

great fame or reputation

His outstanding performance in the Olympic Games won him great renown.

In your pocket or purse, carry 10 to 20 cards so you can use them at odd moments: standing in line, waiting for gas, eating lunch alone, and so on. Test yourself by looking at the word and trying to remember the meaning. Then turn the card over and check yourself. The next time you review the flash cards, use the backs of the cards: Read the definition and see if you know the word. You should also try to spell the word, so that you will be able to use it in writing. Don't be discouraged if you forget the word. The average person needs about seven self-testing sessions to master a new word. Space the sessions several hours or days apart rather than rushing through them all at once. When you feel that you have mastered a particular word, put its card in another, less frequently reviewed pile at home. This will prevent the pile you carry with you from growing too large.

REVIEW WORDS

Below are the Review Words for this chapter. We will use these words to practice the skills taught in this chapter.

conform (kən fôrm′) *v.*   1. to become the same or similar   2. to be in accord or agreement [the house *conforms* to specifications]   3. to behave in a conventional way, esp. in accepting without question customs, traditions, prevailing opinions, etc.

delectable (dē lek′tə bəl, di-) *adj.*   very pleasing; delightful; now esp., pleasing to the taste; delicious; luscious

egocentric (ē′gō sen′trik, eg′o-) *adj.*   viewing everything in relation to oneself; self-centered

enunciate (ē nun′sē āt′, i-) *v.*   to pronounce words, esp. clearly and distinctly; articulate

judicious (jōō dish′əs) *adj.*   having, applying, or showing sound judgment; wise and careful

ornate (ôr nāt′) *adj.*   heavily ornamented or adorned, often to excess

penitence (pen′i təns) *n.*   the state of being sorry for doing wrong; repentance

pitfall (pit′fôl′) *n.*   an unsuspected difficulty, danger, or error that one may fall into

requisite (rek′wə zit) *adj.*   required, as by circumstances; necessary for some purpose; indispensable [the *requisite* supplies for a journey]

valiant (val′yənt) *adj.*   1. full of or characterized by valor or courage; brave   2. resolute; determined [made a *valiant* effort]

fat, āpe, cär; ten, ēven; is, bīte; gō, hôrn, tōōl, look; oil, out; up, fʉr; get; joy; yet; chin; she; thin, *th*en; zh, leisure; ŋ, ring; ə for *a* in *ago*, *e* in *agent*, *i* in *sanity*, *o* in *comply*, *u* in *focus*; ′ as in *able* (ā′b′l)

EXERCISE 1: REVIEW WORDS IN CONTEXT

Fill in each blank with the word that correctly completes the sentence. Check your answers in the back of the book.

conform	egocentric	judicious	penitence	requisite
delectable	enunciate	ornate	pitfall	valiant

1. Movie stars, famous musicians, politicians, and others in the public eye receive so much attention that they can easily become _____.

2. The middle class is perceived as more likely to _____ to conventional standards of behavior than are either the upper or the lower classes.

3. Drug or alcohol addiction is a _____ that ruins the careers of many famous people.

4. Most people find chocolate _____.

5. The _____ number of jurors is twelve.

6. She was so touched by her husband's _____ for the way he behaved at the party that she forgave him everything.

7. Historically, poor people used plain, simple clothing and furnishings; those of the wealthy were _____.

8. _____ use of rewards and punishments can change almost anyone's behavior.

9. Public speakers must learn to _____ clearly so they can be understood by everyone.

10. After his injury, he made a _____ effort to learn to use his legs again.

EXERCISE 2: REVIEW WORDS

A. For each of the following words, write a definition and a sentence, both in your own words.

1. penitence

   a. Definition _____

   b. Sentence _____

2. requisite

   a. Definition _____

   b. Sentence _____

3. delectable

   a. Definition _____

   b. Sentence _____

4. enunciate

   a. Definition _____

   b. Sentence _____

5. conform

   a. Definition _____

   b. Sentence _____

B. For each of the following words, make up a mnemonic device—for example, a word association, a visual association, or a rhyme.

1. valiant _____

2. ornate _____

3. pitfall _____

4. judicious _____

5. egocentric _____

See the back of the book for sample answers.

NEW WORDS I

Below is the first list of New Words for this chapter. Make up a mnemonic device
for each one and compare them with the samples in the back of the book.

depict (di pikt′) *v.*   1. to represent in a drawing, painting, sculpture, etc.; portray; picture
2. to picture in words; describe

Mnemonic _____

deplete (di plēt′) *v.*   1. to gradually use up the resources, strength, etc.   2. to empty wholly
or partly

Mnemonic _____

excruciating (iks′kroo′shē āt′iŋ) *adj.*   1. causing intense physical or mental pain; agonizing
2. intense or extreme [with *excruciating* attention to detail]

Mnemonic _____

furor (fyoor′ôr) *n.*   1. fury; rage; frenzy   2. (*a*) a great, widespread outburst of admiration or
enthusiasm; craze; rage (*b*) a state of excitement or confusion; commotion or uproar

Mnemonic _____

negate (ni gāt′) *v.*   1. to deny the existence or truth of   2. to make ineffective

Mnemonic _____

renown (ri noun′) *n.*   great fame or reputation; celebrity

Mnemonic _____

satiate (sā′shē āt′) *v.*   to provide with more than enough, so as to weary or disgust; glut; surfeit

Mnemonic _____

semblance (sem′bləns) *n.*   1. outward form or appearance; aspect   2. the look or appearance
of something else; resemblance   3. a likeness, image, representation, or copy
4. false, assumed, or deceiving form or appearance   5. mere empty show; pretense

Mnemonic _____

utilitarian (yoo til′ə ter′ē ən) *adj.*   1. of or having to do with utility   2. stressing usefulness
over beauty or other considerations   3. made for or aiming at utility

Mnemonic _____

vilify (vil′ə fī′) *v.*   to use abusive or slanderous language about someone; defame

Mnemonic _____

fat, āpe, cär; ten, ēven; is, bīte; gō, hôrn, tool, look; oil, out; up, fʉr; get; joy; yet; chin; she; thin, *th*en; zh, leisure; ŋ, ring; ə for *a* in *ago, e* in *agent, i* in *sanity, o* in
comply, u in *focus;* ' as in *able* (ā′b'l)

Fill in each blank with the word that best completes the sentence. Check your answers in the back of the book.

| depicting | excruciating | negated | satiate | utilitarian |
| depleted | furor | renown | semblance | vilified |

1. It takes 100 pounds of hay per day to _____ an elephant.

2. The Spanish Inquisition, which began in 1478, was known for the _____ tortures inflicted on converted Jews and Muslims who were considered insincere in their faith.

3. From 1840 to 1845 John Banvard painted a 16,000-foot canvas _____ 1,200 miles of landscape from the mouth of the Mississippi River to New Orleans.

4. In the Irish potato famine the food supply became _____.

5. Leonardo da Vinci achieved such _____ as a painter, sculptor, architect, musician, poet, philosopher, inventor, biologist, astronomer, geologist, and mathematician that some people think he must have come from another planet.

6. Industrial designers attempt to combine beauty with function in _____ objects like toasters and computers.

7. In recent years the media have earned a reputation for stirring up a _____ over the marital infidelities of political candidates.

8. In Greek myth, Sisyphus was forced by the gods to repeatedly push a heavy rock to the top of a steep hill only to have his efforts _____ when it rolled down again.

9. The mopoke, a bird of the Australian bush, has the _____ of a tree branch when sitting on a limb of the ti tree.

10. Benedict Arnold, a general in the American Revolution, has been _____ by generations of Americans because he arranged to betray West Point to the British.

NEW WORDS II

Make up a good sentence using each of the New Words below.

conscientious (kän′shē en′shəs) *adj.*   1. governed by, or made or done according to, what one knows is right; scrupulous; honest   2. showing care and precision; painstaking

Sentence _____

dire (dīr) *adj.*   1. arousing terror or causing extreme distress; dreadful; terrible   2. calling for quick action; urgent [a *dire* need]

Sentence _____

equivocal (i kwiv′ə kəl) *adj.*   1. that which can have more than one interpretation; having two or more meanings; purposely vague, misleading, or ambiguous [an *equivocal* reply]   2. uncertain; undecided; doubtful [an *equivocal* outcome]   3. suspicious; questionable [*equivocal* conduct]

Sentence _____

fortitude (fôrt′ə tōōd′) *n.*   the strength to bear misfortune, pain, etc., calmly and patiently; firm courage

Sentence _____

insolent (in′sə lənt) *adj.*   boldly disrespectful; impudent

Sentence _____

lament (lə ment′) *v.*   1. to feel or express deep sorrow for; mourn or grieve for   2. to regret deeply —*n.*   an outward expression of sorrow; lamentation; wail

Sentence _____

militant (mil′i tənt) *adj.*   1. at war; fighting   2. ready and willing to fight; esp., vigorous or aggressive in support or promotion of a cause —*n.*   a militant person

Sentence _____

refute (ri fyōōt′) *v.*   1. to prove (a person) to be wrong   2. to prove (an argument or statement) to be false or wrong, by argument or evidence

Sentence _____

resplendent (ri splen′dənt) *adj.*   shining brightly; full of splendor; dazzling; splendid

Sentence _____

wary (wer′ē) *adj.*   1. cautious, on one's guard   2. characterized by caution [a *wary* look]

Sentence _____

fat, āpe, cär; ten, ēven; is, bīte; gō, hôrn, tōōl, look; oil, out; up, fʉr; get; joy; yet; chin; she; thin, *th*en; zh, leisure; ŋ, ring; ə for *a* in *ago, e* in *agent, i* in *sanity, o* in *comply, u* in *focus;* ' as in *able* (ā′b'l)

Circle the letter before the word or phrase that best defines the italicized word in each sentence. Check your answers in the back of the book.

1. The female puffin, a northern sea bird, may make the most *conscientious* mother in the world—she stuffs her chick with food until it outweighs her.

   PUFFIN
   (to 13 1, 2 in. long)

   a. intelligent   b. hardworking   c. neglectful   d. angry

2. Disagreeing with a dictator can have *dire* consequences.

   a. serious   b. minor   c. humorous   d. happy

3. In order to protect their privacy, movie stars often give *equivocal* answers to questions about their personal lives.

   a. lying   b. stupid   c. unclear   d. wordy

4. It takes a lot of *fortitude* to be honest when people don't want to hear the truth.

   a. strength   b. fear   c. enjoyment   d. freedom

5. Rude or *insolent* remarks will not be tolerated by employers.

   a. disrespectful   b. flattering   c. courteous   d. depressed

6. During the Republican administrations of the 1980s, liberals had reasons to *lament* their losses on issues like civil rights, abortion rights, and environmental protection.

   a. celebrate   b. weep over   c. resent   d. fight over

7. *Militant* warlords ruled 17th century Japan.

   a. gentle   b. annoying   c. loving   d. aggressive

8. Tobacco companies have tried to *refute* the idea that the connection between smoking and lung cancer has been proved.

   a. uphold   b. disprove   c. agree with   d. help

9. The *resplendent* Taj Mahal, built of white marble inlaid with semiprecious stones, was built between 1639 and 1648 by Shah Jehan as a tomb for his beloved wife, Mumtaz Mahal.

   a. large   b. old   c. magnificent   d. expensive

10. Animals in northern Mexico are *wary* of the elephant tree which gives off a spray as foul smelling as a skunk's.

    a. careful   b. secretive   c. sick   d. protective

Write T or F in the blank. Check your answers in the back of the book.

_____ 1. A wolf in sheep's clothing has the semblance of a coyote.

_____ 2. A militant will go to any length to avoid a conflict.

_____ 3. A writer can depict scenes.

_____ 4. You would lament winning a bet.

_____ 5. An unknown person is renowned.

EXERCISE 6: ANALOGIES

A word analogy is a puzzle in which two sets of words are compared. The two words in the first set have some kind of relationship to each other. You have to recognize the relationship in order to fill in the blank in the second set. Analogies use two mathematical symbols—:, which means *is to*, and ::, which means *as*. For example:

night : day :: dark : _____

This example reads: night *is to* day *as* dark *is to* _____. You must decide on the relationship of the first two words. *Night* and *day* are opposites. Therefore, the word in the blank must be the opposite of *dark*. The answer is *light*. There are two kinds of relationships in the analogies that follow. Either the words mean the same thing or they are opposites. Fill in the blanks and check your answers in the back of the book.

1. requisite : necessary :: negate : _____   a. argue b. accept c. agree d. deny

2. conform : rebel :: insolent : _____   a. polite b. nasty c. cruel d. sad

3. egotistic : self-centered ::   a. cowardice b. cheerfulness
   fortitude : _____   c. courage d. happiness

4. valiant : brave :: furor : _____   a. calm b. noise c. depth d. concern

5. delectable : nasty ::   a. enjoyable b. painful c. dangerous
   excruciating : _____   d. careful

EXERCISE 7: MATCHING MEANINGS

Write the letter of the word that means the opposite of the word in the first column.
Check your answers in the back of the book.

_____	1.	deplete	a.	careless
_____	2.	conscientious	b.	prove
_____	3.	refute	c.	stockpile
_____	4.	vilify	d.	starve
_____	5.	satiate	e.	praise

EXERCISE 8: WORD CONTRASTS

In each group below circle the word that does not mean what the others mean.
Check your answers in the back of the book.

1. equivocal   unclear   confusing   straightforward
2. wary   foolhardy   reckless   careless
3. resplendent   dazzling   splendid   dull
4. utilitarian   useful   useless   practical
5. dire   urgent   terrible   unimportant

EXERCISE 9: SENTENCE COMPLETION

Complete each sentence in your own words. Sample answers are provided in the
back of the book.

1. Everyone wants *conscientious* employees because _____
   _____.

2. Some groups object to TV shows that *depict* acts of violence; others _____
   _____.

3. When you *deplete* your savings, _____
   _____.

4. Telling lies can have *dire* consequences, such as _____
   _____.

5. Politicians will make *equivocal* statements as long as _____
   _____.

6. Besides *excruciating* pain, arthritis can cause _____ _____.

7. Not everyone has the *fortitude* to _____ _____.

8. Even though he knew the decision would cause a *furor*, _____ _____.

9. Before you make an *insolent* remark, _____ _____.

10. He didn't know whether to *lament* the decision or _____ _____.

11. A *militant* approach is sometimes best; however, _____ _____.

12. Unless you want to *negate* all our work, _____ _____.

13. If we don't *refute* Jim's argument, _____ _____.

14. His *renown* grew as a result of _____ _____.

15. Her gown was *resplendent,* except that _____ _____.

16. Alison's urge to shop was impossible to *satiate;* consequently, _____ _____.

17. He had the *semblance* of a kindly old uncle, but _____ _____.

18. It has *utilitarian* purposes, too—for example, _____ _____.

19. Jason likes to *vilify* Jane, especially _____ _____.

20. Although we must be *wary* around Christine, _____ _____.

aggrandize (ə gran′dīz, ag′rən-) *v.*   to make or seem to make greater, more powerful, richer, etc.

copious (kō′pē əs) *adj.*   1. very plentiful; abundant   2. full of information

eclectic (ek lek′tik) *adj.*   1. selecting from various systems, styles, doctrines, or sources   2. composed of material gathered from various sources, systems, etc.—*n.*   a person who uses eclectic methods in philosophy, science, or art

emulate (em′yə lāt′) *v.*   1. to try to equal or surpass, esp. to imitate or copy with a view to equal or surpass   2. to rival successfully

enmity (en′mə tē) *n.*   the bitter attitude or feelings of an enemy or of mutual enemies; hostility; antagonism

incisive (in sī′siv) *adj.*   1. cutting into   2. sharp; keen; penetrating; acute [an *incisive* mind]

indefatigable (in′di fat′i gə bəl) *adj.*   that which cannot be tired out; not yielding to fatigue; untiring

pastoral (pas′tər əl) *adj.*   1. of shepherds or their work or way of life   2. characteristic of rural life; idealized as peaceful, simple, and natural   3. of a pastor or his duties

rapacious (rə pā′shəs) *adj.*   1. taking by force; plundering   2. greedy or grasping; voracious   3. living on captured prey; predatory

razed (rāzd) *v.*   torn down completely; leveled; demolished

---

fat, āpe, cär; ten, ēven; is, bīte; gō, hôrn, tōōl, look; oil, out; up, fʉr; get; joy; yet; chin; she; thin, *th*en; zh, leisure; ŋ, ring; ə for *a* in *ago, e* in *agent, i* in *sanity, o* in *comply, u* in *focus;* ′ as in *able* (ā′b′l)

EXERCISE 10: ADVANCED WORDS IN CONTEXT

Fill in each blank with the word that correctly completes the sentence. Check your answers in the back of the book.

aggrandize	eclectic	enmity	indefatigable	rapacious
copious	emulate	incisive	pastoral	razed

1. The ancient city of Carthage was _____ in 146 B.C. by the Roman general Scipio Africanus Minor.

2. Generally considered the greatest woman athlete of modern times because she excelled at baseball, basketball, track, and golf, Babe Didrikson provides a model for girls to _____.

3. Fraternity parties are occasions on which beer is available in _____ amounts.

4. Modern clothing styles tend to be _____, borrowing ideas for fabrics, colors, and designs from many historical periods.

5. Mark Twain's _____ wit made him a master of satire.

6. Marie Antoinette, queen of France from 1774 until her execution in 1793, earned the _____ of the French people for her famous solution to the bread famine, "Let them eat cake."

7. The _____ island of Molokai Hawaii, was chosen as the site of a government leper colony because it was largely uninhabited.

8. One day in 1936 the _____ Jesse Owens tied the world record in the 100-yard dash; 10 minutes later he broke the world record in the broad jump; 9 minutes later he broke the world record for the 220-yard dash; and 45 minutes later he broke the world record for the 220-yard hurdles.

9. The robber barons at the turn of the century justified their _____ practices by the theory of social Darwinism, which holds that the strong rise to the top because they are superior.

10. Some people will spend thousands of extra dollars for a car with a more prestigious brand name because they think an expensive car will _____ their status.

EXERCISE 11: OWN WORDS

It is not enough just to learn the words in this book. Your needs will be different from the needs of other students, since you will come into contact with different words in your classes and in your life. Each chapter in this book has a page on which you are asked to write ten words that you believe you need to learn. You may have seen them in your textbooks, in newspapers or magazines, or in other sources. Try to choose words that occur often rather than words you will probably rarely see. Write your first ten words in the spaces provided below. Then pronounce each word, put the definition in your own words, use the word in a sentence, and put it on a flash card for regular review.

1. _____   6. _____

2. _____   7. _____

3. _____   8. _____

4. _____   9. _____

5. _____   10. _____

chapter 3
USING THE CONTEXT

Reprinted by permission of Tribune Company Syndicate, Inc.

In the last chapter we mentioned that you know about 40,000 words by the time you are an adult. How did you learn most of these words? You probably did not look up every word in the dictionary. The easiest and most common way to learn and to remember new words is by using the *context*. Learning through context is guessing the meaning of a word based on the way it is used. You may not know the meaning of *subterranean,* but if you saw the sentence "Because the water was subterranean, we had to dig a well," you would immediately know that *subterranean* means "underground." The phrase "dig a well" provided the needed context for guessing the meaning of the word.

Types of Context Clues

Your success at guessing the meaning of an unfamiliar word depends upon the amount of context provided in the sentence and your ability to recognize the context clues. For example, if the previous sentence had been "The water was subterranean," you would have had too few clues and too many possible meanings to make a good guess. You might have logically concluded that the water was cold, dirty, hot, or even nonexistent.

Using the context efficiently can save endless hours of work. Inefficient use of context clues can make you overly dependent on the dictionary. Constantly stopping to use the dictionary breaks your train of thought and reduces your comprehension.

The italicized words in the following sentences are taken from the New Words for this chapter, so they may be unfamiliar to you. Use the context to figure out their meanings before reading the answer.

1. Calvin Coolidge, also known as "Silent Cal," was our most *taciturn* president.

    a. nontalkative   b. intelligent   c. clumsy   d. easygoing

    The answer is *a.* The context (*silent*) in this sentence gave you the **definition** of the word *taciturn.* Either the definition can be a *synonym,* as in this example, or it can consist of several words.

2. France's border with Germany, considered secure when the forts of the Maginot Line were built, proved *vulnerable* to enemy attack when German forces simply flew over the barrier.

    a. protected   b. dangerous   c. defenseless   d. useless

    The answer is *c.* The context of the sentence provided the clue by means of **contrast.** In other words, you knew from the sentence that the meaning of *vulnerable* had to contrast with the meaning of *secure.* In the following example, the contrast is in the form of an *antonym:* "Some of the people on the assembly line did jobs that were sloppy, but others did jobs that were *meticulous.*"

3. The American Indian wore moccasins of soft leather so that he could move quietly through the forest, often wore animal skins to conceal his scent, and used a bow and arrow rather than a noisier weapon, all to keep from frightening off the game he hunted; in short, he was a *stealthy* hunter.

    a. poor b. quick c. careless d. sneaky

    The answer is *d*. In this case the context provided a **summary** clue to the meaning of the word *stealthy*. *Stealthy* summed up all the ideas that went before.

4. Big packages or a six-foot Christmas tree and a large turkey are examples of the *ponderous* items we have to handle at Christmastime.

    a. easy b. impossible c. bulky d. small

    The answer is *c*. In this case the words *bulky, six-foot,* and *large* offer **examples** of things that are *ponderous.*

5. Taking a TV set to the repair shop for the sixth time in one month would produce *ire* in anyone.

    a. fear b. anger c. insanity d. happiness

    The answer is *b*. Even if you don't have a TV set, you can draw on general **experience** with repair problems as a clue to the meaning of *ire*. Anyone placed in a similar position would probably become very angry at the inconvenience and the cost.

REVIEW WORDS

Below are the Review Words for this chapter. We will use these words to practice the skills taught in this chapter.

aesthetic (es thet′ik) *adj.*   1. of beauty   2. sensitive to art and beauty; showing good taste; artistic

apprehend (ap′re hend′, -ri-) *v.*   1. to take into custody; capture or arrest   2. to take hold of mentally; perceive; understand   3. to anticipate with anxiety; dread

elapse (ē laps′, i-) *v.*   slip by; pass; said of time

ethical (eth′i kəl) *adj.*   of or conforming to moral standards

homicide (häm′ə sīd′; *also* hō′mə-) *n.*   any killing of one human being by another

perimeter (pə rim′ə tər) *n.*   the outer boundary of a figure or area

perturb (pər tʉrb′) *v.*   to cause to be alarmed, agitated, or upset; disturb or trouble greatly

uncanny (un kan′ē) *adj.*   1. mysterious or unfamiliar, esp. in such a way as to frighten or make uneasy; eerie; weird   2. so remarkable, acute, etc. as to seem weird

velocity (və läs′ə tē) *n.*   quickness or rapidity of motion or action; swiftness; speed

zeal (zēl) *n.*   intense enthusiasm, as in working for a cause

fat, āpe, cär; ten, ēven; is, bīte; gō, hôrn, tōōl, look; oil, out; up, fʉr; get; joy; yet; chin; she; thin, *th*en; zh, leisure; ŋ, ring; ə for *a* in *ago, e* in *agent, i* in *sanity, o* in *comply, u* in *focus;* ′ as in *able* (ā′b′l)

Fill in each blank with the word that correctly completes the sentence. Check your answers in the back of the book.

aesthetic	elapsed	homicide	perturbed	velocity
apprehension	ethical	perimeter	uncanny	zeal

1. One of today's controversial issues is the use of the death penalty for serious crimes such as _____.

2. You can use a stopwatch to determine the number of _____ seconds during a race.

3. Collectors often buy paintings with an eye to their investment value as well as their _____ value.

4. You need to use pegs around the _____ of a tent to keep it from blowing away.

5. Several people have surfaced who bear an _____ resemblance to Elvis Presley.

6. When facing oral surgery, most people feel _____.

7. You may be able to determine the _____ of a car at the moment of impact by measuring the skid marks.

8. Do not _____ yourself; I will take care of the problem.

9. Many people question the ability of professional associations, such as the American Bar Association for lawyers and the American Medical Association for doctors, to properly punish their own members for _____ violations.

10. Political _____ is more often found among young adults than among the middle-aged.

Use the context to fill in the blanks in the following mystery story with the Review Words below. Then solve the mystery.

aesthetic   elapsed   homicide   perturbed   velocity
apprehend   ethical   perimeter   uncanny   zeal

The Case of the Misleading Monet

Inspector Keane viewed the painting with _____ apprecia-
tion. Unfortunately, a bullet hole in the canvas spoiled an otherwise beautiful
original by Monet. In addition, the bottom corner of the frame that formed the
_____ of the painting had been shattered by a bullet.

The night before, the gardener at the estate had heard gunshots and, shortly
afterward, a man was seen running out the door of the house. The gardener was not
quite sure of the time that had _____ between the sound of the
shots and the moment he saw the running figure.

Inspector Keane had been called to the scene of the crime not only because of
his _____ for solving mysteries but also because this was the home
of his old college friend Colonel Bowbridge. Apparently no _____
had been committed, and the colonel said that none of the valuable silver, antiques, or
paintings he owned were missing from his home. Inspector Keane had never had a
case in which someone had broken into a house just to destroy a valuable painting.

He reviewed the evidence, trying to find a clue to the mystery. The
_____ of the two bullets, based on the depth they had penetrated
into the wall, told Keane that whoever had fired the bullets was very near the painting
when he pulled the trigger. If only one shot had been fired, Keane might have
concluded it was an accident, but the second shot in the same direction proved there
was a reason. But who would want to destroy the painting and the frame? Although
the thought _____ him, Keane had to consider that his old
friend might have destroyed the painting to collect the insurance on it. His
_____ practices prevented him from discounting any suspects, but,
fortunately, the facts did not support his suspicion. If the first shot had destroyed the
painting, then why the second shot? Then, Keane's _____ mind
took a strange turn. Suppose the sequence of shots were reversed. Suppose the in-

truder intended to shoot at the frame and had destroyed the painting as a decoy. Keane examined the frame. It was hollow, and around the splintered corner he saw something sparkling.

By the time the colonel entered the room, Keane was already on his way to

_____ the criminal. Who was the criminal and why had he de-
10
stroyed the Monet?

Solution

The criminal was the man who had sold Bowbridge the frame for the painting. He had been smuggling diamonds into the country in hollow frames. Keane knew that the frame for such an expensive painting should be made from only the finest wood and should be solid, not hollow.

Check your answers in the back of the book. If any of the Review Words are unfamiliar to you, use the methods discussed in Chapter 2 to make them part of your vocabulary.

NEW WORDS I

For each of the New Words that you don't already know, use the four memory techniques described in Chapter 2 to learn it.

audacious (ô dā′shəs) *adj.*   1. bold or daring; fearless   2. not restrained by a sense of shame or propriety; rudely bold; brazen

coerce (kō urs′) *v.*   1. to restrain by force   2. to compel to do something   3. to bring about by using force; enforce

eminent (em′ə nənt) *adj.*   1. standing high by comparison with others, as in rank or achievement; renowned; exalted; distinguished   2. outstanding; remarkable; noteworthy [a man of *eminent* courage]   3. rising above other things or places; high; lofty

flaunt (flônt) *v.*   1. to make a gaudy, conspicuous, or defiant display   2. to show off proudly, defiantly, or rashly [to *flaunt* one's guilt]

irony (ī′rə nē, ī′ər nē) *n.*   1. an expression in which the intended meaning of the words is the opposite of their usual sense [the *irony* of calling a stupid plan "clever"]   2. an event or result that is the opposite of what is expected [the *irony* of the firehouse burning down]

prudent (prōō′d′nt) *adj.*   1. capable of exercising sound judgment in practical matters, esp. as concerns one's own interests   2. cautious or discreet in conduct; not rash   3. managing carefully and with economy

staid (stād) *adj.*   sober; sedate; steady and settled

stringent (strin′jənt) *adj.*   rigidly controlled, enforced, etc.; strict; severe

thwart (thwôrt) *v.*   to hinder, obstruct, frustrate, or defeat (a person, plans, etc.)

tractable (trak′tə b'l) *adj.*   1. easily managed, taught, or controlled; obedient   2. easily worked; capable of being changed, molded, trained; adaptable; pliable

---

fat, āpe, cär; ten, ēven; is, bīte; gō, hôrn, tōōl, look; oil, out; up, fur; get; joy; yet; chin; she; thin, *th*en; zh, leisure; ŋ, ring; ə for *a* in *ago, e* in *agent, i* in *sanity, o* in *comply, u* in *focus;* ′ as in *able* (ā′b'l)

EXERCISE 3: FILL-IN

Fill in each blank with the word that correctly completes the sentence. Check your answers in the back of the book.

audacious	eminent	irony	staid	thwart
coerce	flaunt	prudent	stringent	tractable

1. During the 1980s it was considered desirable to _____ one's wealth by driving fancy cars and wearing expensive jewelry.

2. People who are grossly overweight should go on a _____ diet to lose their excess pounds, since they have increased chances of high blood pressure, heart attacks, strokes, and diabetes.

3. Thomas Edison, who invented the light bulb and motion picture camera, among other things, is probably the most _____ American inventor.

4. It is an _____ that Albert Einstein, the most famous scientist in the world, was considered stupid by his childhood teachers.

5. _____ people are careful not to get sunburned because the damage to the blood vessels caused by even a moderately severe sunburn can take from 4 to 15 months to heal.

6. It might seem _____ to give a woman a perfume made of sweat and deer oil, but Chanel #5, a famous fragrance, contains the sweat from an Abyssinian cat and musk from a Siberian deer.

7. Judges and accountants are thought to be more _____ than actors, dancers, and musicians.

8. President Theodore Roosevelt began a policy under which the government could _____ giant corporations into allowing free competition.

9. Ex-President Richard Nixon was accused of trying to _____ the investigation of the Watergate break-in by erasing the tapes that might have proven his involvement.

10. Our presidents are in a difficult position because we do not wish them to be so _____ that they cannot make their own decisions, but we do wish them to be responsive to public opinion.

amiable (āʹmē ə bəl, āmʹyə bəl) *adj.*   having a pleasant and friendly disposition; good-natured

ascent (ə sentʹ) *n.*   1. the act of rising or climbing   2. an advancement, as in rank, fame, etc.   3. (*a*) a way leading up; upward slope (*b*) the amount of such slope [an *ascent* of three degrees]

gist (jist) *n.*   the essence or main point, as of an article or argument; core

ire (īr) *n.*   intense anger; rage; fury

meticulous (mə tikʹyoo ləs, -yə-) *adj.*   extremely or excessively careful about details; precise; finicky; too particular; fussy

ponderous (pänʹdər əs) *adj.*   1. very heavy   2. unwieldy because of weight   3. seeming heavy; bulky; massive   4. labored and dull [a *ponderous* joke]

presumptuous (prē zumpʹchoo əs, pri-; -chə wəs) *adj.*   too bold or forward; taking too much for granted; showing overconfidence or arrogance

stealthy (stelʹthē) *adj.*   characterized by secret or artfully sly action or behavior

taciturn (tasʹə tʉrnʹ) *adj.*   almost always silent, not liking to talk; uncommunicative

vulnerable (vulʹnər ə bəl) *adj.*   1. that which can be wounded or injured   2. (*a*) open to criticism or attack [a *vulnerable* reputation] (*b*) easily hurt, as by unfavorable criticism; sensitive (*c*) affected by a specific influence, temptation, etc. [*vulnerable* to political pressure]   3. open to attack by armed forces

fat, āpe, cär; ten, ēven; is, bīte; gō, hôrn, tōol, look; oil, out; up, fʉr; get; joy; yet; chin; she; thin, *th*en; zh, leisure; ŋ, ring; ə for *a* in *ago*, *e* in *agent*, *i* in *sanity*, *o* in *comply*, *u* in *focus*; ' as in *able* (āʹb'l)

Circle the letter before the word or phrase that best defines the italicized word in
each sentence. Check your answers in the back of the book.

1. Politicians are expected to be *amiable* in public, but Theodore Roosevelt holds a record for
   shaking hands with 8,513 people at one White House party in 1907.

   a. hazardous   b. friendly   c. funny   d. lengthy

2. When asked why he made his famous *ascent* of Mt. Everest, Sir Edmund Hillary said he
   climbed the highest mountain in the world because it was there.

   a. decline   b. fall   c. agreement   d. climb

3. The *gist* of the defendant's alibi was that his client could not have murdered his wife
   because he was in Guatemala at the time of her death.

   a. core   b. circumstance   c. verdict   d. plot

4. People feel *ire* when they go to pick up their car at the time promised, and find that the
   mechanic hasn't even looked at it yet.

   a. happiness   b. anger   c. fright   d. sorrow

5. Oriental rugs are made with *meticulous* attention to detail.

   a. sloppy   b. intelligent   c. cheap   d. careful

PENGUIN
(to 4 ft. high)

6. The 90-pound emperor penguin may be *ponderous* and slow on land, but it is
   as weightless in the water as any other bird is in the air.

   a. light   b. helpless   c. heavy   d. fast

7. The bad actor was so *presumptuous* that he arrived at the Academy Awards banquet with a
   prepared acceptance speech, whereas the winner was so modest that he never thought of
   preparing a speech at all.

   a. modest   b. quiet   c. talented   d. overconfident

8. Probably the greatest recorded robbery occurred when four *stealthy* thieves took 19
   paintings worth over $19 million from a home in Ireland.

   a. poor   b. quick   c. careless   d. sneaky

9. Actors Gary Cooper and John Wayne fit the old male stereotype of being strong and
   taciturn.

   a. quiet   b. talkative   c. stupid   d. bossy

10. Feminists are looking for men who are less unemotional and more sensitive and *vulnerable*.

    a. resistant   b. safe   c. open   d. attractive

EXERCISE 5: TRUE-FALSE

Write T or F in the blank. Check your answers in the back of the book.

_____ 1. Ironic statements are often cutting.

_____ 2. Immunizations make you less vulnerable to diseases.

_____ 3. People who are coerced into doing something do it willingly.

_____ 4. Stealthy people do things openly.

_____ 5. When you make an ascent you rise.

EXERCISE 6: ANALOGIES

Complete the second pair of words so they have the same relationship as the first.
Check your answers in the back of the book.

1. zeal : enthusiasm :: staid : _____   a. rowdy   b. spoiled   c. rich   d. serious

2. perimeter : circumference ::   a. unknown   b. prominent
   eminent : _____   c. uncomfortable   d. social

3. ethical : dishonest :: stringent :   a. strict   b. liberal   c. dishonest
   _____   d. pleasant

4. apprehend : catch :: gist : _____   a. thought   b. core   c. accessory
                                        d. goal

5. perturbed : composed ::   a. careful   b. careless   c. thoughtless
   meticulous : _____   d. boring

EXERCISE 7: MATCHING MEANINGS

Write the letter of the word that means the opposite of the word in the first column.
Check your answers in the back of the book.

_____ 1. thwart   a. wary

_____ 2. flaunt   b. talkative

_____ 3. audacious   c. foolish

_____ 4. taciturn   d. assist

_____ 5. prudent   e. camouflage

EXERCISE 8: WORD CONTRASTS

In each group, circle the word that does not mean what the others mean. Check your answers in the back of the book.

1. ire   fury   rage   calmness
2. ponderous   massive   light   unwieldy
3. amiable   discourteous   ill-mannered   rude
4. presumptuous   respectful   brash   overconfident
5. tractable   flexible   obedient   headstrong

EXERCISE 9: SENTENCE COMPLETION

Complete each sentence in your own words. Sample answers are provided in the back of the book.

1. If you are an *amiable* person, _____

   _____.

2. An *ascent* of Mt. Everest would be exciting, although _____

   _____.

3. Talking back to a policeman is not only *audacious* _____

   _____.

4. You might feel *coerced* if _____

   _____.

5. When an *eminent* American dies, _____

   _____.

6. A rich man might *flaunt* his wealth by _____

   _____.

7. If you cannot understand the *gist* of an argument, _____

   _____.

8. I would react with *ire* if _____

   _____.

9. It is a form of *irony* when _____

   _____.

10. A bank teller must be *meticulous* when counting out money; otherwise, _____
_____ .

11. An example of a *ponderous* task is _____
_____ .

12. Bill was so *presumptuous* that just after he met Cathy _____
_____ .

13. Before *prudent* people go out to buy a car, _____
_____ .

14. Dating a *staid* person might be boring because _____
_____ .

15. One thing a *stealthy* robber might do is _____
_____ .

16. Some bosses have very *stringent* standards; consequently, _____
_____ .

17. A *taciturn* woman would probably not be comfortable if _____
_____ .

18. While it might be heroic to try to *thwart* a bank robbery, _____
_____ .

19. Many private schools accept only *tractable* youngsters because _____
_____ .

20. I am most *vulnerable* to a cold when _____
_____ .

admonish (əd män′ish, ad-) *v.*   1. to warn   2. to express mild disapproval of   3. to urge or advise strongly   4. to inform or remind, by way of a warning

cursory (kur′sə rē) *adj.*   hastily, often superficially done; performed rapidly with little attention to detail

detriment (de′trə mənt) *n.*   1. damage; injury; harm   2. anything that causes damage or injury

empirical (em pir′i kəl) *adj.*   1. relying or based solely on experiment and observation rather than theory [the *empirical* method]   2. relying or based on practical experience without reference to scientific principles [an *empirical* remedy]

inordinate (in ôr′də nit, -ôrd′′n it) *adj.*   lacking restraint or moderation; too great or too many; immoderate

mitigate (mit′ə gāt′) *v.*   to make or become milder, less severe, less rigorous, or less painful; moderate

peruse (pə rōoz′) *v.*   1. to read carefully or thoroughly; study   2. to read: now often implying a casual or leisurely reading

ruse (rōoz) *n.*   a trick, scheme, or plan, esp. a sly or artful trick to achieve a goal

sporadic (spə rad′ik, spə-) *adj.*   1. happening from time to time; not constant or regular; occasional   2. widely separated from others, scattered, or isolated in occurrence; appearing singly, apart, or in isolated instances

ubiquitous (yōo bik′wə təs) *adj.*   (seemingly) present everywhere at the same time

fat, āpe, cär; ten, ēven; is, bīte; gō, hôrn, tōol, look; oil, out; up, fur; get; joy; yet; chin; she; thin, *th*en; zh, leisure; ŋ, ring; ə for *a* in *ago, e* in *agent, i* in *sanity, o* in *comply, u* in *focus;* ' as in *able* (ā′b'l)

EXERCISE 10: ADVANCED WORDS IN CONTEXT

Fill in each blank with the word that correctly completes the sentence. Check your answers in the back of the book.

admonish   detriment   inordinate   peruse   sporadic
cursory   empirical   mitigate   ruse   ubiquitous

1. Based solely on _____ evidence of what occurred when he clamped off arteries versus what happened when he clamped off veins, Harvey determined that arteries carried blood away from the heart and that veins carried blood to the heart.

2. Many people feel that there is an _____ amount of violence on TV.

3. It is controversial whether the cholesterol in eggs, which was once considered a _____ to one's health, is as harmful as was thought.

4. After police broke up the riot in South Africa, the neighborhood was quiet except for the sound of _____ gunfire.

5. You should _____ the fine print of contracts before signing.

6. Perhaps the most famous _____ of all time was the Trojan Horse myth, by which the ancient Greeks finally won their nine-year war against Troy.

7. During tax season we often feel the IRS is _____, watching each of us carefully as we fill out our tax returns.

8. Today doctors _____ young mothers not to give solid foods to babies too early because of concern about allergic reactions.

9. Aspirin, which was originally developed to reduce fever and _____ minor aches and pains, is now thought by doctors to reduce the incidence of heart attacks in men.

10. After practicing for several weeks, the singer needed only a _____ glance at the music to perform it well.

This first crossword puzzle in the book reviews the New Words from Chapter 2. We suggest that you use a pencil in case you change your mind about your answers. The clues marked with an asterisk (*) have answers from the New Words from Chapter 2. Check your answers in the back of the book.

Across

*1. Painstaking
10. Less than two
11. Abbr. for *bachelor of science*
12. Past tense of *bite*
14. Indefinite article used before words beginning with vowels
*16. Urgent
*17. Strength
21. Same as 18 Down
23. Debtor's note
24. Abbr. for *television*
*26. Portray
*27. Aggressive
30. Lincoln's nickname
32. Burning
*34. To glut
37. Chemical symbol for *gold*
39. Abbr. for *foot*
40. Abbr. for *bachelor of arts* (alt.)
42. Dined
*43. Cautious
*45. Fame
46. Group of actors in a play or film
47. Abbr. for *junior*

Down

1. Fit in
2. Abbr. for *Old Norse*
3. Antonym of *far*
4. Abbr. for *Citizens Band*
5. Contraction for "*is not*"
6. Abbr. for *New Brunswick*
7. To become weary
8. Third-person singular pronoun
*9. Practical
*13. To prove wrong
15. Abbr. for *New Testament*
18. Either . . . _____
19. Same as 8 Down
20. Special eating program
22. 3.1416
24. Initials of Sir Thomas Lawrence (Lawrence of Arabia)
*25. To slander
26. Initials of David Niven
28. Abbr. for *Irish Republican Army*
29. Insect
31. Exist
32. Abbr. for *Alcoholics Anonymous*
*33. Outburst of excitement
34. Past tense of *see*
35. Preposition meaning *on, in, near,* or *by*
36. Organs for hearing
38. Malt beverage popular in fraternities
41. Wager
44. Abbr. for *recreational vehicle*

Find ten unfamiliar words in books, magazines, and newspapers. On line *a,* write the sentence in which you found the word. Circle the word. Using the context of the sentence, guess the meaning of the word and write your definition on line *b.* Check the meaning in the dictionary to see whether you are right. If your definition is wrong or incomplete, write a corrected definition on line *c.*

1. a. _____

    b. _____

    c. _____

2. a. _____

    b. _____

    c. _____

3. a. _____

    b. _____

    c. _____

4. a. _____

    b. _____

    c. _____

5. a. _____

    b. _____

    c. _____

6. a. _____

    b. _____

    c. _____

7. a. _____

    b. _____

    c. _____

8. a. _____

    b. _____

    c. _____

9. a. _____

    b. _____

    c. _____

10. a. _____

     b. _____

     c. _____

chapter 4

GETTING THE MOST FROM YOUR DICTIONARY

Reprinted by permission of Tribune Company Syndicate, Inc.

Everyone knows how to look up definitions, but very few people can use all the valuable material that a good dictionary provides. The dictionary is the one place you can quickly find a word's spelling, pronunciation, etymology, and meaning. This chapter will teach you to use the dictionary effectively.

Dictionary Structure

Below is a sample page from *Webster's New World Dictionary*, Warner Books Paperback Edition.[1] We will refer to this sample in our discussion of the parts of a dictionary.

Main entry without a full pronunciation (see ＊ below)

Main entries

Pronunciation

Spellings of different forms of the word

Part of speech

Multiple entry

Alternate spellings

friendly   [239]   **frost**   *Guide words*

friend'ly *adj.* -li-er, -li-est   1 of or like a friend; kindly   2 not hostile; amicable   3 supporting; helping —**friend'li-ly** *adv.* —**friend'li-ness** *n.*

friend'ship *n.*   1 the state of being friends   2 friendly feeling

frieze (frēz) *n.* [< ML *frisium*] a horizontal band with designs or carvings along a wall or around a room

frig-ate (frig'it) *n.* [< It *fregata*] a fast, medium-sized sailing warship of the 18th and early 19th c.

fright (frīt) *n.* [OE *fyrhto*]   1 sudden fear; alarm   2 something unsightly

fright'en *vt.*   1 to make suddenly afraid; scare   2 to force [*away, off,* etc.] by scaring —**fright'en-ing-ly** *adv.*

fright'ful *adj.*   1 causing fright; alarming   2 shocking; terrible   3 [Colloq.] *a*) unpleasant *b*) great —**fright'ful-ly** *adv.*

frig-id (frij'id) *adj.* [< L *frigus,* coldness]   1 extremely cold   2 not warm or friendly   3 sexually unresponsive: said of a woman —**fri-gid'i-ty** *n.* —**frig'id-ly** *adv.*

Frigid Zone either of two zones (**North Frigid Zone** or **South Frigid Zone**) between the polar circles and the poles

frill (fril) *n.* [< ?]   1 any unnecessary ornament   2 a ruffle —**frill'y, -i-er, -i-est** *adj.*

fringe (frinj) *n.* [< L *fimbria*]   1 a border of threads, etc. hanging loose or tied in bunches   2 an outer edge; border   3 a marginal or minor part —*vt.* **fringed, fring'ing** to be or make a fringe for —*adj.*   1 at the outer edge   2 additional   3 minor

fringe benefit an employee's benefit other than wages, as a pension or insurance

frip-per-y (frip'ər ē) *n., pl.* **-ies** [< OFr *frepe,* a rag]   1 cheap, gaudy clothes   2 showy display in dress, etc.

Fris-bee (friz'bē) [< "Mother Frisbie's" pie tins] *trademark for* a plastic, saucer-shaped disk sailed back and forth in a simple game —*n.* [*also* **f-**] such a disk

fri-se (frē zā', fri-) *n.* [Fr < *friser,* to curl] an upholstery fabric with a thick pile of loops

Fri-sian (frizh'ən) *n.* the West Germanic language of an island chain, the Frisian islands, along the coast of N Netherlands, West Germany, & Denmark

frisk (frisk) *vi.* [< OHG *frisc,* lively] to frolic —*vt.* [Slang] to search (a person) for weapons, etc. by passing the hands quickly over his clothing

frisk-y (fris'kē) *adj.* **-i-er, -i-est** lively; frolicsome —**frisk'i-ly** *adv.* —**frisk'i-ness** *n.*

frit-ter[1] (frit'ər) *vt.* [< L *frangere,* to break] to waste [money, time, etc.] bit by bit: usually with *away*

frit-ter[2] (frit'ər) *n.* [< L *frigere,* to fry] a small cake of fried batter, usually containing corn, fruit, etc.

friv-o-lous (friv'ə ləs) *adj.* [< L *frivolus*]   1 of little value; trivial   2 silly and light-minded; giddy —**fri-vol-i-ty** (fri väl'ə tē) *pl.* **-ties,** *n.* —**friv'o-lous-ly** *adv.*

frizz or **friz** (friz) *vt., vi.* **frizzed, friz'zing** [Fr *friser*] to form into small, tight curls —*n.* hair, etc. that is frizzed —**friz'zly** or **friz'zy** *adj.*

friz-zle[1] (friz'əl) *vt., vi.* **-zied, -zling** [< FRY[1]] to sizzle, as in frying

friz-zle[2] (friz'əl) *n., vt., vi.* **-zled, -zling** FRIZZ

fro (frō) *adv.* [< ON *frā*] backward; back: now only in TO AND FRO [at TO]

frock (fräk) *n.* [< OFr *froc*]   1 a robe worn by friars, monks, etc.   2 a dress

frog (frôg, fräg) *n.* [OE *frogga*]   1 a tailless, leaping amphibian with long hind legs and webbed feet   2 a fancy braided loop used to fasten clothing —**frog in the throat** hoarseness

frog'man' *n., pl.* **-men'** one trained and equipped for underwater demolition, exploration, etc.

frol-ic (fräl'ik) *n.* [< MDu *vrō,* merry]   1 a lively party or game   2 merriment; fun —*vi.* **-icked, -ick-ing**   1 to make merry; have fun   2 to romp about; gambol —**frol'ick-er** *n.*

frol'ic-some (-səm) *adj.* playful; merry

from (frum, främ) *prep.* [OE]   1 beginning at; starting with [*from* noon to midnight]   2 out of [*from* her purse]   3 originating with [a letter *from* me]   4 out of the possibility of or use of [kept *from* going]   5 as not being like [to know good *from* evil]   6 because of [to tremble *from* fear]

frond (fränd) *n.* [< L *frons,* leafy branch] the leaf of a fern or palm

front (frunt) *n.* [< L *frons,* forehead]   1 *a*) outward behavior [a bold *front*] *b*) [Colloq.] an appearance of social standing, wealth, etc.   2 the part facing forward   3 the first part; beginning   4 a forward or leading position   5 the land bordering a lake, street, etc.   6 the advanced battle area in warfare   7 an area of activity [the home *front*]   8 a person or group used to hide another's activity   9 [Meteorol.] the boundary between two differing air masses —*adj.* at, to, in, on, or of the front —*vt., vi.*   1 to face   2 to serve as a front [*for*] —**in front of** before —**fron'tal** *adj.*

front-age (frunt'ij) *n.*   1 the front part of a building   2 the front boundary line of a lot or the length of this line   3 land bordering a street, lake, etc.

fron-tier (frun tir') *n.* [see FRONT]   1 the border between two countries   2 the part of a country which borders an unexplored region   3 any new field of learning, etc. —*adj.* of, on, or near a frontier —**fron-tiers'man** (-tirz'mən) *pl.* **-men,** *n.*

fron-tis-piece (frunt'is pēs') *n.* [< L *frons,* front + *specere,* to look] an illustration facing the title page of a book

front office the management or administration, as of a company

front'-run'ner *n.* a leading contestant

front-wheel drive an automotive design in which only the front wheels receive driving power

frost (frôst, fräst) *n.* [OE < *freosan,* freeze]   1 a temperature low enough to cause freezing   2 frozen dew or vapor; rime —*vt.*   1 to cover with frost   2 to cover with frosting

Etymology

Idiomatic expression

Word used in context

Usage

Specialized definition

Cross-reference

Definitions

＊The main entry has accent marks if a full pronunciation is not given.

[1]With permission. From *Webster's New World Dictionary,* Warner Books Paperback Edition. Copyright © 1990 by Simon & Schuster, Inc.

Guide Words

At the top of the page are two *guide words: friendly* and *frost.* These words indicate the first and last words on a page. By using the guide words you can quickly determine whether the word you want is on that page. For example, by using the guide words, you would know that *Frisbee* would be on the page but *frown* would not.

Main Entry[2]

Main entry

frog (frôg, fräg) *n.* [OE *frogga*]   **1** a tailless, leaping amphibian with long hind legs and webbed feet   **2** a fancy braided loop used to fasten clothing —**frog in the throat** hoarseness

The main entry is in boldface type. If a number appears to the right of a main entry, there will be more than one main entry for the word. An example is *fritter.*

frit-ter¹ (frit′ər) *vt.* [< L *frangere,* to break] to waste (money, time, etc.) bit by bit: usually with *away*
frit-ter² (frit′ər) *n.* [< L *frigere,* to fry] a small cake of fried batter, usually containing corn, fruit, etc.

Multiple entries occur when the words have significantly different meanings and perhaps origins. The main entry also gives alternate spellings of a word. For example, *arrant* is a variation of *errant.*

ar-rant (ar′ənt) *adj.* [var. of ERRANT] out-and-out; notorious

If a spelling is marked *Brit.,* as in the word *vigour,* it is not a standard spelling for Americans.

vig-or (vig′ər) *n*   [< L *vigere,* be strong] active force or strength; vitality; energy Brit., etc. sp. **vig′our** —**vig′or-ous** *adj.* —**vig′or-ous-ly** *adv.*

The syllabication, indicating where you would break the word in writing, is indicated in this dictionary by hyphens, as in the word *fruition.*

fru-i-tion (froo ish′ən) *n.* **1** the bearing of fruit **2** a coming to fulfillment; realization

---

[2]Except where otherwise indicated, dictionary excerpts in this chapter are from *Webster's New World Dictionary,* Pocket Edition (Victoria Neufeldt, Editor-in-Chief) (New York: Simon & Schuster, Inc., 1990). Reprinted with permission © 1990 by Simon & Schuster, Inc.

Pronunciation

Pronunciations

frog (frôg, fräg) **n.** [OE *frogga*]   **1** a tailless, leaping amphibian with long hind legs and webbed feet   **2** a fancy braided loop used to fasten clothing —**frog in the throat** hoarseness

The symbols in parentheses after the main entry tell you how to pronounce the word. The pronunciation guide is located either at the bottom of the page, as in our sample, or, in some cases, at the front of the dictionary. Use of the pronunciation guide was discussed in Chapter 2 as a method of remembering new words. Since the symbols used in one dictionary may be different from those used in another dictionary, you will save time if you familiarize yourself with the guide in the dictionary you will be using.

Sometimes you will see only a portion of the pronunciation, as in the word frolicsome.

frol′ic·some (-səm) **adj.** playful; merry

This means that the first syllable, *frolic* is pronounced as in the previous main entry.

If the word can be pronounced more than one way, both pronunciations are given. For example, the first syllable in *fructose* can be pronounced to rhyme either with *luck* (fruk′) or with *look* (frook′).

fruc·tose (fruk′tōs′, frook′-) **n.** [< L *fructus*, fruit + OSE] a sugar found in sweet fruits and in honey

Sometimes multiple pronunciations correspond to different parts of speech. For example, the word *insult* is pronounced *in sult′* when used as a verb ("Don't insult my intelligence") and *in′sult* when used as a noun ("That statement is an insult to my intelligence").

in·sult (in sult′; *for n.* in′sult) **vt.** [< L *in-*, on + *salire*, to leap] to subject to an act, remark, etc. meant to hurt the feelings or pride —**n.** an insulting act, remark, etc.

Part of Speech

Part of speech

frog (frôg, fräg) **n.** [OE *frogga*]   **1** a tailless, leaping amphibian with long hind legs and webbed feet   **2** a fancy braided loop used to fasten clothing —**frog in the throat** hoarseness

The part of speech follows the pronunciation. The main symbols you will see are:

n. = noun	A person, place, or thing
v. = verb	An action or event
vt. = transitive verb	Action that affects a person or thing: "I decided to *freeze* the leftover vegetables." A transitive verb requires a direct object to complete its meaning.
vi. = intransitive verb	Action that does not affect a person or thing: "In subzero weather, a person can *freeze* to death." An intransitive verb does not require a direct object to complete its meaning.

freeze (frēz) *vi.* **froze, fro′zen, freez′ing** [OE *freosan*] **1** to be formed into, or become covered with, ice **2** to become very cold **3** to be damaged or killed by cold **4** to become motionless **5** to be made speechless by strong emotion **6** to become formal or unfriendly — *vt.* **1** to form into, or cover with, ice **2** to make very cold **3** to preserve (food) by rapid refrigeration **4** to kill or damage by cold **5** to make motionless **6** to make formal or unfriendly **7** *a)* to fix (prices, etc.) at a given level by authority *b)* to make (funds, etc.) unavailable to the owners —*n.* **1** a freezing or being frozen **2** a period of freezing weather —**freeze out 1** to die out through freezing, as plants **2** [Colloq.] to keep out by a cold manner, competition, etc. —**freeze over** to become covered with ice —**freez′a·ble** *adj.*

adj. = adjective	Modifies the noun or pronoun
adv. = adverb	Modifies a verb, adjective, or other adverb

Some words can be used in several parts of speech; an example is *front*.

front (frunt) *n.* [< L *frons*, forehead] **1** *a)* outward behavior [a bold *front*] *b)* [Colloq.] an appearance of social standing, wealth, etc. **2** the part facing forward **3** the first part; beginning **4** a forward or leading position **5** the land bordering a lake, street, etc. **6** the advanced battle area in warfare **7** an area of activity [the home *front*] **8** a person or group used to hide another's activity **9** *Meteorol.* the boundary between two differing air masses —*adj.* at, to, in, on, or of the front —*vt., vi.* **1** to face **2** to serve as a front (*for*) —**in front of** before —**fron′tal** *adj.*

Etymology

> **frog** (frôg, fräg) **n.** [OE *frogga*]   1 a tailless, leaping
> amphibian with long hind legs and webbed feet   2 a
> fancy braided loop used to fasten clothing —**frog in the**
> **throat** hoarseness

After the pronunciation and part of speech comes the etymology, or origin of the
word. The symbol < means "derived from." You will find letters such as *L.* for Latin,
Fr. for French, *ME* for Middle English, etc., indicating the language from which the
word is derived. A complete list of abbreviations is located at the front of the dictionary. Some etymologies are especially interesting. For example, look at the etymology for *mouse:*[3]

> **mus-cle** (mus'əl) **n.** [Fr < *musculus*, a muscle, lit., little
> mouse (from the fancied resemblance between the move-
> ments of a mouse and muscle), dim. of *mus*, MOUSE][3]

Definitions

Definitions

> **frog** (frôg, fräg) **n.** [OE *frogga*]   **1** a tailless, leaping
> amphibian with long hind legs and webbed feet   **2** a
> fancy braided loop used to fasten clothing —**frog in the**
> **throat** hoarseness

Some words have more than one definition. If there is more than one definition
under a part of speech, each definition is numbered in boldface type. For example,
the word *frost* has two noun definitions and three verb definitions.

> **frost** (frôst, fräst) **n.** [OE < *freosan*, freeze]   **1** a
> temperature low enough to cause freezing   **2** frozen
> dew or vapor; rime —**vt.**   **1** to cover with frost
> **2** to cover with frosting   **3** to give a frostlike, opaque
> surface to (glass) —**frost'y, -i-er, -i-est, adj.**

The more common words have even more. For example, the word *off* has 21 definitions in the pocket-size edition and many more in the unabridged. Some definitions
also put the word in the context of a sentence or phrase. When technical definitions are given, the technical field is indicated.

Context

> **front** (frunt) **n.** [< L *frons*, forehead]   **1** *a)* outward be-
> havior [a bold *front*] *b)* [Colloq.] an appearance of social
> standing, wealth, etc.   **2** the part facing forward
> **3** the first part; beginning   **4** a forward or leading po-
> sition   **5** the land bordering a lake, street, etc.
> **6** the advanced battle area in warfare   **7** an area of
> activity [the home *front*]   **8** a person or group used to
> hide another's activity   **9** *Meteorol.* the boundary be-
> tween two differing air masses —**adj.** at, to, in, on, or of
> the front —**vt., vi.**   **1** to face   **2** to serve as a front
> (*for*) —**in front of** before —**fron'tal adj.**

Technical definition

Usage

In addition to the definitions, usage will be indicated if it differs from what is acceptable in formal writing. In brackets before the definition you may find terms such as *colloq., slang, archaic,* and *obs.* Colloquial (colloq.) expressions, such as the use of *front* to mean an appearance of high social standing, are used in conversation and informal writing, but not in term papers or formal letters.

> **front** (frunt) ***n.*** [< L *frons, forehead*]   **1** *a)* outward behavior [*a bold front*] *b)* [Colloq.] an appearance of social standing, wealth, etc.

A slang word is even more informal and should not be used in writing assignments.

> **horse opera** [Slang] WESTERN (*n.*)

An archaic or obsolete (obs.) word or definition was used in the past but is rarely or never used today. An example is:

> **how-be-it** (hou bē′it) ***adv.*** [Archaic] however it may be; nevertheless

An *idiomatic* expression is a phrase in which the words do not have their ordinary meaning. For example, *frog in the throat* refers to hoarseness and doesn't mean that you really have an animal in your throat.

Using the Dictionary

Finding the Main Entry

If you don't find a main entry for a word, look under its base word. For example, *frontal* is found under *front.*

> **front** (frunt) ***n.*** [< L *frons, forehead*]   **1** *a)* outward behavior [a bold *front*] *b)* [Colloq.] an appearance of social standing, wealth, etc.   **2** the part facing forward **3** the first part; beginning   **4** a forward or leading position   **5** the land bordering a lake, street, etc. **6** the advanced battle area in warfare   **7** an area of activity [the home *front*]   **8** a person or group used to hide another's activity   **9** *Meteorol.* the boundary between two differing air masses —***adj.*** at, to, in, on, or of the front —***vt., vi.***   **1** to face   **2** to serve as a front (*for*) —**in front of** before —**fron′tal** *adj.*

If you don't find a word you are looking for, try another spelling. For example, try *receive* for *recieve*. For practice, look in a dictionary and try to find the main entries for the following words. Each word listed is either misspelled or part of another entry. If you don't find a main entry for the word, look for its base. If the base is not a main entry, the word is misspelled and you should try another spelling. After you have found the word, put either the correct spelling or the main entry in the space provided.

1. persue _____
2. pettiness _____
3. accross _____
4. ommit _____
5. liberation _____

6. fundamentalist _____
7. protrusion _____
8. discribe _____
9. apreciate _____
10. superstitious _____

Check your answers in the back of the book.

Understanding the Definitions

Finding the entry is your first step. Understanding the word's definition is the second step.

Don't be frustrated when you find a word that is defined by an even more difficult word. If, for example, you are looking up *snide,* you may find a definition you don't understand, such as:

> **snide** (snīd) *adj.* [prob. < Du dial] slyly malicious or deri-
> sive

You could look up *malicious* or *derisive.* Malicious is defined as

> **ma·li·cious** (mə lish′əs) *adj.* having, showing, or caused by
> malice; spiteful —**ma·li′cious·ly** *adv.*

Malice is defined as

> **mal·ice** (mal′is) *n.* [< L *malus,* bad]   **1** active ill will;
> desire to harm another   **2** *Law* evil intent

Therefore, *snide* means slyly harmful or spiteful. *Derisive* is found under *deride*, which is defined as

> **de-ride** (di rīd′) *vt.* **-rid′ed, -rid′ing** [< L *de-*, down + *ridere*, to laugh] to laugh at in scorn; ridicule **—de-ri′sion** (rizh′ən) *n.* **—de-ri′sive** (-ri′siv) *adj.* **—de-ri′sive-ly** *adv.*

Therefore a snide remark is one that is used to slyly ridicule or laugh at another person.

Using the Pronunciation Guide

To test your understanding of the pronunciation guide, complete the following exercise. If you need help, use your dictionary.

fat, āpe, cär; ten, ēven; is, bīte; gō, hôrn, tō͞ol, look; oil, out; up, fur; get; joy; yet; chin; she; thin, *th*en; zh, leisure; ŋ, ring; ə for *a* in *ago*, *e* in *agent*, *i* in *sanity*, *o* in *comply*, *u* in *focus*; ′ as in *able* (ā′b'l)

1. Fill in the definitions in your own words:

   project   a. präj′ekt _____

   b. prə jekt′ _____

2. In each sentence, circle the correct pronunciation of *transports:*

   a. She went into *transports* over her new fur coat.

   (trans′pôrts   trans pôrts′)

   b. The railroad *transports* goods across the country.

   (trans′pôrts   trans pôrts′)

3. Fill in the correct part of speech

   a. kən test′ _____

   b. kän′test _____

Check your answers in the back of the book.

Choosing the Correct Definition

When you come to a word with several meanings, such as *train,* you have to use the context in which the word appeared in order to choose the correct definition. Using the entry for *train,* fill in the blanks before the following sentences with the number of the corresponding definition. The first one has been done for you. Use the part of speech to help you choose the correct definition.

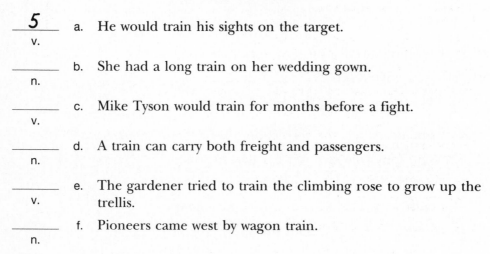

train (trān) *n.* [< L *trahere,* to pull]   **1** something that drags along behind, as a trailing skirt   **2** a group of followers; retinue   **3** a procession; caravan   **4** any connected order; sequence [a *train* of thought]   **5** a line of connected railroad cars pulled by a locomotive —*vt.*   **1** to guide the growth of (a plant)   **2** to guide the mental, moral, etc. development of; rear   **3** to instruct so as to make proficient   **4** to make fit for an athletic contest, etc.   **5** to aim (a gun, etc.) —*vi.* to undergo training —**train-ee** (trān ē′)

___**5**___   a.   He would train his sights on the target.
v.

_____   b.   She had a long train on her wedding gown.
n.

_____   c.   Mike Tyson would train for months before a fight.
v.

_____   d.   A train can carry both freight and passengers.
n.

_____   e.   The gardener tried to train the climbing rose to grow up the
v.   trellis.

_____   f.   Pioneers came west by wagon train.
n.

Check your answers in the back of the book.

When you look up a word, make a habit of checking the pronunciations, etymology, and all meanings. Try to put the definition(s) in your own words and use the word in a sentence. This will help you remember the word and make it a part of your vocabulary.

Types of Dictionaries

The first English dictionary, *A Table Alphabetical Conteyning and Teaching the True Writing and Understanding of Hard Usuall English Words,* published in 1604, contained about 3,000 words. Today, dictionaries come in three sizes: pocket, desk, and unabridged. A pocket-size edition has the fewest entries, and the entries include fewer definitions, fewer examples of usage, and fewer illustrations. Pocket editions typically contain about 50,000 of the most common words. Desk dictionaries may contain 150,000 entries. Unabridged dictionaries, which are usually seen in libraries, may contain 450,000 entries. Here are excerpts from the entries for the same word, *crowd,* in the three types of dictionaries.

Pocket[4]

crowd (kroud) *vi.* [OE *crudan*]   1 to push one's way (*into*)   2 to throng —*vt.*   1 to press or push   2 to fill too full; cram —*n.*   1 a large number of people or things grouped closely   2 the common people; the masses   3 [Colloq.] a set; clique —

Desk[5]

crowd[1] (kroud) *vi.* [ME. *crouden* < OE. *crudan*, to press, drive, akin to MHG. *kroten*, to oppress < IE. base **greut-*, to compel, press, whence Ir. *gruth*, curdled milk, CURD]   1. to press, push, or squeeze   2. to push one's way (*forward, into, through*, etc.)   3. to come together in a large group; throng —*vt.*   1. to press, push, or shove   2. to press or force closely together; cram   3. to fill too full; occupy to excess, as by pressing or thronging   4. to be or press very near to; specif., ☆*Baseball* to stand very close to (the plate) in batting   5. [Colloq.] to put (a person) under pressure or stress, as by dunning or harassing —*n.*   1. a large number of people or things gathered closely together   2. the common people; the masses   3. [Colloq.] a group of people having something in common; set; clique —**crowd (on) sail** to put up more sails in order to increase the ship's speed —**crowd out** to exclude because of insufficient space or time —**crowd′ed** *adj.*

SYN. —**crowd** is applied to an assembly of persons or things in close proximity or densely packed together and may suggest lack of order, loss of personal identity, etc. [*crowds* lined the street]; **throng** specifically suggests a moving crowd of people pushing one another [*throngs* of celebrators at Times Square]; **multitude** stresses greatness of number in referring to persons or things assembled or considered together [a *multitude* arrayed against him]; **swarm** suggests a large, continuously moving group [a *swarm* of sightseers]; **mob**, properly applied to a disorderly or lawless crowd, is an abusive term when used to describe the masses or any specific group of people; **host** specifically suggests a large organized body marshaled together but may be used generally of any sizable group considered collectively [he has a *host* of friends]; **horde** specifically refers to any large predatory band [a *horde* of office seekers]

crowd[2] (kroud) *n.* [ME. *croud* < W. *crwth*, akin to Gael. *cruinn*, curved, round]   1. an obsolete Celtic musical instrument somewhat like a violin but with a shallow, broad body   2. [Brit. Dial.] a violin

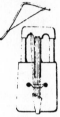

CROWD

¹crowd \'kraud\ *vb* -ED/-ING/-S [ME *crouden*, fr. OE *crūdan* to press, hasten, drive; akin to MLG *krūden* to annoy, MHG *kroten* to press, crowd, annoy, OE *crod* multitude, Norw *kryda* to swarm, MIr *gruth* curds] *vi* **1 a :** to press on : HURRY ⟨~ on one's way⟩ ⟨the ships ~ *ed* northward⟩ **b :** to force a way : appear in a oppressive or importunate manner ⟨ darkness of evening ~*ed* in ⟩ ⟨his heart ~*ed* up into his breast—Pearl S. Buck⟩ **c :** to press close ⟨ the players ~*ed* around the coach⟩ ⟨new cheap labor ~*ing* on the heels of earlier comers—*Amer. Guide Series : Minn.*⟩ **2 :** to collect in numbers: THRONG ⟨memories ~ in from every stage of the journey—Barbara Ward⟩ ⟨policemen warning people not to ~⟩ ~ *vt* **1 :** ENCUMBER, BURDEN, CRUSH, OPPRESS ⟨~ a person's patience with solicitations⟩ ⟨a person ~*ed* to death with titles and honors⟩ **2 a :** to fill by pressing or thronging together : fill or occupy to excess or obstruction ⟨~ a bus with children⟩ ⟨10,000 spectators ~*ing* a stadium⟩ ⟨his mind was ~*ed* with the detail he observed—Nevil Shute⟩ **b :** to press, force, or thrust esp. into a small space or little time : COMPRESS, COMPACT, CRAM ⟨~ children into a bus⟩ ⟨the same wish to ~ meaning is responsible for a good many slurred references—John Berryman⟩ ⟨a multitude of things were ~*ed* together ⟩ **3** *obs* : to confine forcibly : IMPRISON —usu. used with *in* **4 :** PUSH, MOVE, FORCE —usu. used with *off* or *out* ⟨~ a person off the sidewalk⟩ ⟨ we have allowed a false creed to ~ out the real American tradition—Bradford Smith⟩ **5 a :** to urge on : HURRY ⟨we ~*ed* the motor to ten knots—Clifford Gessler⟩ ⟨I ~*ed* him until streams of sweat ran—J.H. Stuart⟩ **b** (1) : to put on (sail) in excess of the usual amount so as to attain maximum speed (2) : INCREASE ⟨the engineer ~*s* steam in the cylinders—Frederick Way⟩ —often used with *on* ⟨~ on speed⟩ **6 :** to put pressure upon (as by solicitation) : dun unreasonably or harshly ⟨I'd never ~*ed* him with questions—J.B. Benefield⟩ **7 :** THRONG, JOSTLE ⟨changes . . . ~ each other in a whirl of confusing images—N.M. Butler⟩ **8 a :** to press close to ⟨one car ~*ing* the car in front⟩ ⟨~*ing* thirty and still not married⟩ **b :** to be a close second to : nearly overtake **c :** to stand close to (the plate) when batting in baseball **9 :** to count on or trust to (luck) unreasonably ⟨~*ing* his luck for all it was worth—F.B. Gipson⟩ **syn** see PACK, PRESS

²crowd \" \ *n* -s **1 a :** a large number of persons esp. when collected into a somewhat compact body without order : THRONG ⟨a ~ of little children⟩ **b :** an unorganized aggregate of people temporarily united in response to a common stimulus or situation in which the individuality of the participants is submerged—compare MOB **2 :** the great body of the people : POPULACE ⟨no man more hated and feared by the ~, the generality of mankind—Edith Sitwell⟩ ⟨all our ideas are ~ ideas—T.H. Ferril⟩ **3 :** a large number of things collected or closely pressed together : MULTITUDE ⟨~*s* of fine silver dust—G.H. Johnston⟩ ⟨ an exciting ~ of incidents—H.C. Webster⟩ ⟨a ~ of wasps, hornets, flies, and gnats—Ellen Glasgow⟩ **4 :** a group of people with something (as a habit, interest, occupation) in common : an exclusive company : SET, CLIQUE ⟨the cocktail ~⟩ ⟨the Hollywood ~⟩ ⟨I don't like him or his ~⟩ ⟨in with the wrong ~⟩ **5 a :** the impressed forward movement of the dipper of a power shovel that forces it into the material to be moved **b :** the mechanism that does the forcing

syn THRONG, PRESS, CRUSH, MOB, ROUT, HORDE: CROWD indicates a massed group of persons, often closely pressed and often with subordination of individualities involved ⟨the *crowd* came pouring out with a vehemence that nearly took him off his legs—Charles Dickens⟩ ⟨we get the real sense of a *crowd* of human beings, animated, as a *crowd,* by an instinct and a genius different from that of any of its particular members—Laurence Binyon⟩ THRONG is closely synonymous with CROWD; occas. it may suggest surging motion or bustling confusion ⟨summer tourists come to join the shopping *throngs* on summer evenings—*Amer. Guide Series: N.H.*⟩ ⟨sailors hung from yards and bowsprits to shout the names of vessels to the bewildered, harried *throng*—Kenneth Roberts⟩ PRESS, not now used so much as formerly, may suggest compact concentration in which movement is difficult ⟨they could not come nigh unto him for the *press*—Mk 2:4 (AV)⟩ CRUSH more strongly stresses compact concentration and difficulty of passage through; it is rarely used without connotation of discomfort ⟨the *crush* was terrific for that time of day . . . for the street was blocked—Virginia Woolf⟩ ⟨a *crush* of dancing couples packed the floor—Hamilton Basso⟩ MOB, usu. derogatory, is likely to indicate a rough crowd composed of lower elements, often one disposed to disorder, riot, or other antisocial action and one abrogating any finer feeling ⟨Oliver was burned in effigy, and Hutchinson's town house was gutted by the *mob*—C.L. Becker⟩ ⟨the *mob,* loudly as they clamored for their own rights, cared nothing for the rights of others—J.A. Froude⟩ ROUT is sometimes a close synonym of MOB; it may suggest a concentration of hectic or disorderly activity in a circumscribed space ⟨the busy *rout* of the street could be seen. He loved the changing panorama of the street—Theodore Dreiser⟩ ⟨a kind of jollity and recklessness which was born in the fort, at the old *routs* and balls—Bruce Hutchison⟩ ⟨a flying *rout* of suns and galaxies, rushing away from the solar system and from one another—E.M. Forster⟩ HORDE may apply to a large surging mass or crowd of rough or savage individuals disposed to predatory or destructive action ⟨*hordes* of desperadoes and gunmen who found the river at this point a convenient crossing—*Amer. Guide Series : Texas*⟩ ⟨*hordes* of sturdy rogues and vagrants—G.E. Fussell⟩ ⟨a *horde* of heavily armed buffoons in big boots went stamping round my decks for hours, poking their great stupid faces into everything—*Times Lit. Supp.*⟩

³crowd \" , 'krüd\ *n* -s [ME *crowde, crouth,* fr. (assumed) MW *crwth* (whence W *crwth* fiddle); akin to MIr *crott* harp, L *curvus* curved—more at CROWN] **1 :** CRWTH **2** *dial Eng* : FIDDLE

⁴crowd \" \ *vi* -ED/-ING/-S *dial Eng* : FIDDLE

As a way of comparing the three types of dictionaries, answer the following questions:

1. How many entries for *crowd* are in the desk dictionary? _____

2. What is the difference between *crowd* and *host?* _____

3. To what language does the etymology go back in the pocket-size edition? _____ In the desk edition? _____

4. How many languages are mentioned in the etymology in the unabridged edition? _____

5. What is the difference between the first and second entries for *crowd* in the desk edition? _____

Check your answers in the back of the book.

Specialized Dictionaries

In addition to general dictionaries, there are also dictionaries that specialize in a particular subject. Here are a few examples:

Dictionary of Slang
Dorland's Illustrated Medical Dictionary
Black's Law Dictionary
Grove's Dictionary of Music and Musicians
Modern Dictionary of Electronics

All dictionaries can be found in the reference section of the library.

Additional Material

Most dictionaries include extra material at the beginning and end. For example, dictionaries we looked at included:

All the nations in the world
Colleges and universities in the United States and Canada
Populations of places in the United States and Canada
Proofreaders' marks
Foreign words and phrases
Tables of weights and measures

Below are the Review Words for this chapter. We will use these words to practice the skills taught in this chapter.

affiliate (ə fil′ē āt′, *for n., usually,* -it) *v.*   to connect or associate (oneself *with*); join —*n.*   an affiliated individual or organization; member

commune (kə myo̅o̅n′; *for n.* käm′yo̅o̅n′) *v.*   to talk together intimately; to be in close rapport [to *commune* with nature] —*n.*   1. a collective farm, as in China   2. a small group of people living communally and sharing in work, earnings, etc.

domestic (də mes′tik) *adj.*   1. of the home or family   2. of or made in one's country   3. tame: said of animals   4. homeloving —*n.*   a maid, cook, etc.

exploit (eks′ploit′; *also, and for v. usually,* eks ploit′, ik sploit′) *n.*   an act remarkable for brilliance or daring; bold deed —*v.*   1. to make use of; turn to account; utilize productively   2. to make unethical use of for one's own advantage or profit, specif. to make profit from the labor of (others) without giving a just return   3. *advertising* to stir up interest in; promote [to *exploit* a product]

extract (*for v.* eks trakt′, ik strakt′; *for n.* eks′trakt′) *v.*   to draw out by effort; pull out [to *extract* a tooth, to *extract* a promise from someone]   2. to remove or separate (metal) from ore   3. to obtain (a substance, esp. an essence or concentrate) by pressing, distilling, using a solvent, etc. [to *extract* juice from fruit] —*n.*   something extracted, specif. (a) a concentrated form, whether solid, viscid, or liquid, of a food, flavoring, etc. [beef *extract*] (b) a passage selected from a book, etc.; excerpt; quotation

graft (graft) *n.*   1. (a) a shoot or bud of one plant or tree inserted into another, where it grows permanently (b) the inserting of such a shoot   2. the transplanting of skin, bone, etc.   3. (a) the dishonest use of one's position to gain money, etc., as in politics (b) anything so gained —*v.*   1. to insert (a graft)   2. to obtain (money, etc.) by graft

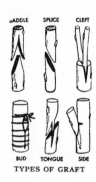

SADDLE   SPLICE   CLEFT

BUD   TONGUE   SIDE
TYPES OF GRAFT

incline (in klīn′; *for n., usually* in′klīn) *v.*   1. to deviate or cause to deviate from a horizontal or vertical position, course, etc.; lean; slope; slant   2. to bend or bow to the body or head   3. (a) to have a particular disposition or bent of mind, will, etc. (b) to have a tendency   4. to have a preference or liking —*n.*   an inclined plane or surface; slope; grade; slant

induce (in dōōs′) *v.*   1. to persuade   2. to bring on [sleep *induced* by drugs]   3. to draw (a conclusion) from particular facts

lapse (laps) *n.*   1. a small error   2. (a) a moral slip (b) a falling into a lower condition   3. a passing, as of time   4. the termination as of a privilege through failure to meet requirements —*v.*   1. to fall into a specified state [he *lapsed* into silence]   2. to backslide   3. to elapse   4. to come to an end; stop   5. to become void because of failure to meet requirements

reserved (ri zurvd′) *v.*   1. kept back, stored up, or set apart for later use or for some special purpose   2. held over to a later time   3. set aside for a special person [to *reserve* a theater seat]   4. kept back or retained for oneself [to *reserve* the right to refuse] —*adj.*   1. kept back or stored up, as for later use or for a special purpose   2. self-restrained, or aloof in speech and manner; reticent; silent   3. restrained and controlled in artistic expression; free from exaggeration or extravagance   4. kept out of action for use in an emergency or for replacing active groups or units, as in sports or warfare

fat, āpe, cär; ten, ēven; is, bīte; gō, hôrn, tōol, look; oil, out; up, fur; get; joy; yet; chin; she; thin, *th*en; zh, leisure; ŋ, ring; ə for *a* in *ago, e* in *agent, i* in *sanity, o* in *comply, u* in *focus;* ′ as in *able* (ā′b′l)

CHAPTER FOUR: GETTING THE MOST FROM YOUR DICTIONARY   **57**

Fill in each blank with the word that correctly completes the sentence. Check your answers in the back of the book.

affiliate	domestic	extract	inclines	lapse
commune	exploits	graft	induce	reserved

1. If a baby is not born within a reasonable time of its due date, the doctors will often _____ labor.

2. His wife was afraid that if she left him he would _____ back into alcoholism.

3. The restaurateur _____ a dozen bottles of the best wine for his personal use.

4. The road _____ uphill and to the east for three miles.

5. Kristina decided not to _____ with any sorority.

6. Most visitors to China ask to visit a _____ .

7. Doctors will _____ skin from the unburned parts of a victim's body to cover the places where the skin is gone.

8. Police historically have been reluctant to intervene in cases of _____ violence, such as wife beating.

9. The plots of the Indiana Jones films revolve around the _____ of the handsome archeologist.

10. Vanilla _____ is commonly used in flavoring foods and drinks.

Five of the Review Words for this chapter (given in italics in the following sentences) have more than one pronunciation. Circle the pronunciation of the word as it is used in the sentence. Check your answers in the back of the book.

1. On June 6, 1896, two men rowed from New York to England in an 18-foot boat—an *exploit* everyone had considered impossible.

    eks′ploit   ik sploit′

2. Funicular railways—railways worked by cables—are common in Switzerland, where the mountainous *inclines* are too steep for ordinary railroads.

    in klīnz′   in′klīnz

3. Tequila is made in Mexico from an *extract* derived from the sap of the mescal cactus.

    ik strakt′   eks′trakt

4. The Teamsters union stopped being an *affiliate* of the AFL-CIO in 1957 when it was expelled as a result of a Senate investigation.

    ə fil′ē āt′   ə fil′ē it

5. The two sisters would *commune* over the telephone for hours on end.

    kə myo͞on′   käm′yo͞on

6. Communist societies claim that capitalist systems *exploit* their workers.

    eks′ploit   ik sploit′

7. The force of her argument *inclines* me to change my mind in her favor.

    in klīnz′   in′klīnz

8. Some dentists will *extract* as many as two million teeth in the course of their careers.

    ik strakt′   eks′trakt

9. Organized crime in the United States is a product of the Prohibition era of the early twentieth century, when such groups as the Al Capone mob of Chicago, the Detroit Purple gang, and the Owney Madden ring of New York City began to loosely *affiliate*.

    ə fil′ē āt′   ə fil′ē it

10. During the 1960s it was common for the teenager of the family to decide to run away from home to live on a *commune*.

    kə myo͞on′   käm′yo͞on

The next five Review Words have multiple meanings. To test your knowledge of the different meanings, we have provided two sentences for each word. Read each sentence, then look back at the Review Word definitions. Identify which meaning would best describe how the word is used (this is similar to the exercise you did with the multiple meanings of the word *train*) and list the number of the definition in the space provided. Be careful to choose a definition under the correct part of speech; we have provided the part of speech below each space. Check your answers in the back of the book.

_____
n.

1. Types of *grafts* include the saddle, splice, cleft, bud, tongue, and side.

_____
n.

2. The 1980 ABSCAM scandal, in which FBI agents posing as middlemen for wealthy Arabs who offered money to U.S. congressmen, is an example of *graft*.

_____
adj.

3. Greta Garbo was the most *reserved* of movie stars; when approached by the media, her typical reply was, "I want to be alone."

_____
adj.

4. The millionaire had a permanently *reserved* table at the city's most elegant restaurant.

_____
v.

5. It is said that buttons were first placed on men's coat sleeves by Frederick the Great of Prussia to *induce* his soldiers to stop wiping their noses on their sleeves.

_____
v.

6. By dropping objects of different weights from the leaning tower of Pisa, Galileo was able to *induce* that objects do not fall at speeds proportional to their weight.

_____
v.

7. By failing to pay his dues, he let his subscription *lapse*.

_____
n.

8. Wiping your mouth on the hostess's tablecloth is a *lapse* in etiquette.

_____
adj.

9. *Domestic* automobiles have faced heavy competition from foreign imports.

_____
adj.

10. The cow is a *domestic* animal.

A. Fill in the following information from the dictionary you are using:

1. Title _____

2. Copyright date _____

3. Hard cover or paperback _____

B. Using your dictionary, find what these abbreviations mean. On the left-hand line write out the word that the abbreviation stands for. On the right-hand line write the definition. The first one has been done for you. Check your answers in the back of the book.

1. etc. _*et cetera*_____   _and so forth_____

2. i.e. _____   _____

3. e.g. _____   _____

4. et al. _____   _____

5. R.S.V.P. _____   _____

6. cf. _____   _____

7. ff. _____   _____

C. Being able to interpret the meaning of symbols used in entries helps you make the most of your dictionary. Find out what each of the following symbols means. Look at the abbreviations list at the front of your dictionary if you can't guess the meaning from the entry. Check your answers in the back of the book.

1. Circle *a* or *b:*
   When you see [D-] in definition 2 does it mean

   > **dem-o-crat** (dem′ə krat′) *n.* **1** one who supports or practices democracy **2** [D-] a Democratic Party member

   a. a member of a political party?
   b. one who believes in democracy?

2. What does [see fol.] mean here? _____

   > **in-stance** (in′stəns) *n.* [see fol.] **1** an example; case **2** a step in proceeding; occasion [in the first *instance*] — *vt.* **-stanced, -stanc-ing** to give as an example; cite —**at the instance of** at the suggestion or instigation of
   > **in-stant** (in′stənt) *adj.* [< L *in-*, in, upon + *stare*, to stand] **1** urgent; pressing **2** imminent **3** immediate **4** concentrated or precooked for quick preparation, as a food or beverage **5** [Archaic] present; current —*n.* **1** a moment **2** a particular moment —**the instant** as soon as

3. Based on the directions in the *roller skate* entry, circle the meaning in the *skate* entry that refers to roller skating.

> **roller skate** SKATE[1] (sense 2) —**roll′er -skate′, -skat′ed, -skat′ing,** *vi.* —**roller skater**
> **skate[1]** (skāt) *n.* [< OFr *eschace,* stilt] **1** a metal runner in a frame, fastened to a shoe for gliding on ice **2** a similar frame or shoe with two pairs of small wheels, for gliding on a floor, sidewalk, etc. —*vi.* **skat′ed, skat′ing** to glide or roll on or as on skates —**skat′er** *n.*
> **skate[2]** (skāt) *n.* [< ON *skara*] any ray fish

4. What does [Pers.] mean in this entry? _____

> **jas-mine** (jaz′min, jas′-) *n.* [< Pers *yāsamin*] any of certain plants of warm regions, with fragrant flowers of yellow, red, or white

5. What does *sing.* mean in this entry? _____

> **da-tum** (dāt′əm, dat′-) *n.* [L, what is given] *sing. of* DATA

6. What does [see prec.] mean in the entry for *vindictive*? _____

> **vin-di-cate** (vin′də kāt′) *vt.* **-cat′ed, -cat′ing** [< L *vis,* force + *dicere,* say] **1** to clear from criticism, blame, etc. **2** to defend against opposition **3** to justify —**vin′di-ca′tion** *n.* —**vin′di-ca′tor** *n.*
> **vin-dic-tive** (vin dik′tiv) *adj.* [see prec.] **1** revengeful in spirit **2** said or done in revenge —**vin-dic′tive-ly** *adv.* —**vin-dic′tive-ness** *n.*

7. What does [< ?] mean in this entry? _____

> **frow-zy** (frou′zē) *adj.* **-zi-er, -zi-est** [< ?] dirty and untidy; slovenly —**frow′zi-ly**

8. What does [Dial.] mean in this entry? _____

> **vict-uals** [vit′′lz] *n. pl.* [< L *victus,* food] [Dial. or Colloq.] articles of food

9. What does [Poet.] mean in this entry? _____

> **oft** (ôft) *adv.* [OE] *chiefly poet. var. of* OFTEN

10. What does *-ties* mean in this entry? _____

> **com-mod-i-ty** (kə mäd′ə tē) *n., pl.* **-ties** [see COMMODE] **1** any useful thing **2** anything bought and sold **3** [*pl.*] staple products, as of agriculture

NEW WORDS I

The New Words in this chapter have multiple meanings.

buoyant (boi′ənt, bōō′yənt) *adj.*   1. having the ability or tendency to float   2. cheerful

countenance (koun′tə nəns, kount″n əns) *n.*   1. facial expression   2. the face   3. approval; support —*v.*   to approve or tolerate

extremity (ek strem′ə tē, ik-) *n.*   1. the outermost part; end   2. the greatest degree   3. great need, danger, etc.   4. an extreme measure   5. [*pl.*] the hands and feet

façade, facade (fə säd′) *n.*   1. the front or main face of a building   2. an imposing appearance concealing something inferior

facet (fas′it) *n.*   1. any of the polished plane surfaces of a cut gem   2. any of a number of sides or aspects, as of a personality —*v.*   to cut or make facets on

facility (fə sil′ə tē) *n.*   1. absence of difficulty   2. skill; dexterity   3. [*usually pl.*] the means by which something can be done   4. a building, etc., that facilitates some activity

franchise (fran′chīz) *n.*   1. any special right or privilege granted by a government   2. the right to vote; suffrage   3. the right to sell a product or service —*v.*   to grant a franchise to

menial (mē′nē əl, mēn′yəl) *adj.*   1. of or fit for servants   2. servile; low —*n.*   1. a domestic servant   2. a servile, low person

patronize (pā′tron īz′, pa′-) *v.*   1. to sponsor; support   2. to treat in a condescending manner   3. to be a regular customer of

prone (prōn) *adj.*   1. lying face downward or prostrate   2. disposed or inclined (*to*) [*prone* to err]

fat, āpe, cär; ten, ēven; is, bīte; gō, hôrn, tōōl, look; oil, out; up, fur; get; joy; yet; chin; she; thin, *th*en; zh, leisure; ŋ, ring; ə for *a* in *ago, e* in *agent, i* in *sanity, o* in *comply, u* in *focus;* ′ as in *able* (ā′b′l)

EXERCISE 5: FILL-IN

Below are the ten New Words you just studied. First, complete the following sentences with the appropriate word. Second, using the definitions on your New Words list, write the number of the proper definition in the blank in front of the sentence number. To help you find the right definition, we have provided the part of speech below that blank. The first one is done for you. Check your answers in the back of the book.

buoyant	extremities	facet	franchise	patronizes
countenances	façade	facility	menials	prone

___1___ 1. Many refugees who were professionals in their own countries have been forced
n.   to take jobs as _____*menials*_____ in the United States.

_____ 2. Liars are _____ to get caught when they can't remember
adj.   what they told to whom.

_____ 3. Frostbite is more likely to attack the _____ than the main
n.   part of the body.

_____ 4. Most waitresses resent it when a customer _____ her by
v.   calling her "honey" or "sweetie."

_____ 5. The early leaders of the feminist movement in the United States—Susan B.
n.   Anthony, Elizabeth Cady Stanton, and others—were disappointed when the

                   Fifteenth Amendment gave the _____ to newly freed black
                   men, but not to women.

_____ 6. Although the eighteenth-century cardinal Mazzofanti never left Italy in his life,
n.
                   he had such a _____ for languages that he spoke 53
                   fluently, another 61 almost as well, and understood 72 additional dialects.

_____ 7. With a frontage of just over four feet, the Green Lantern Restaurant in
n.   Amsterdam, which can seat 88 diners, may be the narrowest restaurant in the
                   world. The narrow frontage comes from the days when a property owner's taxes

                   were based on the width of the _____.

_____ 8. Beard growth differs among different groups of people: The Celts and Slavs have
n.
                   the hairiest _____, the Chinese have but sparse beards, and
                   the American Indians have hardly any facial hair.

_____ 9. Because swimmers are more _____ in salt water than in
adj.   fresh water, swimmers in the extremely salty Great Salt Lake find it impossible to
                   sink.

_____ 10. Before getting married, it is wise to examine every _____ of
n.   the other person's personality.

cavalier (kav′ə lir′) *n.*   1. an armed horseman; knight   2. a gallant gentleman, esp. a lady's escort —*adj.*   1. casual   2. arrogant

chafe (chāf) *vt.*   1. to rub so as to make warm   2. to wear away or make sore by rubbing   3. to annoy; irritate —*vi.*   1. to rub (*on* or *against*)   2. to be vexed

cipher (sī′fər) *n.*   1. the symbol 0; zero   2. a nonentity   3. secret writing based on a key; code   4. the key to such a code

deviate (dē′vē āt′; *for adj. & n.* -it) *v.*   to turn aside (*from* a course, standard, etc.); diverge — *adj.*   deviant —*n.*   a deviant, esp. in sexual behavior

ferment (fʉr′ment; *for v.* fər ment′) *n.*   1. a substance causing fermentation, as yeast   2. excitement or agitation —*v.*   1. to cause or be in the process of fermentation (a change brought about by enzymes that convert sugar into alcohol)   2. to excite or be excited or agitated; seethe

incumbent (in kum′bənt) *adj.*   1. resting (*on* or *upon* one) as a duty or obligation   2. currently in office —*n.*   the holder of an office, etc.

oblique (ə blēk′, ō-) *adj.*   1. slanting   2. indirect or evasive

prevail (prē vāl′, pri-) *v.*   1. to be victorious (*over* or *against*)   2. to succeed   3. to be or become more widespread   4. to be prevalent —**prevail on** (or **upon, with**) to persuade

staunch (stônch, stänch) *adj.*   1. steadfast; loyal   2. strong; solid   3. seaworthy —*v.*   to check the flow of (blood, etc.) from (a cut, etc.); to stop flowing

void (void) *adj.*   1. containing nothing   2. devoid (of) [*void* of sense]   3. ineffective; useless   4. of no legal force —*n.*   1. an empty space   2. a feeling of emptiness —*v.*   1. to empty out   2. to make void; annul

fat, āpe, cär; ten, ēven; is, bīte; gō, hôrn, tōōl, look; oil, out; up, fʉr; get; joy; yet; chin; she; thin, *th*en; zh, leisure; ŋ, ring; ə for *a* in *ago*, *e* in *agent*, *i* in *sanity*, *o* in *comply*, *u* in *focus*; ′ as in *able* (ā′b'l)

Circle the letter before the word or phrase that best defines the italicized word in each sentence. Check your answers in the back of the book.

1. The most famous *cavalier* may be Sir Walter Raleigh: when he and Queen Elizabeth I came to a mud puddle, he placed his cloak in the mud so that she could cross.

   a. warrior   b. rowdy   c. gentleman   d. scholar

2. New shoes often *chafe*, causing blisters.

   a. grip   b. rub   c. pinch   d. smell

3. During wars, messages are often written in *cipher*.

   a. ink   b. numbers   c. secret writing   d. foreign languages

4. One way in which cartoon characters *deviate from* normal people is that they are almost always drawn with only three fingers and a thumb to save time and labor.

   a. imitate   b. resemble   c. copy   d. differ from

5. The oldest alcoholic beverage is mead, a sweet wine made from *fermented* honey.

   a. rotten   b. converted to alcohol   c. converted to sugar   d. agitated

6. In the 1992 presidential election, the *incumbent* was George Bush.

   a. Vice President   b. officeholder   c. voter   d. favorite

7. The building was unusual because it contained *oblique* angles where right angles are expected.

   a. upright   b. horizontal   c. slanting   d. vertical

8. Because Olympic athletes are often so closely matched in skill, it is possible in some events to *prevail* because of luck alone.

   a. lose   b. win   c. cheat   d. surrender

9. Hemophilia is a hereditary condition in which one of the normal blood-clotting factors is missing, making it difficult to *staunch* the flow of blood from even minor cuts.

   a. stop   b. transfuse   c. ease   d. clean

10. People who thought the earth was flat believed that if you got too close to the edge you could fall into *the void*.

    a. the ocean   b. the pit   c. space   d. heaven

EXERCISE 7: TRUE-FALSE

Write T or F in the blank. Check your answers in the back of the book.

_____ 1. A cipher is a large number.

_____ 2. Burger King is a franchise operation.

_____ 3. When a loved one dies you feel a void.

_____ 4. Wealthy people often patronize the arts.

_____ 5. A creative person rarely deviates from the standards of others.

EXERCISE 8: ANALOGIES

In the blank write the letter of the word that best completes each analogy. Check your answers in the back of the book.

1. reserved : quiet :: buoyant : _____   a. depressed   b. lonely   c. friendly
   d. cheerful

2. initiate : begin :: façade : _____   a. reality   b. appearance   c. rear
   d. truth

3. induce : discourage :: prone :   a. upright   b. flat   c. likely
   _____   d. unhappy

4. initiate : expel :: oblique : _____   a. slanting   b. implied   c. begin
   d. acute

5. affiliate : resign :: facility : _____   a. ease   b. building   c. skill
   d. difficulty

EXERCISE 9: MATCHING MEANINGS

Write the letter of the word that means the *opposite* of the word in the first column. Check your answers in the back of the book.

_____	1. staunch	a. royal
_____	2. menial	b. lose
_____	3. cavalier	c. serious
_____	4. chafe	d. disloyal
_____	5. prevail	e. soothe

EXERCISE 10: WORD CONTRASTS

In each group below circle the word that does not mean what the others mean. Check your answers in the back of the book.

1. incumbent   candidate   nominee   applicant
2. countenance   approve   punish   favor
3. facet   aspect   phase   totality
4. extremity   safety   need   distress
5. ferment   excite   quiet   agitate

EXERCISE 11: SENTENCE COMPLETION

Complete each sentence in your own words. Sample answers are provided in the back of the book.

1. Danielle had a very *buoyant* personality until _____
_____.

2. Jesse has a *cavalier* attitude toward studying; consequently, _____
_____.

3. People who *chafe* under the authority of others _____
_____.

4. Timothy was such a complete *cipher* that _____
_____.

5. Although I cannot *countenance* Natalie's behavior, _____
_____.

6. Children who *deviate* from classroom rules _____

_____ .

7. An example of a bodily *extremity* is _____

_____ .

8. Due to his very clever *façade,* _____

_____ .

9. People who have many *facets* to their personality are _____

_____ .

10. If you have a *facility* for math, _____

_____ .

11. When grape juice *ferments* _____

_____ .

12. One of the most famous *franchise* operations is _____

_____ .

13. One of the duties *incumbent* upon citizens is to _____

_____ .

14. *Menial* tasks are often _____

_____ .

15. Some subjects are so sensitive that an *oblique* approach is best; an example is _____

_____ .

16. Instead of *patronizing* discount stores, _____

_____ .

17. Most people expect right to *prevail;* however, _____

_____ .

18. Seth is *prone* to accept most conservative beliefs, provided that _____

_____ .

19. After giving his *staunch* support to the project, _____

_____ .

20. If a contract is *void* _____

_____ .

consort (kän′sôrt; *for v.* kən sôrt′) —*n.* a wife or husband, esp. of a reigning king or queen —*v.* to associate (with)

consummate (kän′sum it; *for v.* kän′sə māt′) *adj.* complete; perfect —*v.* 1. to complete 2. to complete (marriage) by sexual intercourse

dissipate (dis′ə pāt′) *v.* 1. scatter; disperse 2. disappear 3. waste or squander 4. indulge in pleasure to the point of harming oneself

formidable (fôr′mə də bəl) *adj.* 1. causing dread, fear, or awe 2. hard to handle 3. awe-inspiring in size, excellence, etc.; strikingly impressive

forte (fôrt, fōrt) *n.* that which one does particularly well —(fôr′tā, -tē) *adj., adv.* *Music* loud

mercenary (mʉr′sə ner′ē) *adj.* working or done for payment only —*n.* a soldier hired to serve in a foreign army

mundane (mun dān′, mun′dān) *adj.* 1. of the world; worldly 2. commonplace; ordinary

obtuse (äb toos′, əb-) *adj.* 1. not sharp; blunt 2. greater than 90° and less than 180° [an *obtuse* angle] 3. slow to understand or perceive

succulent (suk′yoo lənt) *adj.* 1. full of juice; juicy 2. full of interest, vigor, etc.; not dry or dull 3. *Bot.* having thick, fleshy tissues for storing water, as a cactus —*n.* a succulent plant

viable (vī′ə bəl) *adj.* 1. capable of living 2. workable [*viable* ideas]

fat, āpe, cär; ten, ēven; is, bīte; gō, hôrn, tool, look; oil, out; up, fʉr; get; joy; yet; chin; she; thin, *th*en; zh, leisure; ŋ, ring; ə for *a* in *ago, e* in *agent, i* in *sanity, o* in *comply, u* in *focus;* ′ as in *able* (ā′b′l)

Fill in each blank with the word that correctly completes the sentence. Check your answers in the back of the book.

consort	dissipate	forte	mundane	succulent
consummate	formidable	mercenary	obtuse	viable

1. Rain never falls on parts of the Sahara Desert; although raindrops form, they

   _____ in the heat before they reach the ground.

2. The _____ bigamist was Mrs. Theresa Vaughn of Sheffield, England; she married 62 men during a five-year period without obtaining a divorce from any of them.

3. It is impossible to catch a cold in the winter in Verhoyansk, Siberia; the air is too cold for

   germs to be _____.

4. Motherhood was definitely the _____ of Mrs. Bernard Scheiber of Austria; she had 4 sets of quadruplets, 7 sets of triplets, and 16 pairs of twins—a total of 69 children.

5. While Queen Elizabeth II has had a long, stable relationship with her

   _____, none of her four children has had a lasting marriage.

6. A former soldier without other job skills can sometimes find work as a

   _____ of another country.

7. A 300-pound Sumo wrestler makes a _____ opponent.

8. The aloe vera, a _____ of the lily family, has a gel in its fleshy leaves that is used as an insect repellent and as a treatment for burns.

9. Doing laundry is a _____ task.

10. The most _____ creature ever to live on earth was the stegosaurus, which had a 2½ ounce brain in a 6½ ton body.

This puzzle reviews the New Words from Chapters 2 and 3. The clues marked by an asterisk (*) have answers from those words. Use a pencil so you can erase. Check your answers in the back of the book.

Across

*1. Arrogant
8. Abbr. for *Spain*
9. Negative answer
*10. To cancel out
12. Ant. of *lose*
*14. Very painful
18. Either . . . _____
*19. Open to criticism
24. To make use of
26. Drink related to beer
*27. Strict
30. π
31. Abbr. for *regarding*
32. A brass wind instrument
33. Dog's name
35. To make an effort
37. Archaic form of *you* "God Rest _____ Merry Gentlemen"
38. Finished
40. Abbr. for *New York*
*41. Cautious

Down

*1. Massive
2. Breakfast food
3. Eeny, meeny, miney, _____
4. Abbr. for *teaspoon*
5. Ant. of *down*
6. An organization of workers
7. Boy child
11. What we breathe
*13. Sneaky
15. Put the lid on
16. Ant. of *pro*
*17. Rage
20. Long, thin mark
21. Moved quickly
22. To live or exist
*23. Outstanding
*25. Sober
*28. Something that turns out to be the opposite of what is expected
29. Ant. of *exit* (*v.*)
30. To snoop
34. Nickname for Donald
39. Ant. of *she*

List ten words from your outside reading that you would like to learn, and for each word put the pronunciation, the part of speech, and a simple definition in the spaces below.

1. _____

_____

2. _____

_____

3. _____

_____

4. _____

_____

5. _____

_____

6. _____

_____

7. _____

_____

8. _____

_____

9. _____

_____

10. _____

_____

chapter 5

SUFFIXES

THE LOCKHORNS

"LEROY HAS A WAY WITH WORDS, TOO. HE OFTEN HAS TO EAT THEM."

So far we have discussed two ways to discover the meaning of a word: from its context and by using a dictionary. Now we are going to look at word construction as a means of discovering definitions and remembering meanings. One of the most useful ways to deduce the meanings of unfamiliar words is to analyze the word parts called roots, prefixes, and suffixes. The **root** is the base on which the word is constructed. **Prefixes** are added before the roots to change their meanings. For example, *imprudent* means the opposite of *prudent* because the prefix *im* means "not." **Suffixes** are attached to the ends of roots and usually change the part of speech. However, some suffixes change the meaning of a word as well as the part of speech. For example, by adding the suffix *er* to *commute* it becomes *commuter*, "one who commutes." Suffixes can be attached to whole words, as in comment*ary*, or to parts of words, as in ami*able*. Suffixes will be discussed in this chapter. Prefixes will be discussed in Chapter 6, and Chapters 7, 8, and 9 will cover 30 of the most important roots.

Knowing the most frequently used word parts can help you unlock the meanings of hundreds of new words. For example, the difficult word *triskaidekaphobia* can be easily understood and remembered when broken into its parts:

Word Part	Definition	Examples
tri(s)	three	tripod, triple, trisect
kai	and	(not used in any other English word)
deka (deca)	ten	decade, decimal, decathlon
phobia	fear	claustrophobia, acrophobia

A person who has *triskaidekaphobia* simply has a fear of the number 13 and probably won't go out on Friday the 13th because he believes it to be unlucky.

You can see that learning how to divide and conquer words is very helpful. Just knowing how to recognize suffixes can help solve several word mysteries. For example, you may not realize it but you already know the words *pacifist, aromatic, medicinal, lineage,* and *palatial*. Below we have divided the base words from their suffixes.

Word	Base		Suffix	Suffix Meaning
pacifist	pacify	+	ist	one who
aromatic	aroma	+	ic	like, relating to
medicinal	medicine	+	al	like, relating to
lineage	line	+	age	belonging to, related to
palatial	palace	+	ial	like, relating to

To test your knowledge of suffixes, fill in the missing endings in the mystery below. Check your answers in the back of the book.

The Case of the Missing Blow Gun

Scotland Yard's Inspect_____ Keane was deep in thought. A fam_____ news-
_____1_____2
paper column_____ had been murdered by a most unusu_____ method. The
_____3_____4
only mark on his body was a small punct_____ in the neck obvious_____ made by
_____5_____6
the tiny gray_____ dart on the floor. There was no poss_____ way for so small an
_____7_____8
object to have penetrated the skin so deep_____ unless it had been driv_____ in
_____9_____10
with great force. The only possibil_____ was that the murder_____ used a blow
_____11_____12
gun. An unpleas_____ looking man had been seen leaving the apart_____ about
_____13_____14
the time of the murder but he had been stopped immediate_____ by a sus-
_____15
pic_____ neighbor who thought that he might be a burgl_____. After the neigh-
_____16_____17
bor had discovered the body, he had held the man until the police arrived. Of course,
the man claimed the journal_____ was already dead when he arrived. A search of
_____18
the man's pockets showed the custom_____ collect_____ of objects: a pencil, a
_____19_____20
wallet, some sugar_____ gum, some loose change, and a pipe.
_____21

As the brilli_____ detect_____ sat staring at the body, he grew im-
_____22_____23
pati_____ at his inabil_____ to solve the crime. He had been care_____ to
_____24_____25_____26
notice every detail in the room. Still there was a short_____ of evid_____ and the
_____27_____28
clues were sketch_____ at best. The man's innoc_____ was question_____, but
_____29_____30_____31
the inspector would have to release him unless he could ident_____ the murder
_____32
weapon. Keane was sure that it was an ingen_____ one used by an intellig_____
_____33_____34
crimin_____. At times like these, the inspector enjoyed smoking his pipe. He found
_____35
it helped him concentr_____ and organ_____ his thoughts. With his
_____36_____37
typic_____ thorough_____ he took it apart and cleaned it before filling it with his
_____38_____39
favorite tobacco. He separated the bowl from the stem and with the tal_____ of a
_____40
surgeon he passed a pipe clean_____ through the straight and hollow stem.
_____41

Sudden_____, Keane's attit_____ changed. A child_____ grin appeared
_____42_____43_____44
on his lips. He had the answer to the myst_____. Keane arrested the man on sus-
_____45
pic_____ of murder and sent the pipe to the crime laborat_____ for tests. What
_____46_____47
had Keane realized?

Solution

Keane remembered that the man had a pipe but no matches or tobacco. As the inspector cleaned his own pipe he realized that the hollow stem would make a perfect blow gun.

As you can see from the story, suffixes are used very often. They don't usually change the meaning of the base very much. Their main function is to change a word to a different part of speech—that is, to make the word serve a different function in the sentence. For example, in the sentence "The man wanted to go into politics," the base word *politics* is used as a noun. To use it as an adjective, you would have to say "The man had political ambitions," and to use it as an adverb, "The man was politically inclined." We formed the adjective *political* from the noun by adding the suffix *-al;* we made the adverb by adding *-ly*.

Types of Suffixes

Suffixes That Form Nouns

Base	Suffix	Noun
modify, complicate, exclude	tion, ion, sion	modification, complication, exclusion
bond	age	bondage
rely, coincide	ance, ence	reliance, coincidence
buoyant	cy	buoyancy
utilitarian	ism	utilitarianism
induce	ment	inducement
fort	tude	fortitude
disclose	ure	disclosure
wary	ness	wariness
technical	ity	technicality

The following suffixes form nouns and also change the meaning:

Base	Suffix	Meaning	Noun
logic	ian		logician
agitate, weave, school	or, er, ar	one who, something that	agitator, weaver, scholar
extreme	ist		extremist
psyche	ology	study of	psychology

Suffixes That Form Adjectives

Base	Suffix	Meaning	Adjective
lament, reduce	able, ible	able to be, worthy of being	lamentable, reducible
demon	ic		demonic
silk	en		silken
west	ern		western
child	ish	like, relating to	childish
sketch, like	y, ly		sketchy, likely
Mexico	an		Mexican
desire, labor, advantage	ous, ious, eous	full of, like	desirous, laborious, advantageous
ground	less	without	groundless

Suffixes That Form Nouns or Adjectives

Base	Suffix	Meaning	Noun and Adjective
cup, spite	ful	fullness; full of	cupful (noun) spiteful (adj.)
command, consist	ant, ent	a person or thing that; that has, shows, or does	commandant (noun) consistent (adj.)
station, moment, congratulate	ery, ary, ory	a person or thing connected with; a place for; relating to, connected with	stationery (noun) momentary (adj.) congratulatory (adj.)
persuade, execute, detect	ive	relatedness; like or	persuasive (adj.) executive (noun or adj.) detective (noun)
method, crime, purpose	al, ial	relating to	methodical (adj.) criminal (noun or adj.) proposal (noun)

Suffixes That Form Verbs

Base	Suffix		Verb
example	ify		exemplify
ideal, critic	ize		idealize, criticize
haste	en		hasten
radium	ate		radiate

One Suffix That Forms Adverbs

Base	Suffix		Adverb
staunch	ly		staunchly

Spelling Changes

You probably noticed in the preceding examples that there often are spelling changes when suffixes are added to base words. Although all spelling principles in English have exceptions, here are a few of the most useful. For practice, fill in the blanks following each rule, and check your answers in the back of the book.

1. If a single final consonant in a base has a single vowel before it and if that vowel-consonant combination is in a single syllable or stressed syllable, double the consonant before a suffix beginning with a vowel.

single vowel   single final consonant

re + BEL + ious = rebeLLious

stressed syllable   vowel

    In filling in the following blanks, double the final consonant only if the word meets all four criteria:

(1)   The base has a *single* consonant at the end.
(2)   There is a *single* vowel before the final consonant.
(3)   The vowel-consonant combination occurs in the final *stressed* syllable.
(4)   The suffix begins with a *vowel*.

a.   conform + ity _____

b.   repel + ent _____

c.   sum + ary _____

d.   allot + ment _____

e.   transfer + al _____

2. If a base ends in a silent *e*, drop the *e* before adding a suffix that begins with a vowel.

silent *e* vowel

approximate + ion = approximation

a.   commune + ion _____

b.   oblique + ly _____

c.   extreme + ity _____

d.   survive + al _____

e.   deplete + ion _____

3. When the last two letters of a base are a consonant and a *y*, change the *y* to *i* before adding a suffix.

$$\text{consonant} + y$$
$$\downarrow \quad \swarrow$$
$$\text{controversy} + \text{al} = \text{controversial}$$

a. library + an _____

b. survey + or _____

c. defy + ance _____

d. deploy + ment _____

e. wary + ly _____

4. *able—ible*
When a base is a complete word, the suffix *-able* is usually added. When the base is part of a word, *-ible* is usually added. If the word ends in a silent *e*, drop the *e* and add *-able*.

a. lament _____

b. feas _____

c. aud _____

d. excuse _____

e. elig _____

5. *ary—ery; ant—ent; ance—ence*
There is no clear-cut rule for remembering which of these suffixes to use. You will need to memorize each case individually using mnemonic devices. For example: you might think that *intelligent* men are intelli-*gents*, and *tolerant* people could ignore small ants but would have problems ignoring *taller ants*. Make up a mnemonic device for remembering the spelling of each of the following words.

a. excellence _____

b. adamant _____

c. cemetery _____

d. dictionary _____

e. confident _____

EXERCISE 1: BASE WORDS

Below are ten words from earlier chapters in this book. For each word, write the base word that remains after the suffix is removed. Some of the words have spelling changes. If you need help, use your dictionary. Check your answers in the back of the book.

1. conscientious _____

2. ethical _____

3. stealthy _____

4. taciturn _____

5. enigmatic _____

6. extremity _____

7. lamentation _____

8. patronize _____

9. requisite _____

10. negative _____

REVIEW WORDS

Below are the Review Words for this chapter. We will use these words to practice the skills taught in this chapter.

acknowledgment (ak naľij mənt, ək-) *n.*   1. an admission or confession   2. something given in acknowledging, as an expression of thanks   3. recognition of the authority or claims of

differentiate (dif´ər en´shē āt´) *v.*   1. to become or make unlike; to develop new characteristics or differences   2. to perceive or express the difference in; distinguish between

distinctive (di stiŋk´tiv) *adj.*   making distinct; distinguishing from others; characteristic

idealize (ī dē´əl īz´) *v.*   to make ideal, think of or represent as ideal; regard or show as perfect or more nearly perfect than is true

motivate (mōt´ə vāt´) *v.*   to provide with, or effect a cause of action, incentive, or goal; incite or impel

populous (păp´yoo ləs, -yə-) *adj.*   full of people; crowded or thickly populated

remedial (ri mē´dē əl) *adj.*   1. providing, or intended to provide, a remedy   2. *Educ.* designating or of any special course of study for helping students overcome deficiencies in specific skills, abilities, or knowledge [*remedial* reading]

remotely (ri mōt´lē) *adv.*   distantly or from afar in terms of space, time, connection, relation, or relevance

resourceful (ri sôrs´fəl, -zôrs´-) *adj.*   full of resource; able to deal promptly and effectively with problems, difficulties, etc.

solidify (sə lid´ə fī´) *v.*   to make or become solid, hard, firm, compact, united, etc.

fat, āpe, cär; ten, ēven; is, bīte; gō, hôrn, tool, look; oil, out; up, fur; get; joy; yet; chin; she; thin, *th*en; zh, leisure; ŋ, ring; ə for *a* in *ago*, *e* in *agent*, *i* in *sanity*, *o* in *comply*, *u* in *focus*; ' as in *able* (ā´b'l)

EXERCISE 2: REVIEW WORDS IN CONTEXT

Fill in each blank with the word that correctly completes the sentence. Check your answers in the back of the book.

acknowledgment   distinctive   motivate   remedial   resourceful
differentiate   idealize   populous   remotely   solidify

1. _____ courses are offered in basic subjects like reading, writing, and math.

2. Most people are not even _____ interested in learning to play the harpsichord.

3. Zebras have a very _____ coloration.

4. Money will _____ people to do things they would not ordinarily do.

5. Water will _____ at a lower temperature if it contains salt.

6. Children _____ their mothers and fathers until they are old enough to see parental flaws.

7. As cities become more _____, crime tends to increase.

8. She wrote an _____ in the front of her book, thanking those who helped her write it.

9. In life or death matters, people can become very _____.

10. Wine experts can _____ between different vintages from the same vineyard by taste and smell.

EXERCISE 3: REVIEW WORDS—PARTS OF SPEECH

Using your knowledge of suffixes, change each Review Word to the part of speech given below the blank. Check your answers in the back of the book.

1. populous   _____
                                        verb

2. differentiate   _____
                                      adjective

3. remedial   _____
                                        noun

4. idealize   _____
                                       adverb

5. remotely   _____
                                      adjective

6. acknowledgment   _____
                                        verb

7. resourceful   _____
                                        noun

8. distinctive   _____
                                       adverb

9. solidify   _____
                                      adjective

10. motivate   _____
                                        noun

EXERCISE 4: ADDING SUFFIXES

Add the suffix to the base word. Use your spelling rules as guides. Check your answers in the back of the book.

1. stealthy + ness   _____
2. obtuse + ly   _____
3. abhor + ent   _____
4. chafe + ing   _____
5. admire + able   _____
6. conform + ist   _____
7. zeal + ous   _____
8. admit + ance   _____
9. equivocal + ly   _____
10. adverse + ary   _____

Some of the words below are spelled incorrectly. Using your spelling rules as guides, find the incorrectly spelled words and write them correctly in the blanks. Check your answers in the back of the book.

1. occurrence _____
2. fashionible _____
3. useable _____
4. replacment _____
5. prevailling _____

6. varyance _____
7. completness _____
8. individualism _____
9. finallize _____
10. closeness _____

alarmist (ə lärm′ist) *n.*   1. one who spreads alarming rumors   2. one who anticipates the worst

categorical (kat′ə gôr′i kəl) *adj.*   1. positive; unconditional; without any doubt   2. in a specific scheme of classification

compensatory (kəm′pen′sə tôr′ē) *adj.*   1. making up for; counterbalancing   2. making amends (for)

compliant (kəm plī′ənt) *adj.*   tending to give in to others; yielding

exhaustive (eg zôs′tiv, ig-) *adj.*   leaving nothing out; thorough

fatalism (fāt′′l iz′əm) *n.*   the belief that all events are determined by one's destiny and are therefore inevitable

fixation (fiks ā′shən) *n.*   an obsession; a strong unhealthy feeling (about) or love (for)

holistic (hō lis′tik) *adj.*   total; complete

lineage (lin′ē ij) *n.*   1. descent from an ancestor   2. ancestry; family

rationalize (rash′ən əl īz′) *v.*   1. to devise a reasonable-sounding explanation for one's acts or beliefs (usually in self-deception)   2. to make or be reasonable

fat, āpe, cär; ten, ēven; is, bīte; gō, hôrn, tōōl, look; oil, out; up, fʉr; get; joy; yet; chin; she; thin, *th*en; zh, leisure; ŋ, ring; ə for *a* in *ago, e* in *agent, i* in *sanity, o* in *comply, u* in *focus;* ′ as in *able* (ā′b'l)

Fill in each blank with the word that best completes the sentence. Check your answers in the back of the book.

alarmist	compensatory	exhaustive	fixation	lineage
categorical	compliant	fatalism	holistic	rationalize

1. The belief of astrologers that the stars affect what happens to us is a type of _____.

2. After the environmental candidate's passionate speech about the seriousness of losing the rain forests, his opponent labeled him an _____.

3. Rewards and punishments are used at times by all parents to make their children more _____.

4. Some men have such a _____ on women's legs that they really do not care what a woman's face looks like or what her mind contains.

5. After World War I, Germany had to give such enormous _____ payments to the Allies that its economy was ruined; this became one cause of World War II.

6. If we _____ our mistakes rather than admitting them, we will not be able to learn anything from them.

7. _____ medicine believes that medical specialists, who focus on specific organs, may be missing the larger picture.

8. According to Scottish tradition, a kilt can be worn only by a man who can trace his _____ from a specific clan.

9. Sherlock Holmes solved his cases as a result of careful and often _____ attention to detail.

10. There are three _____ divisions for all natural objects: animal, vegetable, and mineral.

enormity (i nôr′mə tē, ē-) *n.*   extremely large size or extent; hugeness; vastness

enviable (en′vē ə bəl) *adj.*   good enough to be envied or desired

erroneous (ər ō′nē əs, e rō′-, i-) *adj.*   containing an error; mistaken; wrong

hindrance (hin′drəns) *n.*   a person or thing that stops; an obstacle

inflammatory (in flam′ə tôr′ē) *adj.*   arousing excitement, anger, etc. [an *inflammatory* speech]

sensuous (sen′shoo əs) *adj.*   1. of, derived from, or perceived by the senses [soft, *sensuous* music]   2. enjoying sensation

soundness (sound′nes) *n.*   1. freedom from defect, damage, or decay   2. stability   3. valid reasoning

technicality (tek′ni kal′ə tē) *n.*   a minute point, detail, etc., brought to bear on a main issue [convicted on a *technicality*]

therapeutic (ther′ə pyoot′ik) *adj.*   serving to cure or heal or to preserve health [*therapeutic* abortion]

transitory (tran′sə tôr′ē, -zə-) *adj.*   not enduring; temporary; fleeting

fat, āpe, cär; ten, ēven; is, bīte; gō, hôrn, tool, look; oil, out; up, fʉr; get; joy; yet; chin; she; thin, *th*en; zh, leisure; ŋ, ring; ə for *a* in *ago*, *e* in *agent*, *i* in *sanity*, *o* in *comply*, *u* in *focus;* ′ as in *able* (ā′b′l)

Circle the letter before the word or phrase that best defines the italicized word in
each sentence. Check your answers in the back of the book.

1. The *enormity* of the damage done by an overly critical parent to a child's self-esteem has
    been described by many psychologists.

    a. dullness   b. expense   c. hugeness   d. unimportance

2. People who wish to live long lives find the 200-year span of some fish in
    the sturgeon family *enviable*.

    STURGEON
    (to 7 ft. long)

    a. frightening   b. terrible   c. satisfying   d. desirable

3. It is *erroneous* to believe that we are electing our president when we vote every four years;
    we are really electing representatives to the Electoral College, who meet in December to
    elect the leader of our country.

    a. correct   b. wrong   c. stupid   d. common

4. Because men of the Middle Ages found buttons on the right side *a hindrance* to drawing
    their swords in battle, they moved their coat buttons to the left side.

    a. a help   b. an obstacle   c. a shield   d. a substitute

5. When you argue with your husband or wife, you should avoid *inflammatory* remarks that
    just make the other person angry and don't solve the problem.

    a. arousing   b. wonderful   c. complimentary   d. boring

6. Most Romans found eating sweet onions for dessert a *sensuous* experience and looked
    forward to doing so.

    a. pleasing to the mind   b. smelly   c. pleasing to the senses   d. humorous

7. If the foundations of your house are attacked by termites or dry rot, the *soundness* of the
    house may eventually be affected.

    a. stability   b. weakness   c. flexibility   d. life

8. Because the man had begun running before the signal to start the race, he was
    disqualified on a *technicality*, even though he came in first.

    a. correction   b. mistake   c. detail   d. exception

9. Once considered by doctors to be an old wives' tale, the *therapeutic* effects of hot chicken
    soup on people with colds have been proven scientifically.

    a. deadly   b. nonexistent   c. healing   d. lasting

10. The fact that 99.9 percent of all animal species disappeared from the earth before the
    coming of humans indicates that life forms are *transitory*.

    a. present   b. dying   c. unchanging   d. temporary

EXERCISE 8: TRUE-FALSE

Write T or F in the blank. Check your answers in the back of the book.

_____ 1. People generally refuse to accept compensatory payments after an accident at work.

_____ 2. People who believe in fatalism believe they can determine their own futures.

_____ 3. An alarmist is usually worried about something.

_____ 4. Most of us rationalize our actions at some time in our lives.

_____ 5. People in prison are in an enviable situation.

EXERCISE 9: ANALOGIES

In previous analogy exercises you looked for pairs of words that were synonyms or antonyms. This exercise contains a new type of analogy. The relationship of the pairs of words is *classification:example*. That is, the second word of each pair is an example of the first:

car : Ford :: vegetable : lettuce

Determine which of the three types of analogies is used in each group below, and then fill in the blank to make the second pair agree with the first. Check your answers in the back of the book.

1. solidify : liquefy :: fixation : _____

    a. obsession b. fondness c. sex
    d. dislike

2. competent : unqualified :: enormity : _____

    a. normalness b. closeness c. smallness
    d. largeness

3. communicable disease : measles :: sensuous experience : _____

    a. problem b. tasting wine c. hatred
    d. taking a test

4. type of correspondence : letters :: therapeutic aid : _____

    a. muscles b. injuries c. bandages
    d. unemployment insurance

5. scholarly : studious :: lineage : _____

    a. race b. friends c. ancestry
    d. grandmother

EXERCISE 10: WORD CONTRASTS

In each group below circle the word that does not mean what the others mean.
Check your answers in the back of the book.

1. compliant   conforming   rebelling   assenting
2. hindrance   obstruction   stoppage   help
3. transitory   permanent   changeless   constant
4. soundness   sturdiness   durability   instability
5. inflammatory   soothing   angering   arousing

EXERCISE 11: MATCHING MEANINGS

Write the letter of the word that means the opposite of the word in the first column.
Check your answers in the back of the book.

_____ 1. technicality   a. flawless

_____ 2. exhaustive   b. conditional

_____ 3. holistic   c. superficial

_____ 4. erroneous   d. generality

_____ 5. categorical   e. specialized

EXERCISE 12: SENTENCE COMPLETION

Complete each sentence in your own words. Sample answers are provided in the
back of the book.

1. You should not act like an *alarmist* when your children have minor accidents, because _____
   _____.

2. You may *categorically* deny you caused an accident; however, _____
   _____.

3. A *compensatory* payment is needed when _____
   _____.

4. One should always be *compliant* with a police officer because _____
   _____.

5. Assessing the *enormity* of a problem is important before _____
   _____.

6. Beauty is an *enviable* attribute; nevertheless, _____
_____ .

7. *Erroneous* information can lead to _____
_____ .

8. Scientists are doing *exhaustive* research to find a cure for AIDS because _____
_____ .

9. Believers in *fatalism* think that _____
_____ .

10. If you have a food *fixation,* _____
_____ .

11. Having young children wash dishes is often more of a *hindrance* than a help since _____
_____ .

12. *Holistic* doctors treat the whole body because _____
_____ .

13. It is unwise to make an *inflammatory* remark to a professor during class because _____
_____ .

14. Proof of a show dog's *lineage* is essential in order to _____
_____ .

15. A person can *rationalize* cheating on his or her income tax forms, but _____
_____ .

16. An example of a *sensuous* experience would be _____
_____ .

17. The *soundness* of your school's English program depends on many things, including _____
_____ .

18. Courts sometimes make decisions based on a *technicality* of the law, and so _____
_____ .

19. Hot water can have a *therapeutic* effect on swollen joints; thus, _____
_____ .

20. A *transitory* condition changes quickly whereas _____
_____ .

ADVANCED WORDS

abysmal (ə biz′məl) *adj.*   1. of or like a bottomless gulf; not measurable   2. very bad [*abysmal* poverty]

codify (käd′ə fī, kō′də fī) *v.*   to arrange (laws, etc.) systematically

enigmatic (en′ig mat′ik) *adj.*   mysterious; puzzling; baffling

fabricated (fab′ri kāt′id) *adj.*   1. made, constructed, etc.; manufactured   2. made up (a story, lie, etc.); invented

idolatry (ī däl′ə trē) *n.*   worship of idols; excessive devotion to or reverence for some person or thing

monastic (mō nas′tik, mə-) *adj.*   of or characteristic of monks or nuns

provident (präv′ə dənt) *adj.*   1. providing for future needs or events; exercising or characterized by foresight   2. prudent

severance (sev′ər əns, sev′rəns) *n.*   a separation, division, or breaking off

solicitous (sə lis′ə təs) *adj.*   1. showing care or concern [*solicitous* for her welfare]   2. desirous; eager [*solicitous* to make friends]

strictures (strik′chərs) *n.*   1. adverse criticisms   2. limiting or restricting conditions

fat, āpe, cär; ten, ēven; is, bīte; gō, hôrn, tōol, look; oil, out; up, fur; get; joy; yet; chin; she; thin, *th*en; zh, leisure; ŋ, ring; ə for *a* in *ago, e* in *agent, i* in *sanity, o* in *comply, u* in *focus;* ′ as in *able* (ā′b'l)

Fill in each blank with the word that correctly completes the sentence. Check your answers in the back of the book.

abysmal	enigmatic	idolatry	provident	solicitous
codify	fabricated	monastic	severance	strictures

1. Squirrels demonstrate _____ behavior when they store nuts for the winter.

2. The results of the reading test were _____; 80% of the class performed below grade level.

3. Conservative politicians do not appear very _____ about the welfare of the homeless.

4. The Dewey decimal system in one of the systems used to _____ books in libraries.

5. A hundred years ago female teachers in the United States were expected to lead _____ lives, which included remaining unmarried.

6. The _____ expression on the Mona Lisa has fascinated viewers since the time of Leonardo da Vinci.

7. In 1910 four Englishman _____ a wild story about being Abyssinian princes; they were so convincing that the most important battleship in the British navy gave them a royal greeting.

8. Within the _____ of corporate life, some find it difficult to express their creativity.

9. Some devoted fans of Elvis Presley have reached the stage of _____.

10. A _____ of diplomatic relations between the two countries followed the terrorist attack.

EXERCISE 14: CROSSWORD PUZZLE

Fill in the puzzle using a pencil. The clues with asterisks (*) refer to New Words
from previous chapters. Check your answers in the back of the book.

Across

- *1. Faces
- 9. Indefinite article
- 10. Abbr. for *orange juice*
- 11. First person pl. pronoun
- *12. To empty
- *14. Indirect
- 15. A brand of cola
- 16. Abbr. for *feet*
- *17. Mourn
- 18. To hang in the air
- 21. Ant. of *yes*
- 22. Tool for chopping
- *23. Great need or danger
- 24. Metal container
- 25. Sound of laughter
- 26. Abbr. for *centimeter*
- *29. To succeed
- 32. Chemical symbol for *helium*
- 33. Female pronoun
- 35. Chemical symbol for *radium*
- 36. Abbr. for *Connecticut*
- 37. To pass away
- *38. To sponsor
- *41. Main point
- 42. Ant. of *out*
- 43. Uncovers
- *44. Excitement
- 45. A trick

Down

- *1. Gentleman
- 2. Yoko
- 3. To indicate agreement with the head
- 4. Abbr. for *Tijuana*
- 5. To catch or arrest
- 6. Sound made by a horse
- *7. Purposely unclear
- 8. Root vegetable
- 13. Person confined in an institution
- 14. Prefix meaning *eight*
- 15. Abbr. for *registered nurse*
- *16. The right to vote
- 19. Preposition
- 20. Mickey, Minnie, and Mighty
- 25. To strike
- 27. Is introduced to
- *28. To irritate
- *29. Inclined
- 30. Past tense of *run*
- 31. Lowest or highest card
- 33. Abbr. for *Spain*
- 34. French for *and*
- *37. Very serious
- 39. Edge of a glass
- 40. Suffix meaning *one who,* as in scient_____
- 41. Vapor
- 43. Abbr. for *bushel*

EXERCISE 15: OWN WORDS

From your outside reading choose ten words you would like to learn that contain
suffixes studied in this chapter. Write the word, the part of speech, the base from
which the word came, and a brief definition.

Word	Part of Speech	Base	Definition

1. _____
2. _____
3. _____
4. _____
5. _____
6. _____
7. _____
8. _____
9. _____
10. _____

chapter 6

PREFIXES

© 1974 "Peanuts" is reprinted by permission of UFS, Inc.

Whereas a suffix is added to the end of a word or word base and has the primary function of changing its part of speech, a prefix goes in front of the base and changes its meaning. For example, the root *cede* (also spelled *ceed* and *cess*) means "to go" or "to yield." In the list below we have added prefixes to this root. Notice how the meanings change.

Prefix	Meaning	Word	Definition
ac	to	accede	yield to
con	with, together	concede	yield (go with)
ex	out, beyond	exceed	go beyond
inter	between	intercede	go between
pre	before	precede	go before
pro	forward	proceed	go forward
re	back	recede	go back
suc	under	successive	following (going under)

Though you may not realize it, breaking words into recognizable parts is something you already know how to do quite well. Most of us do this automatically whenever we encounter a new word. The more word parts you know, the faster your vocabulary will develop. This is why people who know one of the foreign languages based on Latin (Spanish, French, Italian, Portuguese, and Romanian) have an advantage on vocabulary tests over those who do not. More than half of our English words are derived either directly from Latin or from Latin through Old French. In some cases, the English word conveys the individual meanings of its parts, as in the word *intercede*, which means "go between." In other cases, the meaning of the word has changed over time so that the meanings of the separate parts no longer add up to the meaning of the whole, although they do provide a clue, as in *successive*.

Some prefixes have more than one meaning. For example, *in* sometimes means "not," as in *inaccurate*, and sometimes means "very" (*invaluable* means very valuable). When you are unsure which meaning applies, you can use the context to figure it out or look up the derivation in the dictionary.

Spelling Variations

Word parts have also changed in terms of spelling over the past 2,000 years. For example, the prefix *sub* means "under." However, it changes to *suc* before *c* (succeed), *suf* before *f* (suffer), *sup* before *p* (suppose), and *sus* before *c, p,* or *t* (suspect). The main reason for these changes is that it's difficult for English speakers to pronounce words such as *subcede* and *subfer*. Several other prefixes follow the same principle of changed spelling to reflect changes in pronunciation. Usually the last letter of the prefix changes to match the first letter of the base. The prefix *ad,* meaning "to," changes to *ac* before *c* (accept), *af* before *f* (affect), *ag* before *g* (aggravate), *an* before *n* (annex), *ap* before *p* (appear), *ar* before *r* (arrive), *as* before *s* (assembly), *at* before *t* (attend), and *a* before *sc, sp,* and *st* (aspect).

Types of Prefixes

Prefixes can be grouped by meaning. Learning them in groups helps you remember them.

Negative Prefixes

The following prefixes have negative meanings.

Prefix	Meaning	Examples
ant, anti	against	antonym, antisocial
contra, contro, con	against	contradict, controversial, contrast
ob, oc (before c)	against	obstacle, occasion
of (before f)		offend
op (before p)		opponent
o (before m)		omission
dis, dif (before f)	not, apart	discontinue, differentiate
in, im (before p, b, m)	not	interminable, immobile
il (before l)		illogical
ir (before r)		irresponsible
mal	bad, wrong, ill	malicious, malfunction
non, n	not	nonprofit, neither
un	not, reverse of an action	unbiased, undo
mis	wrong	mislead, mispronounce

Placement Prefixes

Another group of prefixes identifies the placement or direction of things: whether they are down, behind, in front, between, and so on.

Prefix	Meaning	Examples
ab, a	away, down, from	absence, amoral
de	away, down, from	deviate, demerit
ad, ac (before c or q)	to	administer, accumulate
af (before f)		affection
ag (before g)		aggrandize
an (before n)		annex
ap (before p)		appeal
ar (before r)		arrange
as (before s)		assemble
at (before t)		attach
a (before sc, sp, st)		ascend, aspect, astound
con, com (before b, p, m)	with, together	concurrent, commune
co (before a vowel)		cooperative
col (before l)		collateral
cor (before r)		correspondence

ex, extra	out, former, beyond	expel, ex-wife, extraordinary
e (before b, d, g, l, m, n, r, v)		emit
ec (before c or s)		eccentric, ecstasy
ef (before f)		effective
in, en	into, very, inside	ingenious, encompass
em, im (before b, p, m)		embrace, implicit
intro, intra	in, within	introduce, intramural
inter	between	interim, intercept
para	alongside, beyond	paragraph, paraphrase
per	through, by, thorough	per annum, perspective
pro, pur	forward, before, for	prospect, pursuit
re, retro	back	reverse, retroactive
sub, suc (before c)	under, below	subversive, succumb
suf (before f)		suffice
sup (before p)		support
sus (before c, p, t)		sustain
super, sur	above, beyond	superlative, surpass
trans	across	transact

Time Prefixes

Another group of prefixes specifies the location of things in time: whether they are before, after, and so on.

Prefix	Meaning	Examples
post	after	posterior, posterity
pre	before	premonition, preliminary
re	again	reconcile, reimburse

Miscellaneous

Prefix	Meaning	Examples
bene	good	benediction, benefactor
di	two, twice, double	dilemma, diverse
equi	equal	equivocal, equitable

EXERCISE 1: PREFIX FILL-IN

To check your understanding of the 29 common prefixes discussed in this chapter, complete the following exercise by providing your own example (one not given in the preceding list) for each prefix. Try to select a word that will help you remember what the prefix means. For example, a good mnemonic for *mal* might be *malpractice* because it means *bad* practice. Check in a dictionary that provides word origins to be sure your word is based on the right prefix.

Prefix	Meaning	Example
a, ab	away, from, down	_____
ad, ac, af, ag, an, ap, ar, as, at, a	to	_____
ant, anti	against	_____
bene	good	_____
con, com, co, col, cor	with, together	_____
contra, contro, con	against	_____
de	from, away, down	_____
di	two, twice, double	_____
dis, dif	apart, not	_____
equi	equal	_____
ex, extra, e, ec, ef	out, former, beyond	_____
in, en, em, im, intra, intro	into, very	_____
il, im, il, ir	not	_____
inter	between	_____
mal	bad, wrong, ill	_____
mis	wrong	_____
n, non	not	_____
ob, oc, of, op, o	against	_____
para	alongside, beyond	_____
per	through, by, thorough	_____
post	after	_____
pre	before	_____
pro, pur	before, forward, for	_____
re	again	_____
re, retro	back	_____
sub, suc, suf, sup, sus	under, below	_____
super, sur	above, beyond	_____
trans	across	_____
un	not, reverse of an action	_____

EXERCISE 2: REVIEW WORDS—PREFIXES

Before you look at the definitions for the Review Words on the next page, use the prefixes in this chapter to fill in the blanks below. Check your answers on the next page.

Review Word	**Definition**
1. _____compass	to go *into* (contain)
2. _____im	*between* times (meanwhile)
3. _____annum	*by* year (annual)
4. _____lative	*above* all others (supreme)
5. _____erior	*after* (behind, rear)
6. _____monition	*fore*warning
7. _____concile	get *back* together
8. _____phrase	*beyond* what is said (reword)
9. _____icious	having *bad* intentions
10. _____diction	*good* words (blessing)

REVIEW WORDS

Below are the Review Words for this chapter. We will use these words to practice the skills taught in this chapter.

benediction (ben′ə dik′shən) *n.* a blessing

encompass (en kum′pəs) *v.* 1. to shut in all around; surround; encircle 2. to contain; include

interim (in′tər im) *n.* the period of time between; meantime

malicious (mə lish′əs) *adj.* having, showing, or caused by malice; spiteful; intentionally mischievous or harmful

paraphrase (par′ə frāz′) *n.* a rewording of the meaning expressed in something spoken or written —*v.* to reword

per annum (pər an′əm) *adj.* by the year; annually

posterior (päs tir′ē ər) *adj.* 1. later; following after; subsequent 2. at or toward the rear; behind —*n.* the buttocks

premonition (prem′ə nish′ən, prē-) *n.* a feeling that something, esp. something bad, will happen; foreboding

reconcile (rek′ən sīl′) *v.* 1. to make friendly again or win over to a friendly attitude 2. to settle (a quarrel or dispute) or to agree 3. to make (arguments, ideas, texts, accounts, etc.) consistent, compatible, etc.; bring into harmony 4. to make content, submissive, or acquiescent (to) [to become *reconciled* to one's lot]

superlative (sə pur′lə tiv; *also* soo-, sōō-) *adj.* 1. superior to or excelling all other or others; of the highest kind, quality, degree, etc.; supreme 2. excessive or exaggerated 3. *Gram.* designating or of the extreme degree of comparison of adjectives and adverbs; expressing the greatest degree of the quality or attribute expressed by the positive degree; usually indicated by the suffix -*est* (*hardest*) or by the use of *most* with the positive form (*most beautiful*) —*n.* 1. the highest or utmost degree; acme; height; peak 2. something superlative 3. *Gram.* (a) the superlative degree (b) a word or form in this degree

fat, āpe, cär; ten, ēven; is, bīte; gō, hôrn, tōol, look; oil, out; up, fur; get; joy; yet; chin; she; thin, *th*en; zh, leisure; ŋ, ring; ə for *a* in *ago, e* in *agent, i* in *sanity, o* in *comply, u* in *focus;* ' as in *able* (ā′b'l)

Fill in each blank with the word that correctly completes the sentence. Check your answers in the back of the book.

benediction	interim	paraphrase	posterior	reconcile
encompass	malicious	per annum	premonition	superlative

1. Opposing candidates often try to spread _____ rumors about each other.

2. The word *humanities* is used to _____ all the branches of learning concerned with human thought and relations, as distinguished from the sciences; especially literature, philosophy, and history.

3. On the day he was assassinated, Caesar's wife begged him not to go to the Senate because of a _____ she had.

4. Because of inflation, the _____ income of the average worker can increase while his or her standard of living decreases.

5. The separated couple decided to _____ instead of divorce because they could not afford to support two separate households.

6. You must cite your sources when you _____ another person as well as when you quote him or her.

7. Many people want religious weddings because they believe that the _____ of the clergy will increase their chances of having a successful marriage.

8. A "couch potato" sits on his or her _____ for hours every day.

9. The word *baddest* has been used in slang as a _____, meaning "best."

10. I plan to become a registered nurse, but in the _____ I'm gaining experience by working as a nurse's aide.

adhere (ad hir′) *v.*   1. to stick fast; stay attached   2. to give allegiance or support (*to*)

contraband (kän′trə band′) *n.*   smuggled goods —*adj.*   illegal to import or export

digress (dī gress′, di-) *v.*   to turn aside, esp. from the main subject, in speaking or writing

discrepancy (di skrep′ən sē) *n.*   disagreement; inconsistency

intrinsic (in trin′sik, -zik) *adj.*   belonging to the real nature of a thing; not dependent on external circumstances; essential

misgiving (mis giv′iŋ) *n.*   a disturbed feeling of fear, doubt, etc.

per se (pur sā, sē′) *adj.*   by (or in) itself; intrinsically

predecessor (pred′ə ses′ər) *n.*   a person preceding or coming before another, as in office

prolific (prō lif′ik, prə-) *adj.*   1. producing many young or much fruit   2. creating many products of the mind

subservient (səb sur′vē ənt) *adj.*   1. that is of service, esp. in a subordinate capacity   2. submissive; servile

fat, āpe, cär; ten, ēven; is, bīte; gō, hôrn, tōol, look; oil, out; up, fur; get; joy; yet; chin; she; thin, *th*en; zh, leisure; ŋ, ring; ə for *a* in *ago, e* in *agent, i* in *sanity, o* in *comply, u* in *focus;* ′ as in *able* (ā′b'l)

EXERCISE 4: FILL-IN

Fill in each blank with the word that best completes the sentence. Check your answers in the back of the book.

adhere   digress   intrinsic   per se   prolific
contraband   discrepancy   misgivings   predecessor   subservient

1. In an "aside" an actor will _____ from the action of the play and speak directly to the audience.

2. People in some "service" jobs, such as waitresses, gardeners, hairdressers, and chauffeurs, are expected to be more _____ than those in jobs such as physicians and attorneys.

3. The amount of money you earn _____ is not the only determinant of your lifestyle; expenses are equally important.

4. U.S. silver coins minted before 1965 contain 90 percent silver; because of inflation their _____ value currently varies between 10 and 40 times their face value.

5. Most animals would have _____ about jumping into a crocodile's mouth, but the crocodile never bites the little Egyptian plover; it allows the bird to pick its teeth clean of uneaten food after each meal.

6. Lope de Vega, born in 1562, was extremely _____: the great Spanish dramatist wrote about 1500 plays, as well as many poems and prose works.

7. Because survivors of the Donner party, trapped in the Sierra Nevada in 1846 and driven to cannibalism, did not _____ to the same story about what happened to the missing members, the facts were discovered.

8. Gerald Ford was the first U.S. president to gain office because of the resignation of his _____, Richard Nixon.

9. U.S. Customs officials use dogs in the baggage terminals of international airports, to sniff for drugs and other _____.

10. Many gangsters, such as Al Capone, were never convicted of any major crimes, but because of the _____ between the amount of money their crimes earned them and the amount they reported to the Internal Revenue Service, they were finally jailed for income tax evasion.

cohesion (kō hē′zhən) *n.*   tendency to stick together

equilibrium (ē′kwi lib′rē əm) *n.*   a state of balance between opposing forces

extrinsic (eks trin′sik, -zik) *adj.*   not essential; not intrinsic; external

inequity (in ek′wi tē) *n.*   inequality; injustice

intersperse (in′tər spʉrs′) *v.*   1. to put here and there; scatter   2. to vary with things scattered here and there

malign (mə līn′) *v.*   to speak evil of; slander —*adj.*   1. malicious   2. evil   3. very harmful

obnoxious (əb näk′shəs, äb-) *adj.*   very unpleasant; offensive

retaliate (ri tal′ē āt′) *v.*   to return like for like, esp. injury for injury

transpire (tran spīr′) *v.*   1. to give off vapor, moisture, etc., as through pores   2. to become known   3. to take place

uninhibited (un′in hib′it id) *adj.*   free to express oneself; not checked or repressed

fat, āpe, cär; ten, ēven; is, bīte; gō, hôrn, to͞ol, look; oil, out; up, fʉr; get; joy; yet; chin; she; thin, *then*; zh, leisure; ŋ, ring; ə for *a* in *ago, e* in *agent, i* in *sanity, o* in *comply, u* in *focus;* ′ as in *able* (ā′b'l)

Circle the letter before the word or phrase that best defines the italicized word in
each sentence. Check your answers in the back of the book.

1. The Medici family was *cohesive* enough to dominate Florence from the 15th century until
   1737, producing three popes, two queens of France, and several cardinals of the Roman
   Catholic Church, even though it had numerous illegitimate offspring and a tendency of
   some of its members to assassinate other members.

   a. united   b. nice   c. hostile   d. honest

2. The symbol of justice is old-fashioned scales in states of *equilibrium.*

   a. trade   b. balance   c. power   d. harm

3. Some psychologists say that the use of *extrinsic* rewards such as prizes and treats with
   schoolchildren undermines their love of learning for its own sake.

   a. internal   b. external   c. expensive   d. frequent

4. The *inequity* between the sizes of Earth and Saturn is vividly understood when you realize
   that more than 600 Earths would fit inside Saturn.

   a. agreement   b. balance   c. unfairness   d. inequality

5. She likes to *intersperse* jokes throughout her lectures, to break up the monotony.

   a. laugh at   b. scatter   c. hide   d. enjoy

6. It is common for political candidates to *malign* their opponents instead of discussing the
   real issues.

   a. praise   b. distrust   c. slander   d. bribe

7. Poor table manners, such as chewing with your mouth open, can make you *obnoxious* to
   others.

   a. sad   b. awful   c. fun   d. silly

8. King Henry VIII of England *retaliated against* the pope's refusal to grant him a divorce
   from the first of his six wives by breaking with Rome and founding the Church of
   England.

   a. obeyed   b. argued with   c. gave in to   d. got even with

9. Animals perspire; plants *transpire.*

   a. give off vapor   b. wilt   c. turn brown   d. die

10. Isadora Duncan, pioneer American modern dancer, dazzled European audiences with her
    uninhibited dances based on Greek classical art, which she performed barefoot wearing an
    adaptation of the Greek tunic and many colorful scarves.

    a. expressive   b. tap   c. formal   d. Spanish

EXERCISE 6: TRUE-FALSE

Write T or F in the blank. Check your answers in the back of the book.

_____ 1. Goods imported without a duty are contraband.

_____ 2. Absent-minded professors never digress when they lecture.

_____ 3. At a certain age everyone finds gray hairs interspersed with those of the original color.

_____ 4. Food per se cannot guarantee good health, but a poor diet can make you sick.

_____ 5. When a thing transpires, it dies.

EXERCISE 7: ANALOGIES

Each analogy below is one of the three types you have already worked with. First, decide if the words in the first pair are synonyms, antonyms, or classification : example. Then choose the word that best completes the analogy. Check your answers in the back of the book.

1. encompass : exclude ::
   malign : _____
   a. dangerous b. smear c. ill
   d. praise

2. per annum : income tax ::
   prolific : _____
   a. sparse b. children c. rabbit
   d. plentiful

3. posterior : rear :: inequity : _____
   a. injustice b. evil c. wealth
   d. fairness

4. premonition : hunch ::
   equilibrium : _____
   a. scales b. inequity c. balance
   d. imbalance

5. malicious : friendly ::
   discrepancy : _____
   a. profit b. noise c. argument
   d. agreement

EXERCISE 8: MATCHING MEANINGS

Write the letter of the word that means the opposite of the word in the first column. Check your answers in the back of the book.

_____	1. retaliate	a.	detachment
_____	2. misgiving	b.	external
_____	3. intrinsic	c.	forgive
_____	4. predecessor	d.	faith
_____	5. cohesion	e.	follower

EXERCISE 9: WORD CONTRASTS

In each group below, circle the word that does not mean what the others mean. Check your answers in the back of the book.

1. uninhibited   expressive   restricted   free
2. subservient   dominant   superior   powerful
3. adhere   stick   unite   separate
4. obnoxious   pleasing   nice   sweet
5. extrinsic   intrinsic   inborn   essential

EXERCISE 10: SENTENCE COMPLETION

Complete each sentence in your own words. Sample answers are provided in the back of the book.

1. When you do not *adhere* to the rules of the game, _____
   _____.

2. *Cohesion* among members of a group can be increased by _____
   _____.

3. Each year customs officials seize *contraband* such as _____
   _____.

4. Speakers will *digress* from their main points when _____
   _____.

5. If there is a *discrepancy* between the figures on your tax return and the IRS's figures, _____
   _____.

6. What caused me to lose my *equilibrium* was _____

   _____.

7. *Extrinsic* rewards given by teachers include _____

   _____.

8. Women complain of *inequities* in their salaries compared with those of men; in fact, _____

   _____.

9. *Interspersed* with the roses were _____

   _____.

10. Learning has *intrinsic* rewards, such as _____

    _____.

11. Although candidates commonly *malign* their opponents, _____

    _____.

12. I had *misgivings* about my appointment with Darryl; consequently, _____

    _____.

13. One of the most *obnoxious* things I have ever seen was _____

    _____.

14. It isn't wealth *per se* that determines social class, it's also _____

    _____.

15. Ronald Reagan was the *predecessor* of _____

    _____.

16. Chelsea was such a *prolific* songwriter that _____

    _____.

17. Three historical figures who were opposed to *retaliation* were _____

    _____.

18. Some jobs require *subservience;* for instance, _____

    _____.

19. The events in the story actually *transpired* in _____

    _____.

20. *Uninhibited* behavior is usually increased by _____

    _____.

ADVANCED WORDS

abscond (əb skänd´) *v.*   to leave hastily and secretly, esp. to escape the law

antithesis (an tith´ə sis) *n.*   1. a contrast or opposition, as of ideas   2. the exact opposite

corroborate (kə räb´ə rāt´) *v.*   to confirm; support

demented (di ment´id) *adj.*   mentally ill; insane; out of one's mind

dichotomy (dī kät´ə mē) *n.*   division into two parts

dissonance (dis´ə nəns) *n.*   1. an inharmonious combination of sounds; discord   2. any lack of harmony or agreement

extraneous (ik strā´nē əs) *adj.*   1. coming from outside; foreign   2. not pertinent; irrelevant

non sequitur (nän sek´wi tər) *n.*   1. conclusion that does not follow from the premise   2. remark having no bearing on what has just been said

paragon (par´ə gän, -gən) *n.*   a model of perfection or excellence

rescind (ri sind´) *v.*   to revoke or cancel (a law, etc.)

fat, āpe, cär; ten, ēven; is, bīte; gō, hôrn, tōōl, look; oil, out; up, fʉr; get; joy; yet; chin; she; thin, *th*en; zh, leisure; ŋ, ring; ə for *a* in *ago, e* in *agent, i* in *sanity, o* in *comply, u* in *focus;* ´ as in *able* (ā´b'l)

EXERCISE 11: ADVANCED WORDS IN CONTEXT

Fill in each blank with the word that correctly completes the sentence. Check your answers in the back of the book.

abscond	corroborate	dichotomy	extraneous	paragon
antithesis	demented	dissonance	non sequitur	rescinded

1. Niccolo Machiavelli, in his classic book on power politics, *The Prince,* written in the 16th century, says that a politician must seem to be religious, humane, and honest, but if he is to be successful, he must in reality be the _____ of what he seems.

2. Some of Einstein's theories were so far in advance of their time that scientists are only recently finding the evidence to _____ them.

3. The greatest case of welfare fraud on record was engineered by a gypsy, Anthony Moreno, who, by forging birth certificates and school records, invented 3,000 children for whom he collected more than $6 million from the French social security system before he managed to _____ to Spain.

4. Because there are two opposing parties, American political debate usually involves more _____ than harmony.

5. Before the age of tranquilizers, the mentally ill looked and acted much more _____ than they do now.

6. After her third marriage in 1501, Lucrezia Borgia, illegitimate daughter of Pope Alexander VI, gained a reputation as a _____ of nobility and kindness despite her family's involvement in murder plots, incest, and vice.

7. Before the Twenty-first Amendment to the U.S. Constitution _____ Prohibition in 1933, there was a period of uncontrolled illegal drinking (often of inferior and dangerous beverages) and lawbreaking.

8. You should erase all _____ marks on machine-scored answer sheets because the machine will score them as wrong answers.

9. The candidate was known for his illogical speech; one _____ followed the other.

10. There was a _____ between the designer's haute couture (high fashion) section and her ready-to-wear division, which produces dresses to sell in department stores.

Fill in the puzzle in pencil. The words with asterisks (*) refer to New Words from previous chapters. Check your answers in the back of the book.

Across

*1. Absolute, as in a statement
11. Same as 5 Down
*12. Extreme
13. Move around
14. Marilyn's initials
15. Abbr. for *electrical engineer*
16. Postscript
17. Abbr. for *lawyer*
18. Payment for transportation
20. Frequency modulation
*21. Cancel
24. Former
25. Farm animal
27. Use a chair
29. Chemical symbol for *osmium*
31. Abbr. for *southeast*
32. We
*33. Spreader of frightening rumors
34. Sixth sense
35. Same as 16 Across
36. Same as 8 Down
38. Sick
*39. New-age medicine
42. Abbr. for *railroads*
44. Alt. spelling for prefix meaning *in*, as in _____compass
45. Abbr. for *I have*
46. Sweet potato
47. Abbr. for *American Bar Association*
50. Ant. of *close*
*51. Immensity
*53. Side or angle
54. Same as 27 Across
55. English for *sí* or *oui*

Down

*1. Adj. form of *compensate*
2. Weapons
3. Short for Edgar
*4. Main idea
5. Either . . . _____
6. Crimson
7. Abbr. for *civil service*
8. Prefix meaning *to*, as in _____tach
*9. Heredity
*10. Anger
*15. Thorough
17. *Ante meridiem*
*18. Preoccupation; obsession
19. *Anno Domini*
*20. Acceptance of events as inevitable
22. Old English
*23. Yielding
26. Abbr. for *teaspoon*
28. Irreg. spelling of prefix meaning *not*, as in _____legal
30. Antonym of *bro*
*31. Sober in manner
37. Initials of poet Eliot
39. Uses the ears
40. Gratuity
41. 100 in the dollar
43. Ancient Egyptian god
48. Derek or Diddley
49. Ant. of *miss*
50. Yiddish exclamation
51. Same as 15 Across
52. Abbr. for *mile*

List ten words from your outside reading that you would like to learn. Try to choose words containing prefixes that will help you learn the definitions.

1. _____

2. _____

3. _____

4. _____

5. _____

6. _____

7. _____

8. _____

9. _____

10. _____

MIDTERM REVIEW

Review Words: Chapters 2–6

A. Sentence Completions

Circle the word that best completes the sentence.

1. When a person _____ clearly, he or she is easy to understand. (enunciates, communes)

2. A guilty person feels _____. (velocity, penitence)

3. Washing dishes is a _____ chore. (superlative, domestic)

4. A _____ person copes well with problems. (resourceful, perturbed)

5. After shearing, it is hard to _____ between a sheep and a goat. (paraphrase, differentiate)

6. Fame and fortune _____ some people to work hard. (motivate, idealize)

7. Water _____ at 0 degrees Centigrade. (solidifies, inclines)

8. Courses in _____ math are offered to first-year college students. (remote, remedial)

9. If you don't renew, your subscription will _____. (encompass, lapse)

10. Vanilla is an _____ from a bean. (extract, affiliate)

B. True-False

If the sentence is true, write T in the blank. If the sentence is false, write F in the blank.

_____ 1. A judicious person watches out for pitfalls.

_____ 2. Things are made ornate for aesthetic reasons.

_____ 3. A benediction is malicious.

_____ 4. A person who commits homicide should be apprehended.

_____ 5. A premonition is an uncanny feeling.

_____ 6. Graft is ethical.

_____ 7. The first astronauts received acknowledgment for their exploits.

_____ 8. Delectable foods induce people to overeat.

_____ 9. After the requisite number of years elapse, you become eligible for retirement.

_____ 10. The more you conform, the more distinctive you will be.

C. Multiple Choice

Circle the letter preceding the word that is closest in meaning to the numbered word.

1. posterior   a. rear   b. front   c. side   d. top
2. per annum   a. daily   b. weekly   c. monthly   d. yearly
3. reconcile   a. disagree   b. fight   c. agree   d. separate
4. interim   a. beginning   b. meanwhile   c. end   d. finish
5. encompass   a. exclude   b. include   c. forbid   d. bar
6. valiant   a. brave   b. cowardly   c. complete   d. incomplete
7. perimeter   a. center   b. top   c. bottom   d. edge
8. populous   a. empty   b. quiet   c. crowded   d. dull
9. reserved   a. quiet   b. loud   c. busy   d. angry
10. zeal   a. boredom   b. laziness   c. sadness   d. enthusiasm

Check your answers in the back of the book.

New Words: Chapters 2–6

A. Sentence Completions

Circle the word that best completes the sentence.

1. _____ people are secretive. (Stealthy, Vulnerable)

2. A man of _____ is famous. (fortitude, renown)

3. A(n) _____ has no value. (cipher, irony)

4. _____ items are made to be practical. (Utilitarian, Compensatory)

5. A large meal will _____ most appetites. (patronize, satiate)

6. When you have an inner-ear infection, you can lose your _____ . (equilibrium, fixation)

7. If an item is marked $5, but the salesperson asks for $7, you should question the _____. (inequity, discrepancy)

8. _____ meals need to look and smell good as well as taste good. (Prolific, Sensuous)

9. People who make _____ statements don't take a position. (equivocal, buoyant)

10. People with poor circulation have cold _____. (extremities, franchises)

11. Mental hospitals should be _____. (therapeutic, chafing)

12. If you _____ the flow of blood, you stop it. (intersperse, staunch)

13. Countries often go to war to _____ for some minor incident. (retaliate, coerce)

14. Grapes must be _____ before they can become wine. (fermented, rationalized)

15. Power and glory are _____. (transitory, holistic)

16. The _____ of his crime made life imprisonment seem a small price to pay. (enormity, semblance)

B. Synonyms and Antonyms

If the words in each pair are synonyms, write S in the blank. If they are antonyms, write A in the blank.

_____	1.	compliant	tractable
_____	2.	vilify	malign
_____	3.	amiable	obnoxious
_____	4.	hindrance	facilitation
_____	5.	predecessor	incumbent
_____	6.	conscientious	cavalier
_____	7.	intrinsic	extrinsic
_____	8.	uninhibited	staid
_____	9.	presumptuous	audacious
_____	10.	negate	refute

C. True-False

If the sentence is true, write T in the blank. If it is false, write F in the blank.

_____ 1. Ire can disturb one's countenance.

_____ 2. Subservient people often do menial jobs.

_____ 3. After exhaustive research, you might be able to trace your lineage back 100 years.

_____ 4. Many people find resplendent possessions to be enviable.

_____ 5. A cohesive argument is filled with digressions.

_____ 6. Taciturn people tend to flaunt their beliefs in public.

_____ 7. Being insolent to your boss can have an inflammatory effect and get you fired.

_____ 8. When well written, the gist of an argument is an oblique statement.

_____ 9. One can lament behind a cheerful façade.

_____ 10. A categorical denial that there is contraband aboard a ship may stop the Coast Guard from searching the vessel.

_____ 11. Being able to depict a scene per se does not make a painter a great artist.

_____ 12. A mountain-climbing team must make stringent safety checks before beginning an ascent.

_____ 13. A fatalist believes that destiny will always prevail over individual will.

_____ 14. A law may be voided because of a technicality.

D. Fill-in

Using the words below, fill in the blanks in the story. Use each word only once.

adhere	dire	facet	misgivings	soundness
alarmists	eminent	furor	ponderous	thwarted
depleted	erroneous	meticulously	prone	transpired
deviate	excruciating	militant	prudent	wary

Did the Channel Really Burn?

In September of 1940, a story circulated throughout war-torn England that the

British had _____ the _____ Germans' attempt
                        1   2

to invade England across the English Channel. The rumor claimed that the English

had set the channel on fire to destroy the approaching German ships.

The closeness of England to occupied France made the British

_____ of the possibility of attack. To make matters worse,
      3
_____ kept the country in a _____ by warning
      4   5
that the constant air attacks were a sign of forthcoming invasion. People in
_____ circumstances are _____ to believe stories
      6   7
that _____ people would otherwise question. Many believed the
      8
rumor that _____ metal pipes had been _____
            9   10
laid below the ocean so that the military could flood the coastal waters with gasoline
and set the sea on fire with just the touch of a button. In fact, such a plan had been
proposed but was quietly abandoned when _____ scientists, after
                                              11
making thorough studies of every _____ of the project, expressed
                                        12
very strong _____ about the _____ of the idea.
            13   14
Under any circumstances, such a feat was not even remotely possible because of the
_____ English fuel supply. However, this fact did little to stop the
      15
rumor. To make matters worse, there were supposed to be eyewitnesses. Everyone
knew someone who had seen a charred German corpse that had surely suffered an
_____ death in the burning sea. Even later, many people would not
      16
_____ from their _____ accounts of what
      17   18
had _____. Today there are English people who still
      19
_____ to the false belief that the Channel was once set ablaze to
      20
stop the German invasion of the island by sea.

Check your answers in the back of the book.

Advanced Words: Chapters 2–6

A. Sentence Completions

Circle the word that best completes the sentence.

1. When a person sheds _____ tears, he or she cries a lot. (mundane, copious)

2. An _____ statement is perplexing. (enigmatic, incisive)

3. A quick reading is _____. (mitigating, cursory)

4. Something unnecessary is _____. (dissipated, extraneous)

5. When a building is demolished, it is _____. (corroborated, razed)

6. When one does particularly well at something, that thing is called his or her _____. (forte, consort)

7. If something is workable, it is _____. (perused, viable)

8. When you exercise sound judgment by providing for your future, you are being _____. (provident, eclectic)

9. _____ pay is given when you leave a company. (Severance, Ubiquitous)

10. When you _____ an order, you withdraw it. (rescind, abscond)

B. True-False

If the sentence is true, write T in the blank. If the sentence is false, write F in the blank.

_____ 1. Most people consider a rapacious person to be a paragon of virtue.

_____ 2. An abysmal performance on a job would be a detriment to one's record.

_____ 3. Police will often use whatever empirical evidence is found at the scene of a crime to tell if a witness was actually there or if he or she fabricated the story.

_____ 4. A person who makes only sporadic tries at achieving a goal may be described as indefatigable.

_____ 5. The top French restaurants are expensive because the preparation of succulent dishes requires inordinate effort on the part of the chefs.

_____ 6. A parent who is solicitous about a child's teeth will admonish him not to eat candy.

_____ 7. The antithesis of idolatry is contempt.

_____ 8. Constant dissonance between co-workers might lead to enmity.

_____ 9. People generally consider a person who always speaks in non sequiturs to be demented.

_____ 10. When a ruler imposes formidable strictures on his subjects, he is likely to be loved by them.

C. Multiple Choice

Circle the letter preceding the word that is closest in meaning to the numbered word.

1. dichotomy   a. talent b. division c. shield d. similarity

2. consummate   a. highest b. partial c. weakest d. minor

3. monastic   a. unnecessary b. legal c. abstaining d. hidden

4. aggrandize   a. hide b. increase c. reduce d. damage

5. emulate   a. believe b. copy c. consult d. misunderstand

6. obtuse   a. dull b. clear c. smart d. forceful

7. ruse   a. discovery b. surprise c. trick d. attack

8. pastoral   a. extraordinary b. harsh c. rural d. cautious

9. codify   a. arrange b. scatter c. destroy d. confuse

10. mercenary   a. teacher b. soldier c. substitute d. leader

Check your answers in the back of the book. Circle the words you missed on the lists inside the front and back covers of this book. Use either the lists inside the covers or flash cards to memorize the words before you take the Midterm Exam.

chapter 7

ROOTS I

Archie

The English language has two main sources: Anglo-Saxon and Latin.

Anglo-Saxon Roots

From the fifth century A.D. until the Norman Conquest in 1066, England was ruled by the Anglo-Saxons, who spoke a Germanic dialect. The languages of these tribes formed Old English, the basis of our language. Most of the short, simple, and practical words in modern English (such as *land, rain, crops, cow,* and *ox*) come from Anglo-Saxon words.

Latin Roots

Most of the longer, more complicated words in our language came from Latin or from Greek through Latin. They came into English from four main sources.

In the first century B.C. Julius Caesar sent **Roman** troops throughout western Europe. In 55 B.C. he conquered the British Isles and his troops remained for nearly 500 years. A more important source was **Christianity,** which came to Britain during the Anglo-Saxon rule; with it came the Latin-speaking priests and their Latin ceremonies. Words such as *sanctuary, ceremony,* and *charity* came into use. Also, the words *paradise, bible,* and *bishop* (which the Christians had taken from the Greek) became a part of the English language. When William the Conqueror and his **Norman French** troops invaded England in 1066, English underwent a third change. The Normans, who spoke Old French, began to dominate the political life of the country. Although Anglo-Saxon remained the language of the common people, Old French, which was directly derived from Vulgar Latin (the everyday form of Latin spoken by the Roman troops occupying Europe), became the language of power. Old French gave us most of our words about government and war. From it we took *prince, state, jury, money, property,* and *battle.*

The combination of Anglo-Saxon, Norman French, and Latin formed a new language called Middle English, which was spoken in England between A.D. 1100 and 1500. An example of a word that entered English at this time was *avoid.* In Latin the word was *exvacare.* Old French picked up the word as *esvuidier,* which became the Anglo-French word *avoider* and finally the Middle English word *avoiden.*

The English language's final source of Latin (and Greek) came in the 15th century with the **Renaissance.** The Renaissance witnessed a revival of interest in the study of classical Latin and Greek learning, and Latin became the formal language of communication among educated people in Europe. Frequently, English would adopt from Latin the same word that it had adopted hundreds of years before from Old French. The results became known as *doublets*—that is, two different words from the same source. For example, the words *dual* and *double* both have to do with two and both come from Latin. However, notice the differences in their derivations.[1]

---

du·al (-əl) *adj.* [L. *dualis* < *duo,* TWO] **1.** of two **2.** having or composed of two parts or kinds, like or unlike; double; twofold [a *dual* nature] —*n. Linguis.* **1.** *same as* DUAL

dou·ble (dub''l) *adj.* [ME. < OFr. < L. *duplus,* lit., two-fold (akin to Gr. *diploos*) < *duo,* TWO + -*plus* < IE. *pel-,* to fold, whence L. *plicare,* to fold: cf. SIMPLE, HAPLO-,

---

[1]With permission. From *Webster's New World Dictionary,* Third College Edition. Copyright © 1988 by Simon & Schuster, Inc.

Dual came to English directly from Latin, but *double* came indirectly through Old French.

Word Analysis

A **root** is a group of letters that forms a unit with a particular meaning. To this base you can generally add different prefixes and suffixes to change its meaning or part of speech. Knowing the major roots can help you unlock numerous unknown words. For example, if you had never seen the word *impede* before, you still might have some idea of its meaning because you could think of words with *ped* in them such as *pedestrian* and *pedal*. You could therefore guess that *impede* has something to do with *foot*. In Chapter 6 you learned that *im* means "in" in words such as *imprison* and *import*. So, you could make an educated guess that *impede* has to do with holding the foot in place. In fact, *impede* means to hinder the progress of; to obstruct; to delay.

When you learn to make these kinds of mental associations between familiar and unfamiliar words your vocabulary will increase rapidly. For example, the prefixes and suffixes added to the root *cede, ceed, cess,* (see Chapter 6) unlock dozens of words. The next three chapters will assist you in learning some of the most useful roots in English. Once you understand how to identify these roots, you should attempt to recognize new ones as you read. You can discover the meaning of new roots by using a dictionary that includes word etymologies. You will begin to see that many words spring from the same root and form a family. Also, remembering the meaning of one root is far easier than remembering individually the meanings of the several dozen words that may derive from that root. Therefore, learning roots not only helps you recognize unfamiliar words but also serves as a mnemonic device to remember meanings of words.

Remembering Roots

A good way to remember the meaning of a word part is to relate it to words you already know. For example, you could try to remember that *cede* means "to go or yield" by thinking of the words *proceed* or *recede*. Another mnemonic device is visualization. For instance, to remember *press, prim, prin* (to press or squeeze) you might picture a little old lady pressing *press* words.

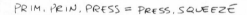

PRIM, PRIN, PRESS = PRESS, SQUEEZE

New Roots

Here are several of the words derived from the root *press, prim, prin,* which is taught in this chapter. The words on the left are common words that you can use as mnemonics to remember the meaning of the root. The words on the right are New Words and Advanced Words for this chapter.

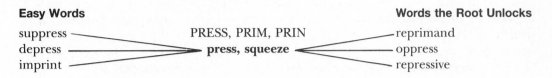

Easy Words		Words the Root Unlocks
suppress	PRESS, PRIM, PRIN	reprimand
depress	**press, squeeze**	oppress
imprint		repressive

Another root is *plac, plea:* "please, calm."

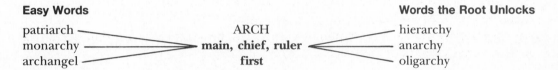

Easy Words		Words the Root Unlocks
placid	PLAC, PLEA	placate
pleasure	**please, calm**	complacent
pleasant		implacable

As a mnemonic for *plac, plea* you might picture a *plac*id walk on the beach bringing you *plea*sure because it is so *calm* and *plea*sant.

A third root is *arch:* "main, chief, ruler, first."

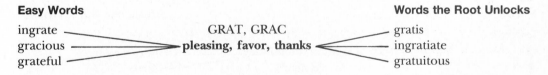

Easy Words		Words the Root Unlocks
patriarch	ARCH	hierarchy
monarchy	**main, chief, ruler**	anarchy
archangel	**first**	oligarchy

Picture an *arch*angel telling a mon*arch* that the king is not the *main ruler,* God is.

A fourth root is *grat, grac:* "pleasing, favor, thanks."

Easy Words		Words the Root Unlocks
ingrate	GRAT, GRAC	gratis
gracious	**pleasing, favor, thanks**	ingratiate
grateful		gratuitous

Picture the *grate*ful Pilgrims sitting down at the first *Thanks*giving saying *grace* for all of the *pleasing* food.

A fifth root is *al, alt:* "other."

Easy Words		Words the Root Unlocks
alien	AL, ALT	altercation
alibi	**other**	alienate
alternative		altruist

Picture some *al*iens from *other* planets giving you no *alt*ernative but to fly away with them in their flying saucer.

A sixth root is *gen, gin:* "birth, race, kind, origin."

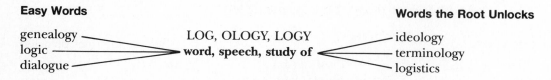

Easy Words

homogeneous
ingenious
genuine

GEN, GIN
birth, race, kind, origin

Words the Root Unlocks

congenial
congenital
progeny

Picture an in*gen*ious scientist combining *genes* to make a new *race* of babies *born* from test tubes.

A seventh root is *log, ology, logy:* "word, speech, study of."

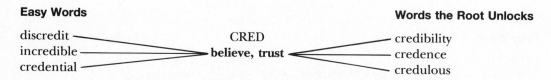

Easy Words

genealogy
logic
dialogue

LOG, OLOGY, LOGY
word, speech, study of

Words the Root Unlocks

ideology
terminology
logistics

Picture a boy on a *log study*ing psych*ology* so he can give a *speech* about it in class the next day.

An eighth root is *cred:* "believe, trust."

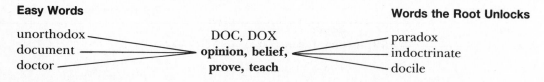

Easy Words

discredit
incredible
credential

CRED
believe, trust

Words the Root Unlocks

credibility
credence
credulous

Picture yourself having to go through an in*cred*ible amount of trouble trying to make someone *believe* who you are so you can use your *cred*it cards.

A ninth root is *doc, dox:* "opinion, belief, prove, teach."

Easy Words

unorthodox
document
doctor

DOC, DOX
opinion, belief,
prove, teach

Words the Root Unlocks

paradox
indoctrinate
docile

Picture a *doc*tor trying to give a patient his *opinion* on what is wrong while the patient asks to see a *doc*ument proving that the doctor is a real M.D.

The last root in this chapter is *rog:* "ask, seek."

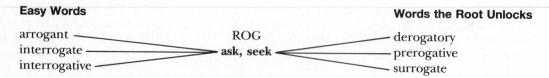

Easy Words

arrogant
interrogate
interrogative

ROG
ask, seek

Words the Root Unlocks

derogatory
prerogative
surrogate

Picture an ar*rog*ant inter*rog*ator *ask*ing you a lot of questions.

To check your understanding of the ten common roots discussed in this chapter, provide your own example (one not given in the previous list) for each root. Try to pick a word that will help you remember what the root means. Check in a dictionary that provides word origins to be sure your word is based on the right root.

Root	Definition	Example
press, prim, prin	press, squeeze	_____
plac, plea	please, calm	_____
arch	main, chief, ruler, first	_____
grat, grac	pleasing, favor, thanks	_____
al, alt	other	_____
gen, gin	birth, race, kind, origin	_____
log, ology, logy	word, speech, study of	_____
cred	believe, trust	_____
doc, dox	opinion, belief, prove, teach	_____
rog	ask, seek	_____

EXERCISE 2: REVIEW WORDS—ROOTS

Before you look at the definitions for the Review Words on the next page, use the roots in this chapter to fill in the blanks below. Check your answers on the next page.

1. ___ ___ ien   someone from another place
2. homo ___ ___ ___ eous   the same in structure; the same kind
3. genea ___ ___ ___ ___   the study of family descent
4. sup ___ ___ ___ ___ ___   to put or press down by force
5. ___ ___ ___ ___ id   calm; quiet
6. dis ___ ___ ___ ___ it   to cast doubt on one's believability
7. ar ___ ___ ___ ant   full of or due to pride (above asking questions)
8. unortho ___ ___ ___   not conforming to the usual beliefs
9. in ___ ___ ___ ___ e   an ungrateful person (one who does not give thanks)
10. patri ___ ___ ___ ___   the father or chief of a family or tribe

REVIEW WORDS

Below are the Review Words for this chapter. We will use these words to practice the skills taught in this chapter.

alien (āl′yən, āl′ē ən) *adj.* 1. belonging to another country or people; foreign 2. strange, not natural [cruel words *alien* to his lips] 3. opposed or repugnant [beliefs *alien* to one's religion] 4. of aliens —*n.* 1. a foreigner 2. a foreign-born resident in a country who has not become a naturalized citizen 3. an outsider 4. a hypothetical being in or from outer space, as in science fiction, that may visit or invade the earth

arrogant (ar′ə gənt) *adj.* full of or due to unwarranted pride and self-importance; overbearing; haughty

discredit (dis kred′it) *v.* 1. to show or be a reason for disbelief or distrust; cast doubt on 2. to damage the credit or reputation of; disgrace

genealogy (jē′nē al′ə jē; *often,* -āl-; *also* jen′ē-) *n.* 1. a chart or recorded history of the descent of a person or family from an ancestor or ancestors 2. the science or study of family descent 3. descent from an ancestor; pedigree; lineage

homogeneous (hō′ mō jē′nē əs, -mə-; häm′ō, -ə-) *adj.* 1. the same in structure, quality, etc.; similar or identical 2. composed of similar or identical parts or elements; uniform

ingrate (in′grāt′) *n.* an ungrateful person

patriarch (pā′trē ärk′) *n.* 1. the father and ruler of a family or tribe, as one of the founders of the ancient Hebrew families 2. a person regarded as the founder or father of a colony, religion, business, etc. 3. a man of great age and dignity 4. the oldest individual of a class or group

placid (plas′id) *adj.* undisturbed; tranquil; calm; quiet

suppress (sə pres′) *v.* 1. to put down by force; subdue; quell; crush 2. to keep from appearing or being known, published, etc. [to *suppress* a news story] 3. to keep back; restrain; check [to *suppress* a laugh] 4. *Psychiatry* to consciously dismiss from the mind (unacceptable ideas, impulses, etc.)

unorthodox (un ôr′thə däks′) *adj.* not conforming to the usual beliefs or established doctrines, as in religion, politics, etc.; unapproved or unconventional [*unorthodox* ideas]

---

fat, āpe, cär; ten, ēven; is, bīte; gō, hôrn, to͞ol, look; oil, out; up, fʉr; get; joy; yet; chin; she; thin, *then;* zh, leisure; ŋ, ring; ə for *a* in *ago, e* in *agent, i* in *sanity, o* in *comply, u* in *focus;* ′ as in *able* (ā′b'l)

EXERCISE 3: REVIEW WORDS IN CONTEXT

Fill in each blank with the word that correctly completes the sentence. Check your answers in the back of the book.

alien	discredit	homogeneous	patriarch	suppress
arrogant	genealogy	ingrate	placid	unorthodox

1. Abraham was a _____ in the Bible.

2. E.T. represents a lovable and kind idea of an _____.

3. Dictatorships _____ freedom of speech.

4. Most people's knowledge of their _____ doesn't go back more than three or four generations.

5. Politicians often try to _____ each other.

6. Most parents prefer _____ babies who don't keep them up at night.

7. It is easier to teach a _____ group than one with abilities that vary widely.

8. Rich people are often _____, believing that they are better off than others because they deserve to be.

9. An _____ will look a gift horse in the mouth instead of saying thank you.

10. Because the majority is always conventional, a democracy must take special steps to protect citizens' rights to express _____ views.

NEW WORDS I

alienate (āl′yən āt′, āl′ē ən āt′) *v.* 1. to make unfriendly or to cause to withdraw [his behavior *alienated* his friends] 2. to cause a transference of (affection)

anarchy (an′ər kē, -är′-) *n.* 1. the complete absence of government 2. political disorder; violence; lawlessness

congenital (kən jen′ə təl) *adj.* existing as such at birth [a *congenital* disease]

hierarchy (hī′ər är′ kē, also hī′rär′-) *n.* 1. a group of persons or things arranged in order of rank, grade, etc. 2. church government by clergy in graded ranks 3. the highest officials in such a system

ideology (ī′dē äl′ə jē, id′ē äl′ə jē) *n.* the doctrines or opinions, etc., of an individual, class, etc.

indoctrinate (in däk′trə nāt′) *v.* to instruct in doctrines, theories, beliefs, etc.

ingratiate (in grā′shē āt′) *v.* to bring (oneself) into another's favor

paradox (par′ə däks′) *n.* a statement that seems contradictory, etc., but may be true in fact

prerogative (pri räg′ə tiv) *n.* an exclusive privilege, esp. one peculiar to a rank, class, etc.

terminology (tʉr′mə näl′ə jē) *n.* the terms used in a specific science, art, etc. [legal *terminology*]

fat, āpe, cär; ten, ēven; is, bīte; gō, hôrn, to͞ol, look; oil, out; up, fʉr; get; joy; yet; chin; she; thin, *then*; zh, leisure; ŋ, ring; ə for *a* in *ago, e* in *agent, i* in *sanity, o* in *comply, u* in *focus;* ' as in *able* (ā′b'l)

Fill in the word that best completes the sentence. Check your answers in the back of the book.

alienated	congenital	ideology	ingratiated	prerogative
anarchy	hierarchy	indoctrinate	paradox	terminology

1. According to psychologist A. H. Maslow, a _____ of needs exists such that people must have sufficient food, water, and shelter before they can think of things such as love, beauty, and truth.

2. Deafness caused by the pregnant mother catching German measles is a _____ defect.

3. Nursery rhymes, children's stories, and even television shows that teach moral lessons are ways in which we _____ our children in the moral system of our culture.

4. Sheik Rashid Ben Saeed Al Maktoum _____ himself with Princess Soloman and her family when he spent $44 million on her wedding in Dubai to his son, Mohammed.

5. Computer _____ includes such words as "bit," "byte," "software," and "downtime."

6. It is a _____ that the more love you give away the more you get.

7. It is the _____ of the Queen to be addressed as "your majesty."

8. The unfair tax policies imposed between 1765 and 1775 by King George III of England _____ the American colonists and increased their desire for revolution.

9. Communist _____, which states that the workers own everything, has not worked out well in practice.

10. A state of _____ may exist after a war or other emergency, but government is necessary for the country to run smoothly.

NEW WORDS II

altercation (ôl'tər kā'shən) *n.*   an angry or heated argument; quarrel

complacent (kəm plā'sənt) *adj.*   satisfied; esp. self-satisfied or smug

congenial (kən jēn'yəl) *adj.*   1. kindred; compatible [*congenial* tastes]   2. of the same temperament; friendly [*congenial* people]   3. suited to one's needs; agreeable [*congenial* work]

credence (krēd''ns) *n.*   belief, esp. in the reports or testimony of another [to give *credence* to rumors]

credibility (kred'ə bil'ə tē) *n.*   believability; reliability

derogatory (di räg'ə tôr'ē) *adj.*   1. tending to lessen or impair; detracting   2. belittling

gratis (grat'is, grāt'is) *adv., adj.*   free of charge

oppress (ə pres') *v.*   1. to keep down by the cruel or unjust use of authority   2. to weigh heavily on the mind of; worry

placate (plā'kāt, plak'āt) *v.*   to calm, pacify, or satisfy

reprimand (rep'rə mand') *n.*   a severe or formal scolding —*v.*   to scold severely or formally

fat, āpe, cär; ten, ēven; is, bīte; gō, hôrn, tool, look; oil, out; up, fur; get; joy; yet; chin; she; thin, *th*en; zh, leisure; ŋ, ring; ə for *a* in *ago, e* in *agent, i* in *sanity, o* in *comply, u* in *focus;* ' as in *able* (ā'b'l)

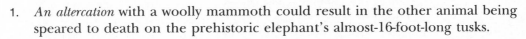

Circle the letter before the word or phrase that best defines the italicized word in each sentence. Check your answers in the back of the book.

1. *An altercation* with a woolly mammoth could result in the other animal being speared to death on the prehistoric elephant's almost-16-foot-long tusks.

   a. an understanding   b. a quarrel   c. a walk   d. a race

2. The *complacent* attitude of "The Muppets" character Miss Piggy amuses audiences but often irritates those around her.

   a. scared   b. uncomfortable   c. stingy   d. self-satisfied

3. Perle Mesta became so famous as the *congenial* hostess of Washington, D.C., parties that a musical comedy, *Call Me Madam,* was written about her.

   a. disgusting   b. longtime   c. agreeable   d. usual

4. In the 17th century many people did not *give credence* to Edmund Halley's statement that the comet he saw in 1682 would appear about every 77 years.

   a. believe   b. distrust   c. listen to   d. think about

5. Albert Einstein's *credibility* as a physicist was so well established that scientists accepted his theory of relativity, $E = mc^2$, even though no one was able to actually prove it for years.

   a. believability   b. dishonesty   c. income   d. thinking

6. Disguising *a derogatory* remark as a joke does not prevent it from hurting the victim.

   a. a foolish   b. a humorous   c. an uncomplimentary   d. a flattering

7. It is not proper to expect a doctor, lawyer, or accountant to provide his or her services *gratis* even if he or she is a friend.

   a. frequently   b. quickly   c. nightly   d. free

8. History has seen many cases of people overthrowing one government that was *oppressing* them only to find that their new government was just as bad or worse.

   a. persecuting   b. helping   c. judging   d. ignoring

9. If your boss is angry at you, it is wise to find a way to *placate* him or her.

   a. upset   b. anger   c. stimulate   d. soothe

10. It is humiliating to your children when you *reprimand* them in front of their friends.

    a. influence   b. scold   c. praise   d. meet

Write T or F in the blank. Check your answers in the back of the book.

_____ 1. Computer programmers use special terminology.

_____ 2. It is paradoxical to say that bravery is often a form of cowardice.

_____ 3. In a situation of anarchy there is little government control.

_____ 4. Congenital defects occur after birth.

_____ 5. Oppressed people have very little freedom.

EXERCISE 7: ANALOGIES

In previous exercises of this type you learned how to find pairs of words that were synonyms, were antonyms, or had the relationship of classification : example. This exercise contains those types of analogies plus a new type. In this kind of analogy the relationship of the pairs of words is *cause : effect:* The first word describes something that not only precedes the second in time but also causes it.

drought : dead crops :: paradox : surprise

Determine which of the four kinds of analogies is used in each group below, and then fill in the blank to make the second pair agree with the first. Check your answers in the back of the book.

1. placid : calm :: hierarchy : _____   a. disorder   b. names   c. rank
                                          d. anger

2. homogeneous : same ::   a. satisfied   b. unhappy   c. angry
   complacent : _____   d. bad

3. arrogant : humble ::   a. irritating   b. pleasing   c. honest
   ingratiating : _____   d. believable

4. ingrate : anger ::   a. credit   b. belief   c. satisfaction
   indoctrination : _____   d. disbelief

5. alien : Martian :: ideology : _____ a. communism   b. silence   c. lying
                                          d. trust

EXERCISE 8: MATCHING MEANINGS

Write the letter of the word that means the opposite of the word in the first column.
Check your answers in the back of the book.

1. gratis
2. credibility
3. placate
4. reprimand
5. altercation

a. unbelievability
b. compliment
c. agreement
d. costly
e. infuriate

EXERCISE 9: WORD CONTRASTS

In each group below circle the word that does not mean what the others mean.
Check your answers in the back of the book.

1. congenial   incompatible   sympathetic   harmonious
2. alienate   estrange   unite   distance
3. credence   mistrust   skepticism   disbelief
4. derogatory   praising   degrading   belittling
5. prerogative   obligation   right   privilege

EXERCISE 10: SENTENCE COMPLETION

Complete each sentence in your own words. Sample answers are provided in the back of the book.

1. You are likely to *alienate* someone if _____.

2. An *altercation* may not be avoidable, yet _____.

3. It is frightening to be in a country where there is *anarchy* because _____.

4. As long as a person is *complacent,* _____.

5. You should try to be *congenial* at a party; otherwise, _____.

6. A *congenital* defect can cause the death of a newborn unless _____
_____ .

7. If you give *credence* to politicians, _____
_____ .

8. Our political leaders need to have high *credibility* since _____
_____ .

9. Besides making *derogatory* remarks, an obnoxious person might _____
_____ .

10. When something is *gratis* _____
_____ .

11. Unless you understand the *hierarchy* of command at your job, _____
_____ .

12. Even if you disagree with a person's religious *ideology,* _____
_____ .

13. The army *indoctrinates* new recruits by various methods, including _____
_____ .

14. It is wise to *ingratiate* yourself with a new boss because _____
_____ .

15. Because in a democracy people do not *oppress* others, _____
_____ .

16. It sounds like a *paradox* when someone tells you that _____
_____ .

17. You can *placate* angry parents by _____
_____ .

18. Because in professional football the winner of the coin toss has the *prerogative* to choose which goal his team will defend, _____
_____ .

19. A parent is likely to *reprimand* a child who _____
_____ .

20. If you don't know the *terminology* being used in an article you are reading, _____
_____ .

ADVANCED WORDS

altruism (al′trōō iz əm) *n.*   an unselfish concern for the welfare of others

credulous (krej′ oo ləs, -ə ləs) *adj.*   tending to believe too readily; easily convinced

docile (däs′əl) *adj.*   easy to manage or discipline

gratuitous (grə tōō′i təs, grə tyōō′ i təs) *adj.*   1. given or received free of charge   2. uncalled-for [a *gratuitous* insult]

implacable (im plak′ə bəl, im plā′kə bəl) *adj.*   that which cannot be appeased or pacified; relentless; inflexible

logistics (lō jis′tiks) *n.pl.*   1. the ways in which the details of a particular operation are handled   2. the study or method of moving soldiers, supplying them with food, etc.

oligarchy (äl′i gär′kē) *n.*   1. a form of government in which the ruling power belongs to a few persons   2. a state governed in this way   3. the persons ruling such a state

progeny (präj′ə nē) *n.*   children; offspring

repressive (ri pres′iv) *adj.*   1. holding back; restraining   2. putting down; subduing

surrogate (sur′ə gāt, sur′ə git) *n.*   a deputy or substitute

---

fat, āpe, cär; ten, ēven; is, bīte; gō, hôrn, tōōl, look; oil, out; up, fʉr; get; joy; yet; chin; she; thin, *th*en; zh, leisure; ŋ, ring; ə for *a* in *ago, e* in *agent, i* in *sanity, o* in *comply, u* in *focus;* ′ as in *able* (ā′b′l)

EXERCISE 11: ADVANCED WORDS IN CONTEXT

Fill in each blank with the word that correctly completes the sentence. Check your answers in the back of the book.

altruism	docile	implacable	progeny	repressive
credulous	gratuitous	logistics	oligarchy	surrogate

1. Just before the American Revolution, King George III of England used increasingly stern and _____ measures, such as stationing troops in every large city in the colonies.

2. A psychologist named Ruston found that _____ in children increases with age; young children are less likely to be generous and share their toys.

3. After the age of about 8, children are no longer _____ enough to believe in Santa Claus, the Tooth Fairy, and the Easter Bunny.

4. It is frightening to realize that the offspring of only 2 rats can be responsible for 15,000 _____ in less than a year.

5. Because wild cattle were quite ferocious, it took many centuries of breeding to get the _____ cows we have today.

6. Democracy and _____ are antonyms.

7. Valuable cows may have their fertilized eggs removed and surgically implanted in the uterus of a less valuable _____ that bears the calf.

8. In the book and movie *A Clockwork Orange,* the lead character received enjoyment from _____ violence and therefore never robbed anyone without giving the victim a terrible beating.

9. Many ancient peoples, such as the Greeks and Norsemen, believed that their lives were ruled by _____ gods.

10. The _____ of planning a party for 100 people can be so overwhelming that many people hire party planners.

The clues marked by asterisks (*) refer to New Words from previous chapters.
Check your answers in the back of the book.

Across

*1. Smuggled goods
*10. Fruitful
11. Also
12. Abbr. for *head*
13. Abbr. for *mountains*
14. Material for making roads
17. A single unit
21. Abbr. for *south-southeast*
22. Abbr. for *National Academy of Science*
*23. To speak evil of
*27. Fundamental
29. Abbr. for *district attorney*
30. Sound a cow makes
31. Abbr. for *military*
*32. Offensive
37. Slang for an American soldier
38. Past tense of *say*
39. Chemical symbol for *radium*
43. Abbr. for *extraterrestrial*
44. Prefix meaning *away* or *from*, as in _____dicate, _____stract
*46. Scatter
50. Jacket
52. Abbr. for *Irish Republican Army*
53. Suffix meaning "one who," as in profess_____
54. Abbr. for *Social Security*
*55. Not essential
58. Alt. spelling of prefix meaning "in," as in _____brace
60. Abbr. for tablespoon
61. A large, mooselike deer
*62. Serious

Down

*1. Tendency to stick together
2. Ant. of *young*
3. Chemical symbol for *nickel*
4. Abbr. for *task force*
5. Edge of a glass
6. A main division of a play
7. Alt. spelling of prefix meaning "to," as in _____tendance
8. Ant. of *yes*
9. Opposite of dashes in Morse code
*10. Disposed or inclined
15. Alt. spelling of prefix meaning "to," as in _____semble
*16. Strikes back
18. Chemical symbol for *sodium*
19. Automobile
20. How most sweaters are made
23. Singular of 13 Across (abbr.)
24. Short for limousine
25. Ant. of *out*
26. Abbr. for *general secretary*
28. 12 o'clock P.M.
*29. To turn aside
30. Abbr. for *master of business administration*
33. Same as 25 Down
34. Abbr. for *United States*
35. Tools for cutting down trees
*36. Stuck fast
*40. Polished plane surface of a cut gem
41. Abbr. for *supernova*
*42. Itself (two wds.)
45. Square container
46. Abbr. for *International Trade Relations Board*
47. What many cans are made of
48. One bar in a railroad track
49. Abbr. for *post office*
51. Abbr. for *American Telephone and Telegraph Company*
56. I am; he _____
57. Abbr. for *check*
59. Abbr. for *Michigan*

EXERCISE 13: OWN WORDS

Of the words from your outside reading that you would like to learn, choose ten that contain roots not found in this chapter. Following each number below, write the word, its pronunciation, and a simple definition. In the space labeled "Word Parts," write the parts of the word and their definitions. See the sample below. Use a dictionary for help.

Example: defer (di fur′)—to postpone
de = away, down, from   *fer* = to bear or carry

1. _____

   Word Parts _____

2. _____

   Word Parts _____

3. _____

   Word Parts _____

4. _____

   Word Parts _____

5. _____

   Word Parts _____

6. _____

   Word Parts _____

7. _____

   Word Parts _____

8. _____

   Word Parts _____

9. _____

   Word Parts _____

10. _____

   Word Parts _____

chapter 8

ROOTS II

In the last chapter we discussed the usefulness of word parts in figuring out the meanings of unfamiliar words. For example, the root *cred* comes from the Latin verb *credere,* "to believe or trust." Many words are easy to understand if we know the definition of this root. Examples are *creed, incredible,* and *credence.* However, the derivations of words such as *credit* and *credentials* are less obvious. Their connection with *cred* is that they involve trust or belief in another person. In this case, the etymological meaning, or exact meaning of the word parts, has come to be slightly different from the way the word is currently used. This difference is one reason why you can't always "translate" word parts directly into English. Roots are used as *clues* to meaning, and you always have to check these clues to see whether they fit the context of the sentence or paragraph you're reading.

Variations in Spelling of Roots

Another reason that word parts sometimes don't translate is that the same combination of parts can add up to different words. For example, *avert* and *averse* both come from the same word parts, *a* (away) and *vertere* (to turn), but they have different spellings and slightly different meanings. *Avert* is a verb meaning "to turn away" (to *avert* one's glance from an ugly sight) or "to prevent something from happening" (he apologized to *avert* trouble). *Averse* is an adjective meaning "not willing," "reluctant," or "opposed" (he was *averse* to camping). The reason for the spelling differences is that the words come from different parts of speech in Latin. *Avert* comes from the infinitive, *avertere,* whereas *averse* comes from the past participle, *aversus.* Similarly, the infinitive *praevalere* gave us *prevail,* and the past participle *praevalens* gave us *prevalence.* It is important to remember that these alternate spellings belong to the same root.

Spelling also varies because many words came into English directly from Latin while others came in from the same Latin base but through other languages. For example, the Latin verb *facere,* "to do or make," gave us the English words *manufacture* and *factory.* In Spanish *facere* changed to *hacer,* from which we get *hacienda.* In Italian it became *fare,* from which we get *confetti,* and in French it changed to *faire,* from which we get *affair.* To get an idea of the variety of French and Latin spellings for the same verb, look at the derivations for words based on *facere* shown in the following illustration. You can see that the Latin spellings include *fac, fect,* and *fic,* and that the French spellings include *fair, fet, fit, feat,* and *feit.*

New Roots

The following are ten new roots, with some easy words and some difficult words derived from them.

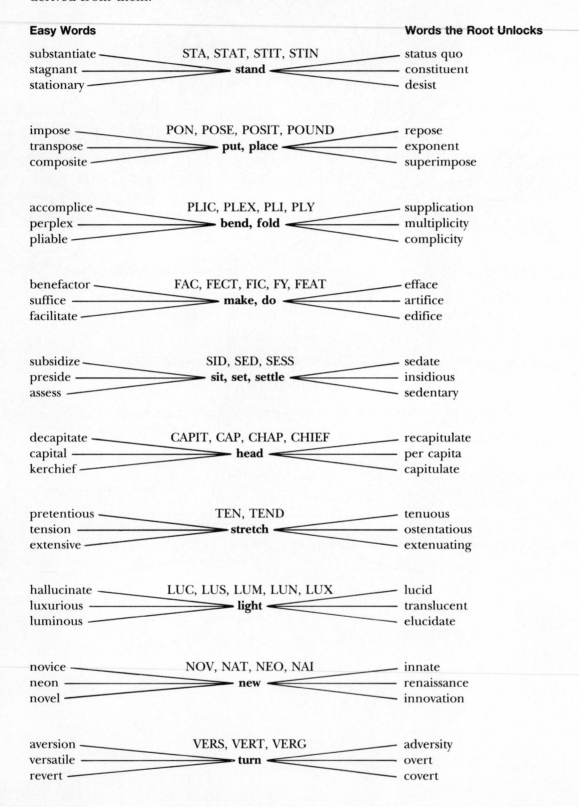

Easy Words   **Words the Root Unlocks**

substantiate   STA, STAT, STIT, STIN   status quo
stagnant   **stand**   constituent
stationary   desist

impose   PON, POSE, POSIT, POUND   repose
transpose   **put, place**   exponent
composite   superimpose

accomplice   PLIC, PLEX, PLI, PLY   supplication
perplex   **bend, fold**   multiplicity
pliable   complicity

benefactor   FAC, FECT, FIC, FY, FEAT   efface
suffice   **make, do**   artifice
facilitate   edifice

subsidize   SID, SED, SESS   sedate
preside   **sit, set, settle**   insidious
assess   sedentary

decapitate   CAPIT, CAP, CHAP, CHIEF   recapitulate
capital   **head**   per capita
kerchief   capitulate

pretentious   TEN, TEND   tenuous
tension   **stretch**   ostentatious
extensive   extenuating

hallucinate   LUC, LUS, LUM, LUN, LUX   lucid
luxurious   **light**   translucent
luminous   elucidate

novice   NOV, NAT, NEO, NAI   innate
neon   **new**   renaissance
novel   innovation

aversion   VERS, VERT, VERG   adversity
versatile   **turn**   overt
revert   covert

For each of the roots below, give an example not previously provided in this chapter. Check the examples in your dictionary to be sure they are from the correct roots.

Root	Meaning	Example
sta, stat, stit, stin	stand	_____
pon, pose, posit, pound	put, place	_____
plic, plex, pli, ply	bend, fold	_____
fac, fect, fic, fy, feat	make, do	_____
sid, sed, sess	sit, set, settle	_____
capit, cap, chap, chief	head	_____
ten, tend	stretch	_____
luc, lus, lum, lun, lux	light	_____
nov, nat, neo, nai	new	_____
vers, vert, verg	turn	_____

Before you look at the definitions of the Review Words on the next page, use the roots in this chapter to fill in the blanks below. Check your answers on the next page.

1. bene _ _ _ tor   one who does good things for others

2. pre _ _ _ tious   showing off (stretching before)

3. sub _ _ _ ntiate   to support or prove (stand under)

4. _ _ _ ice   a person new to a particular occupation, activity, etc.

5. im _ _ _ _   to put or place upon

6. a _ _ _ _ ion   a dislike (a turning away)

7. accom _ _ _ _ e   one who is involved (folded) with another in an illegal act

8. sub _ _ _ ize   to settle a grant upon a person or agency

9. hal _ _ _ inate   to have visions (see halos of light)

10. de _ _ _ _ _ ate   to cut off the head

Below are the Review Words for this chapter. We will use these words to practice the skills taught in this chapter.

accomplice (ə käm′plis) *n.*   a person who knowingly participates with another in an unlawful act; partner in crime

aversion (ə vur′shən) *n.*   an intense or definite dislike; repugnance

benefactor (ben′ə fak′tər) *n.*   a person who has given help, esp. financial help; patron

decapitate (de kap′ə tāt, di-) *v.*   to cut off the head of; behead

hallucinate (hə loo′si nāt′) *v.*   to apparently perceive sights, sounds, etc. that are not actually present; this may occur in certain mental disorders

impose (im pōz′) *v.*   1. to place or set (a burden, tax, fine, etc. *on* or *upon*) as by authority   2. to force (oneself, one's presence or will, etc.) on another or others without right or invitation   3. to pass off; palm off; foist, esp. by deception [to *impose* false cures on unsuspecting patients]

novice (näv′is) *n.*   a person new to a particular occupation or activity, etc.; apprentice; beginner; tyro

pretentious (prē ten′shəs, pri-) *adj.*   1. making claims, explicit or implicit, to some distinction, importance, dignity, or excellence   2. affectedly grand; ostentatious

subsidize (sub′sə dīz′) *v.*   1. to support with a grant of money (a subsidy)   2. to buy the aid or support of with a subsidy, often as a kind of bribe

substantiate (səb stan′shē āt′) *v.*   to show to be true or real by giving evidence; prove; confirm

fat, āpe, cär; ten, ēven; is, bīte; gō, hôrn, tool, look; oil, out; up, fur; get; joy; yet; chin; she; thin, *th*en; zh, leisure; ŋ, ring; ə for *a* in *ago, e* in *agent, i* in *sanity, o* in *comply, u* in *focus;* ′ as in *able* (ā′b′l)

Fill in each blank with the word that correctly completes the sentence. Check your answers in the back of the book.

accomplice	benefactor	hallucinate	novice	subsidize
aversion	decapitate	impose	pretentious	substantiate

1. They say that _____ people show off because they are really insecure.

2. The guillotine was considered a humane punishment in its day because it would _____ people more quickly and cleanly than the executioner's ax would.

3. It is common for schizophrenic patients to _____ that strange voices are talking to them.

4. A rookie cop is a _____ in his profession.

5. Because the rents in Beverly Hills are too high for small businesses like shoe repair shops and dry cleaners, the city has to _____ them so that residents won't lose their services.

6. Many people on both sides of the abortion issue try to _____ their beliefs on others.

7. Bonnie was the _____ of the criminal Clyde Barrows.

8. Most starving artists could use a _____.

9. If you can _____ your alibi, you will go free.

10. Most people feel _____ toward tarantulas.

constituent (kən stich′o͞o ənt) *adj.*   1. necessary in forming or making up a whole; component [a *constituent* part]   2. that can or does appoint or vote for a representative —*n.*   1. a person who appoints another as his agent or representative   2. a member of a constituency, esp. any of the voters represented by a particular official   3. a necessary part or element; component

efface (i fās′, ə-) *v.*   1. to rub out, as from a surface; erase; wipe out [time *effaced* the memory]   2. to make (oneself) inconspicuous; withdraw (oneself) from notice

innate (i nāt′) *adj.*   1. existing naturally rather than acquired; that which seems to have been in one from birth [*innate* talent]   2. existing as a basic attribute [the *innate* humor of a situation]

insidious (in sid′ē əs) *adj.*   1. characterized by treachery or slyness; crafty; wily   2. operating in a slow or not easily apparent manner; more dangerous than seems evident [an *insidious* disease]

multiplicity (mul′tə plis′ə tē) *n.*   1. the quality or condition of having variety or many factors   2. a great number

recapitulate (rē′kə pich′ə lāt′) *v.*   to repeat briefly, as in an outline; summarize

repose (ri pōz′) *v.*   1. to lie at rest   2. to rest from work, travel, exercise, etc.   3. to rest in death or a grave   4. to lie quiet and calm   5. to lie, rest, or be supported [shale *reposing* on a bed of limestone] —*n.*   1. a reposing or resting   2. rest or sleep   3. peace of mind; freedom from worry or troubles   4. calm or ease of manner; composure   5. calm, tranquillity, peace

status quo (stāt′əs kwō, stat′-) *n.*   the existing state of affairs (at a particular time)

supplication (sup′lə kā′shən) *n.*   1. a humble request, prayer, petition, etc.   2. the act of supplicating

translucent (trans lo͞o′sənt, tranz-) *adj.*   partially transparent, as frosted glass

---

fat, āpe, cär; ten, ēven; is, bīte; gō, hôrn, to͞ol, look; oil, out; up, fʉr; get; joy; yet; chin; she; thin, *th*en; zh, leisure; ŋ, ring; ə for *a* in *ago, e* in *agent, i* in *sanity, o* in *comply, u* in *focus;* ′ as in *able* (ā′b'l)

EXERCISE 4: FILL-IN

Fill in each blank with the word that best completes the sentence. Check your answers in the back of the book.

effacing	innate	multiplicity	repose	supplication
constituents	insidious	recapitulate	status quo	translucent

1. In *The King and I*, the young prince of Thailand's first law was that his subjects would no longer have to kneel or bend over in _____; instead they would bow the way Anna, his English teacher, had shown him.

2. Elected officials are supposed to represent the interest of their _____.

3. Before he was shot by the FBI in 1934, John Dillinger was declared "public enemy number one" for a _____ of crimes ranging from bank robbery to murder.

4. The earliest people to _____ on bedsprings were the ancient Greeks, who made them out of leather thongs.

5. Conservatives are people who don't want to change the _____; reactionaries want to return to the past.

6. Some people believe that the personality differences between girls and boys are _____ rather than learned because most nursery school girls prefer to play with dolls and boys with trucks.

7. The _____ plotting of Shakespeare's character Iago caused the destruction of Othello and his wife, Desdemona.

8. _____ glass blocks are sometimes used in building because they provide light without letting outsiders see in.

9. Harold was so self-_____ that no one could remember what he looked like.

10. After the president's State of the Union Address, newscasters will _____ the main points.

adversity (ad vʉr′sə tē, əd-) *n.*   a state of wretchedness or misfortune; poverty and trouble

artifice (ärt′ə fis) *n.*   1. skill or cleverness   2. trickery or slyness   3. a sly or artful trick

exponent (eks pōn′ənt, ik spōn′-) *n.*   1. a person who sets forth, expounds, or promotes (principles, methods, etc.)   2. a person or thing that is an example or symbol (*of* something); representative

lucid (lo͞o′sid) *adj.*   1. transparent   2. designating a period of sanity in a mental disorder   3. clear to the mind; readily understood [*lucid* instructions]   4. clearheaded; logical [a *lucid* thinker]

ostentatious (äs′tən tā′shəs) *adj.*   showy; pretentious

overt (ō vʉrt′, ō′vʉrt) *adj.*   not hidden; open; observable; apparent

per capita (pər kap′i tə) *adj.*   for each person

renaissance (ren′ə säns′) *n.*   1. a new birth; rebirth; revival   2. [R-] the great revival of art, literature, and learning in Europe in the 14th, 15th, and 16th centuries, based on classical sources; it began in Italy and spread gradually to other countries and marked the transition from the medieval world to the modern —*adj.*   [R-] of, characteristic of, or in the style of the Renaissance

sedate (si dāt′) *adj.*   calm, quiet, or composed; esp. serious and unemotional

tenuous (ten′yo͞o əs, -yə wəs) *adj.*   1. slender or fine, as a fiber   2. not substantial; slight; flimsy [*tenuous* evidence]

fat, āpe, cär; ten, ēven; is, bīte; gō, hôrn, to͞ol, look; oil, out; up, fʉr; get; joy; yet; chin; she; thin, *th*en; zh, leisure; ŋ, ring; ə for *a* in *ago*, *e* in *agent*, *i* in *sanity*, *o* in *comply*, *u* in *focus*; ' as in *able* (ā′b'l)

Circle the letter before the word or phrase that best defines the italicized word in each sentence. Check your answers in the back of the book.

1. In Leonardo da Vinci's famous painting, the Mona Lisa has no eyebrows; it was the fashion in *Renaissance* Florence to shave them off.

    a. 1300–1600   b. 1600–1900   c. 1000–1200   d. 500–200 B.C.

2. The Tasaday tribe of cave dwellers in the Philippines, who live without domesticated animals, pottery, wheels, clothes, or agriculture, have the lowest *per capita* income in the world.

    a. individual   b. national   c. tribal   d. family

3. *Exponents* of the Amish faith refuse to bear arms or to take oaths.

    a. enemies   b. businessmen   c. Germans   d. representatives

4. In professions such as sales and politics, where honesty is not always the way to succeed, people learn to use *artifice*.

    a. force   b. bribery   c. sex   d. trickery

5. People tend to associate *sedate* behavior with boring people.

    a. silly   b. self-important   c. emotional   d. serious

6. An argument or theory without any evidence is *tenuous*.

    a. strong   b. strange   c. weak   d. normal

7. As Alzheimer's disease progresses, its victims have fewer and fewer *lucid* intervals.

    a. strong   b. clear   c. friendly   d. loud

8. The saying "Into each life some rain must fall" means that nobody gets through life without some *adversity*.

    a. trouble   b. temptation   c. happiness   d. wealth

9. The invasion of Kuwait by Iraq was an *overt* act of war.

    a. declared   b. financial   c. open   d. hidden

10. The wedding of Catherine de Medici and the duke of Orleans, later King Henry II, in 1533 was extremely *ostentatious;* the wedding cake contained a four-piece orchestra.

    a. small   b. showy   c. large   d. quiet

EXERCISE 6: TRUE-FALSE

Write T or F in the blank. Check your answers in the back of the book.

_____ 1. Revolutionaries want to preserve the status quo.

_____ 2. Most Republicans are exponents of military preparedness.

_____ 3. Families with many dependent children usually have lower per capita incomes than smaller families do.

_____ 4. Stained-glass windows are translucent.

_____ 5. Cellos are usually constituents of rock bands.

EXERCISE 7: ANALOGIES

The analogies below are either synonyms, antonyms, a classification : example pair, or a cause : effect pair. First, decide which type of comparison is used in the first pair of words. Second, find a word from the choices that will make the second pair of words have the same relationship. Check your answers in the back of the book.

1. hallucinatory drug : LSD ::
   ostentatious car : _____

   a. gold Cadillac   b.   white Volkswagen
   c. economy car   d.   expensive car

2. decapitation : death :: adversity :
   _____

   a. happiness   b.   suffering   c.   health
   d. success

3. benefactor : enemy :: lucid :
   _____

   a. clear   b.   bright   c.   intelligent
   d. muddy

4. accomplice : helper ::
   multiplicity : _____

   a. few   b.   expense   c.   many   d.   total

5. pretentious : modest ::
   repose : _____

   a. activity   b.   rest   c.   fear   d.   calmness

EXERCISE 8: MATCHING MEANINGS

Write the letter of the word that means the opposite of the word in the first column.
Check your answers in the back of the book.

1. overt   a. honesty
2. tenuous   b. hysterical
3. sedate   c. preserve
4. efface   d. concealed
5. artifice   e. strong

EXERCISE 9: WORD CONTRASTS

In each group below circle the word that does not mean what the others mean.
Check your answers in the back of the book.

1. innate   natural   inborn   acquired
2. supplication refusal   petition   prayer
3. recapitulate summarize   introduce   repeat
4. insidious   beneficial healthful   good
5. renaissance   decay   rebirth   revival

EXERCISE 10: SENTENCE COMPLETION

Complete each sentence in your own words. Sample answers are provided in the
back of the book.

1. Most of our grandparents can remember times of great *adversity*, such as _____
   _____.

2. Feminists reject the use of "feminine *artifice*" because _____
   _____.

3. Representatives elected by their *constituents* include _____
   _____.

4. Because of air pollution, monuments are being *effaced* _____
   _____.

5. Political conservatives are usually *exponents* of _____
   _____.

6. He showed his *innate* honesty by _____

_____.

7. Lead poisoning is so *insidious* that _____

_____.

8. During *lucid* moments, victims of Alzheimer's disease _____

_____.

9. Because the trade deficit has a *multiplicity* of causes, _____

_____.

10. Some examples of *ostentatious* cars are _____

_____.

11. The sergeant engaged in such *overt* acts of cruelty as _____

_____.

12. Residents of Westchester County, N.Y., have a higher *per capita* income than _____

_____.

13. The summary *recapitulates* _____

_____.

14. In the 1980s there was a *renaissance* of _____

_____.

15. Jeffrey's *repose* was interrupted by _____

_____.

16. *Sedate* people usually wear _____

_____.

17. If you are happy with the *status quo,* _____

_____.

18. The actress's repeated *supplications* to the casting director finally led to _____

_____.

19. His argument contained only the most *tenuous* reasons; in fact, _____

_____.

20. Architects use *translucent* materials such as glass block walls to _____

_____.

capitulate (kə pich′yoo lāt′) *v.*   1. to give up (*to* an enemy) on prearranged conditions; surrender conditionally   2. to give up or give in; stop resisting

complicity (kəm plis′ə tē) *n.*   the fact or state of being an accomplice; partnership in wrong-doing

covert (kō′vərt, kuv′ərt) *adj.*   concealed, hidden, disguised, or secret [a *covert* threat]

desist (di sist′, -zist′) *v.*   to cease (*from* an action); stop; abstain [*desist* from fighting]

edifice (ed′i fis) *n.*   1. a building, esp. a large, imposing one   2. any elaborately constructed institution, organization, etc.

elucidate (i lo͞o′sə dāt′, ə-) *v.*   to make clear (esp. something complicated); explain

extenuating (ik sten′yo͞o āt′iŋ, ek-) *adj.*   characteristic of excuses or other evidence that serves to lessen or seems to lessen the seriousness of (an offense, guilt, etc.) [*extenuating* circumstances]

innovation (in′ ə vā′shən) *n.*   1. something newly introduced; new method, custom, device, etc.; change in a way of doing things   2. the act or process of innovating

sedentary (sed′′n ter′ē) *adj.*   1. of or marked by much sitting around and little travel   2. keeping one seated much of the time [a *sedentary* job]

superimposed (so͞o′pər im pōzd′) *adj.*   put, laid, or stacked on top of something else

fat, āpe, cär; ten, ēven; is, bīte; gō, hôrn, to͞ol, look; oil, out; up, fur; get; joy; yet; chin; she; thin, *th*en; zh, leisure; ŋ, ring; ə for *a* in *ago, e* in *agent, i* in *sanity, o* in *comply, u* in *focus;* ′ as in *able* (ā′b'l)

Fill in each blank with the word that correctly completes the sentence. Check your answers in the back of the book.

capitulate	covert	edifice	extenuating	sedentary
complicity	desist	elucidate	innovation	superimposed

1. The Magna Carta, the most famous document in British constitutional history, forced King John in 1215 to _____ from using his royal power to take away the rights of the people.

2. A writer is more _____ than a bricklayer.

3. Napoleon I had to _____ to the British after the Battle of Waterloo in 1815.

4. Kicking your husband under the table is a _____ way of getting him to change the subject.

5. Ex-President Bush was accused of _____ in the Iran-Contra coverup.

6. An imposing _____ covering 13½ acres, the Vatican Palace is the largest residential palace in the world.

7. X-rays of the Mona Lisa show three _____ versions, all painted by Leonardo, and all completely different.

8. Eyeglasses were a Chinese _____; Marco Polo saw many Chinese wearing them when he visited China in the 13th century.

9. The ancient Greek philosopher Democritus was the first person to _____ atomic theory.

10. Serious crimes can be forgiven if there are _____ circumstances; for example, most people consider stealing permissible when done to save a life.

The clues marked with asterisks (*) refer to New Words from previous chapters.
Check your answers in the back of the book.

Across

*1. To rub
*5. Belief
9. Prefix meaning "to," as in
_____tract
*10. Set of terms
13. Prefix meaning "down," as in
_____cline
14. Abbr. for *Georgia*
15. Ant. of *fro*
*16. Argument
22. Abbr. for *Ohio*
24. Small hotel
25. Indicate agreement
26. Top-quality
27. Abbr. for *Iowa*
29. Same as 3 Down
30. What books are made from
31. Abbr. for *left end* (football)
32. Prefix meaning "with," as in
_____lect
33. Saudi
37. Same as 22 Across
38. Fiber-containing grain
*39. Belittling
41. What Santa brings naughty
children
*42. To calm
48. Sense organ
*49. To keep down

Down

2. Ant. of *love*
3. Dined
4. Type of tree
*5. Friendly
6. Snakelike fish
7. Breakfast food
8. Prefix meaning "with," as in
_____operate
11. To row
*12. Existing at birth
13. Ant. of *don't*
15. Same as 15 Across
17. Falsehood
18. Abbr. for *Tennessee*
*19. Political disorder
20. Toddler
*21. Set of beliefs
22. Abbr. for *Oregon*
*23. Ranking
*26. Contradiction
28. Gorilla, e.g.
34. Prefix meaning "back," as in
_____ject
35. What a ghost says
36. Globes or spheres
37. Same as 22 Down
40. Hole or opening
43. Same as 8 Down
44. Prefix meaning "to," as in
_____peal
45. Thomas Paine's monogram
46. Suffix meaning "one who," as
in bak_____
47. Prefix meaning "to," as in
_____sault

EXERCISE 13: OWN WORDS

Out of the words from your outside reading that you would like to learn, choose ten that contain roots not found in this book. Following each number, write the word, the pronunciation, and a simple definition. In the space labeled "Word Parts," write the parts of the word and their definitions. Use a dictionary if you need help.

1. _____

Word Parts _____

2. _____

Word Parts _____

3. _____

Word Parts _____

4. _____

Word Parts _____

5. _____

Word Parts _____

6. _____

Word Parts _____

7. _____

Word Parts _____

8. _____

Word Parts _____

9. _____

Word Parts _____

10. _____

Word Parts _____

chapter 9

ROOTS III

Drabble

© 1980 "Drabble" is reprinted by permission of UFS, Inc.

Roots in College Courses

As a college student, you see root words constantly. Below is a brief sample of root words commonly used in college classes.

Word Part and Meaning	English	Social Science	Science and Math	Business and Industry	Fine Arts	Other
cap, cept, ceive, cip— to take or seize	capsulize participle reciprocal	perception emancipate capture intercept captive disciple exceptional children	capsule susceptible capacity receptacle conceive concept forceps incapaci- tated transceiver reciprocal	accounts receivable receipt recipient reciprocate reciprocity capacity	captivating receptive perception concept	exception precept discipline capable deceptive misconcep- tion
fac, fect, fec fic—do or make	fiction affective facsimile factual past perfect tense personi- fication	affection deification ratification defector fact fortification ramifications faction defeatist perfectionist malfeasance factorum facilitator de facto ipso facto	infection effect disinfectant factor factorial facula putrefac- tion	deficit factory defect confection manufacture diversifica- tion facsimile sacrifice forfeit modification office face value	benefactor artifact amplifica- tion feature film affectation perfection façade facet facial	self- sufficient unification justification proficiency faulty feasible difficult feat efficient effective ineffectual
luc, lus, lum, lun, lux— light	elucidate allusion lucid Lucifer	hallucinate lucid luminary lunatic illusion delusion lunatic fringe	lumen lunar translunar luminary lumines- cence	luminous paint translucent illuminate	illustration prelude interlude postlude illustrator	lusty luxury elude lustrous disillusion illustrious

Word Part and Meaning	English	Social Science	Science and Math	Business and Industry	Fine Arts	Other
gen, gin— birth, origin, race	genre generaliza- tion gender	progeny genocide genealogy aborigines gentry gentility genesis genius attorney general general assembly generations indigenous origin	hypoaller- genic heteroge- neous homogene- ous oxygen homogenize gene eugenics congenital generic genitals genus gender general practi- tioner	generate generator engineer	genuine genteel photo- genic originality	primo- genitor octogenar- ian ingenious regenerate degenerate genuflect
plic, plex, pli, ply— bend, fold	complex sen- tence explica- tion	complex implicate supplication deploy plight complicity replicate	complica- tion multiplica- tion solar plexus plexus food sup- plement	application plexiglass apartment complex ply plywood pliable pliers display employ duplex supply and demand exploit	supple complex- ion replica duplicate pleat plié	implicit imply explicit implications complicate reply inexplicable complaint perplex simplicity multiplicity
pos, pon, posit, pound —put or place	tranpose correspon- dence exposé expound compound sen- tence preposi- tion possessive appositive purpose exposition expository speak- ing apposition	repondent trial deposi- tion postponement impostor propose repository opposition party proponent depose symposium exponent disposition depository	compost pile transpose supposition decompose mineral deposit compound exponent positron positive charge positive number	position exposure impound disposal proposal repossess bank deposit compound interest post office postage	posture superim- pose composite compo- sure pose stereo compo- nent exposition overexpo- sure composer transpose	presuppose possible repose responsible imposing juxtapose disposed posit

Word Part and Meaning	English	Social Science	Science and Math	Business and Industry	Fine Arts	Other
sta, stit, stin —stand	stationery stanza statement library stacks	standard deviation constitution institution constituent state statesmanship restitution status quo statute statutory circumstantial	static resistance transistor stagnant stamina stabilize stamen statistical stable compound homeostasis statoblast statocyst staunch	mass transit subsistence status estate real estate interstate statement assistant staple establishment stabilizer stadium stator	statuesque statue stanza stage stance stabile	stalwart standard substitute stationary stack

Continuing Study of Roots

Because root words occur so frequently in college textbooks, you will need to continue your study of roots beyond the 30 presented in this book. In the Own Words exercise in this chapter and the two previous chapters, you are asked to choose words that contain roots not found in the book. We suggest that you start your personal roots file by putting the new roots on flash cards. Write the root on the front. On the back write: (1) the meaning of the root, (2) a key word that will help you remember the meaning of the root, and (3) all of the words you find that are based on that root. For example, if you have discovered the root *path* in a*path*etic (without feeling), you might use the word sym*path*y to help you remember that *path* means "feeling," "suffering," or "disease." Think of as many other words as possible that contain the same spelling of the root and check in the dictionary to see if they come from that root. Whenever you come across an unfamiliar word containing the root, write it on the back of the card under your mnemonic word. Note any alternate spellings of the root that you discover, such as *pass* in the word im*pass*ive (no feelings). See the sample flash card on the next page.

    Using flash cards for roots will serve two purposes. First, you will have many of the unfamiliar words grouped by families, so they will be easier to remember than if you had one word on each card. Second, the fact that you are learning the roots themselves will help you understand still more unfamiliar words. You will be taking a shortcut to a good college vocabulary.

Front

path, pass

Back

feeling, suffering, disease (sympathy)

pathos   psychopathic   passionate
pathetic   apathetic   passivism
empathy   neuropathy   pathogenic
sympathy   homeopathy   impatience
pathologist   pathogenic   patient
telepathy   passion   dispassionate
osteopath   passive   hydropathy
apathy   impassive   impassioned
antipathy   compassion
                patience

New Roots

Below are the ten new roots for this chapter, presented with several familiar words and several that you will learn.

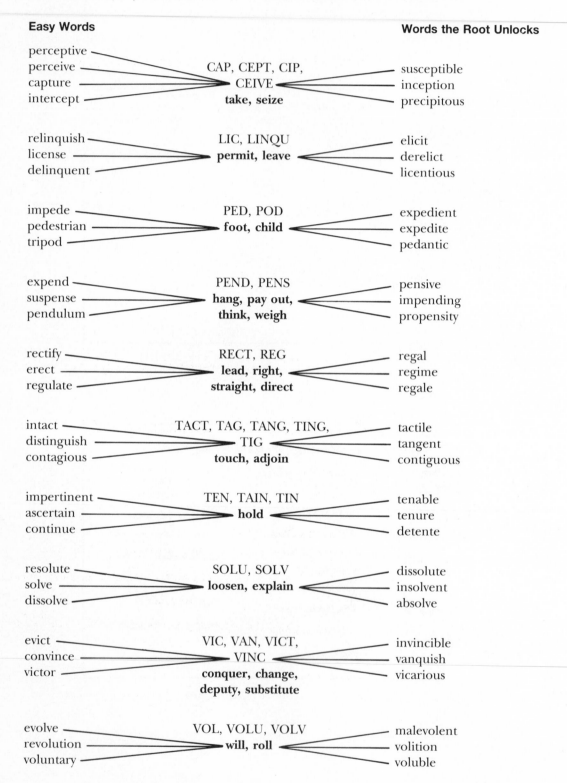

Easy Words

Words the Root Unlocks

perceptive
perceive
capture
intercept

CAP, CEPT, CIP,
CEIVE
take, seize

susceptible
inception
precipitous

relinquish
license
delinquent

LIC, LINQU
permit, leave

elicit
derelict
licentious

impede
pedestrian
tripod

PED, POD
foot, child

expedient
expedite
pedantic

expend
suspense
pendulum

PEND, PENS
**hang, pay out,
think, weigh**

pensive
impending
propensity

rectify
erect
regulate

RECT, REG
**lead, right,
straight, direct**

regal
regime
regale

intact
distinguish
contagious

TACT, TAG, TANG, TING,
TIG
touch, adjoin

tactile
tangent
contiguous

impertinent
ascertain
continue

TEN, TAIN, TIN
hold

tenable
tenure
detente

resolute
solve
dissolve

SOLU, SOLV
loosen, explain

dissolute
insolvent
absolve

evict
convince
victor

VIC, VAN, VICT,
VINC
**conquer, change,
deputy, substitute**

invincible
vanquish
vicarious

evolve
revolution
voluntary

VOL, VOLU, VOLV
will, roll

malevolent
volition
voluble

EXERCISE 1: ROOTS FILL-IN

For each of the roots below, give an example not previously provided in this chapter. Check the examples in your dictionary to be sure they are from the correct roots.

Root	Meaning	Example
cap, cept, cip, ceive	take, seize	_____
lic, linqu	permit, leave	_____
ped, pod	foot, child	_____
pend, pens	hang, pay out, think, weigh	_____
rect, reg	lead, right, straight, direct	_____
tact, tag, tang, ting, tig	touch, adjoin	_____
ten, tain, tin	hold	_____
solu, solv	loosen, explain	_____
vic, van, vict, vinc	conquer, change, deputy, substitute	_____
vol, volu, volv	will, roll	_____

EXERCISE 2: REVIEW WORDS—ROOTS

Before you look at the definitions of the Review Words on the next page, use the roots in this chapter to fill in the blanks below. Check your answers on the next page.

1. e _ _ _ _   to remove (a tenant), by force if necessary

2. e _ _ _ _ e   to develop gradually; unfold (roll out)

3. ex _ _ _ _   to spend, use up, or pay out

4. im _ _ _ e   to hinder or obstruct (keep the feet in place)

5. imper _ _ _ ent   not connected with the matter at hand (not holding to the point)

6. in _ _ _ _   uninjured; kept or left whole; not touched

7. per _ _ _ ive   understanding or becoming aware of (taking through the senses)

8. _ _ _ _ ify   to put right, correct

9. re _ _ _ _ _ ish   to give up (leave again)

10. re _ _ _ _ te   fixed and firm in purpose; determined (explain again)

REVIEW WORDS

Below are the Review Words for this chapter. We will use these words to practice
the skills taught in this chapter.

evict (ē vict′) *v.*   to remove (a tenant) from leased premises by legal procedure, as for failure
to pay rent; to recover (property) through court judgment or superior claim

evolve (ē välv′) *v.*   1. to develop by gradual changes; unfold   2. *Biol.* to develop a species,
organism, or organ from its primitive state to its present or specialized state

expend (ek spend′, ik-) *v.*   1. to spend   2. to consume by using; use up

impede (im pēd′) *v.*   to bar or hinder the progress of; obstruct or delay

impertinent (im purt′'n ənt) *adj.*   1. not pertinent; having no connection with a given matter;
irrelevant   2. not showing proper respect or manners; saucy; insolent; impudent

intact (in takt′) *adj.*   with nothing missing or injured; kept or left whole; sound; entire;
unimpaired

perceptive (pər sep′tiv) *adj.*   able to perceive quickly and easily; having keen insight or
intuition; penetrating

rectify (rek′tə fī′) *v.*   to put or set right; correct; amend

relinquish (ri liŋ′kwish) *v.*   1. to give up or abandon (a plan, policy, etc.)   2. to renounce or
surrender (something owned, a right, etc.)   3. to let go (a grasp, hold, etc.)

resolute (rez′ə loot′) *adj.*   having or showing a fixed, firm purpose; determined; resolved;
unwavering

fat, āpe, cär; ten, ēven; is, bīte; gō, hôrn, tool, look; oil, out; up, fur; get; joy; yet; chin; she; thin, *th*en; zh, leisure; ŋ, ring; ə for *a* in *ago, e* in *agent, i* in *sanity, o* in
comply, u in *focus;* ' as in *able* (ā′b'l)

Fill in each blank with the word that correctly completes the sentence. Check your answers in the back of the book.

| evict | expend | impertinent | perceptive | relinquish |
| evolve | impede | intact | rectify | resolute |

1. Students who are _____ in class risk incurring the ill will of their instructors.

2. Affirmative action is necessary because most white males will not willingly _____ their advantage.

3. Liberals believe that conservatives are trying to _____ progress.

4. Most adolescents are far from _____ when confronted with peer pressure.

5. Lawyers who specialize in landlord-tenant law can help landlords _____ tenants, or they can help tenants who have a complaint against their landlord.

6. Independently wealthy people try to live on the income from their investments, while keeping the principal _____ .

7. Good students will _____ a great deal of effort to earn top grades.

8. When you make a plan, you hope that events will _____ accordingly.

9. A person who is _____ about the feelings of others is likely to do better in business and in love.

10. You should _____ the mistakes you have made.

dissolute (dis′ə lo͞ot′) *adj.*   indulging in pleasure to the point of harming oneself

elicit (i lis′it, ē-) *v.*   1. to draw forth; evoke [to *elicit* an angry reply]   2. to cause to be revealed [to *elicit* facts]

expedient (ik spē′dē ənt, ek-) *adj.*   1. useful for effecting a desired result; convenient   2. based on or guided by self-interest —*n.*   an expedient thing; means to an end

insolvent (in säl′vənt) *adj.*   not solvent; unable to pay debts as they become due; bankrupt

pensive (pen′siv) *adj.*   thoughtful or reflective, often in a melancholy way

regime (re zhēm′, rā zhēm′) *n.*   1. a political or ruling system   2. a system of diet, exercise, etc., for improving health

susceptible (sə sep′tə bəl) *adj.*   easily affected emotionally; having a sensitive nature or sensitive feelings; easily influenced by or affected with [*susceptible* to tuberculosis]

tangent (tan′jənt) *adj.*   that which touches; touching —*n.*   a sudden change to another line of action [to go off on a *tangent*]

tenable (ten′ə bəl) *adj.*   that which can be held, defended, or maintained

tenure (ten′yər, ten′yoor) *n.*   1. the act or right of holding property, an office, etc.   2. the length of time, or the conditions under which, something is held

fat, āpe, cär; ten, ēven; is, bīte; gō, hôrn, to͞ol, look; oil, out; up, fʉr; get; joy; yet; chin; she; thin, *th*en; zh, leisure; ŋ, ring; ə for *a* in *ago, e* in *agent, i* in *sanity, o* in *comply, u* in *focus;* ' as in *able* (ā′b'l)

Fill in each blank with the word that best completes the sentence. Check your answers in the back of the book.

dissolute	expedient	pensive	susceptible	tenable
elicit	insolvent	regime	tangent	tenure

1. Before attending a high school reunion, some people will put themselves on a strict _____ of diet and exercise so they will look their best.

2. Elizabeth II's _____ as queen is for life.

3. The belief that the world is flat is no longer _____ .

4. In geometry, a line touching a curve at only one point is said to be _____ to the curve.

5. Surveys such as the Nielsen polls try to _____ opinions from families who watch television.

6. The Pacific area is the most _____ to volcanic explosions, with 80 percent of all eruptions in the world occurring there.

7. Maximilian II's _____ behavior caused him to lose $36 million at billiards and resulted in his being forced to leave the Bavarian throne.

8. On his expeditions to the Antarctic, Admiral Byrd found it more _____ to spend six months underground in a small shack than to interrupt his explorations to return home.

9. Lenders obtain credit reports on all applicants to screen out those who are _____ .

10. Someone who stares into space in the middle of a party is probably in a _____ mood.

derelict (der′ə likt′) *adj.*   1. deserted by the owner; abandoned   2. neglectful of duty; negligent —*n.*   1. property (especially a ship deserted at sea) that has been abandoned   2. a bum

expedite (eks′pə dīt′) *v.*   to speed up the progress of; hasten; facilitate

impending (im pend′iŋ) *adj.*   about to happen; threatening [*impending* disaster]

inception (in sep′shən) *n.*   the act of beginning; commencement

invincible (in vin′sə bəl) *adj.*   that which cannot be overcome; unconquerable

malevolent (mə lev′ə lənt) *adj.*   wishing evil or harm to others; having or showing ill will; malicious

regal (rē′gəl) *adj.*   of, like, or fit for a king; royal

tactile (tak′təl) *adj.*   of, having, or perceived by the sense of touch

vanquish (vaŋ′kwish, van′kwish) *v.*   to conquer or defeat

volition (vō lish′ən, və lish′ən) *n.*   the act or power of using the will

fat, āpe, cär; ten, ēven; is, bīte; gō, hôrn, tool, look; oil, out; up, fur; get; joy; yet; chin; she; thin, *th*en; zh, leisure; ŋ, ring; ə for *a* in *ago, e* in *agent, i* in *sanity, o* in *comply, u* in *focus;* ′ as in *able* (ā′b′l)

EXERCISE 5: MULTIPLE CHOICE

Circle the letter before the word or phrase that best defines the italicized word in the sentence. Check your answers in the back of the book.

1. A sunken ship is considered *derelict* if the original owners have not tried to find it for 25 years; this means that divers who find treasure on old Spanish galleons are usually allowed to keep it.

   GALLEON

   a. lost   b. abandoned   c. worthless   d. valuable

2. Sending a fax will *expedite* most business, because it isn't necessary to wait for the mail.

   a. prevent   b. begin   c. speed up   d. recover

3. Depression is often accompanied by bad dreams, anxiety, and feelings of *impending* disaster.

   a. terrible   b. unimportant   c. remote   d. coming

4. The *inception* of computers completely changed the nature of office work; for example, it virtually eliminated the typing pool.

   a. introduction   b. end   c. thought   d. expense

5. With the death of Superman it appears that no one at all is *invincible*.

   a. vulnerable   b. unconquerable   c. powerless   d. sneaky

6. Pins are stuck in various parts of voodoo dolls for the *malevolent* purpose of causing another person to feel pain in the same part of the body.

   a. useful   b. evil   c. unusual   d. everyday

7. The *regal* 1981 wedding of Prince Charles and Princess Diana seemed to promise fairy-tale happiness, but it did not work out happily.

   a. royal   b. costly   c. private   d. formal

8. Lack of *tactile* contact with a mother figure makes infant monkeys aggressive and antisocial.

   a. frequent   b. physical   c. emotional   d. continual

9. The soldiers of Julius Caesar *vanquished* most of the barbarian tribes of western Europe during the first century B.C.

   a. surrendered to   b. defeated   c. betrayed   d. fought

10. One way that humans are distinguished from other animals is that they have *volition* rather than being driven entirely by instinct.

    a. dreams   b. emotions   c. will   d. fate

EXERCISE 6: TRUE-FALSE

Write T or F in the blank. Check your answers in the back of the book.

_____ 1. Dissolute people do unwise things.

_____ 2. When you elicit information, you conceal it.

_____ 3. Placing oneself on a regime is almost always harmful.

_____ 4. The tactile senses include the sense of hearing.

_____ 5. When you go off on a tangent, you stray from your subject.

EXERCISE 7: ANALOGIES

In the previous exercises on analogies you learned how to find synonyms, antonyms, classification : example pairs, and cause : effect pairs. This exercise contains one each of those types, plus one new type, in which the relationship is *part : whole*. The first word describes something that is only part of the second thing or idea.

petal : flower :: façade : building

For each group below, decide which of the five kinds of analogies is being used and then fill in the blank to make the second pair agree with the first. Check your answers in the back of the book.

1. impede : block :: pensive : _____   a. thoughtful   b. boring   c. poor
                                           d. outgoing

2. evicting people : being a landlord ::   a. wealth   b. humanity   c. being a king
    regal behavior : _____   d. good parents

3. intact : broken :: expedient :   a. wrong   b. advisable   c. swift
    _____   d. inconvenient

4. solicited items : magazine   a. secretaries   b. writers   c. college
    subscriptions :: tenured jobs : _____   teachers   d. temporary workers

5. impertinence : anger ::   a. action   b. pleasure   c. friendship
    volition : _____   d. sorrow

EXERCISE 8: MATCHING MEANINGS

Write the letter of the word that means the opposite of the word in the first column.
Check your answers in the back of the book.

1. insolvent
2. tenable
3. susceptible
4. invincible
5. derelict

a. defeatable
b. immune
c. cherished
d. rich
e. unbelievable

EXERCISE 9: WORD CONTRASTS

In each group below circle the word that does not mean what the others mean.
Check your answers in the back of the book.

1. expedite   quicken   hasten   retard
2. impending   upcoming   distant   approaching
3. malevolent   kind   sympathetic   lovable
4. inception   origin   onset   completion
5. vanquish   yield   crush   overpower

EXERCISE 10: SENTENCE COMPLETION

Complete each sentence in your own words. Sample answers are provided in the
back of the book.

1. Many people avoid a *derelict* because _____

   _____ .

2. *Dissolute* people often _____

   _____ .

3. A new baby usually *elicits* great joy in the parents; nevertheless, _____

   _____ .

4. It might be *expedient* to buy frozen food; on the other hand, _____

   _____ .

5. If you can *expedite* the renewal of your driver's license by mailing in a form, _____

   _____ .

6. When there is an *impending* hurricane, you should _____ _____ .

7. During the *inception* of a new project at work, _____ _____ .

8. A person might become *insolvent* if _____ _____ .

9. Some drunks think they are *invincible;* therefore, _____ _____ .

10. An example of a mother-in-law being *malevolent* is _____ _____ .

11. If you feel *pensive,* _____ _____ .

12. Princes Diana of England looks *regal* because _____ _____ .

13. Before you go on a strict dietary *regime,* _____ _____ .

14. You might be *susceptible* to a cold even if _____ _____ .

15. The *tactile* sense is especially important when _____ _____ .

16. A teacher who goes off on a *tangent* during a lecture _____ _____ .

17. An idea is *tenable* unless _____ _____ .

18. If you have job *tenure,* _____ _____ .

19. After an army has been *vanquished,* _____ _____ .

20. When you are arrested, if you don't submit of your own *volition,* _____ _____ .

absolve (əb zälv′, ab zälv′, -sälv′) *v.*   1. to free from guilt, duty, etc.   2. to give religious absolution to

contiguous (kən tig′yo͞o əs) *adj.*   1. in contact; touching   2. near; next to

detente (dā tänt′, also dā′tänt′) *n.*   a lessening of tension or hostility, esp. between nations, as through treaties, trade agreements, etc.

licentious (lī sen′shəs) *adj.*   morally unrestrained

pedantic (ped an′tik) *adj.*   emphasizing trivial points of learning

precipitous (pri sip′ə təs) *adj.*   1. steep like a precipice   2. rash; impetuous

propensity (prə pen′sə tē) *n.*   a natural inclination or tendency

regale (ri gāl′) *v.*   to entertain, as with a feast

vicarious (vī ker′ē əs, -kar′-) *adj.*   1. endured or performed by one person in place of another   2. shared in by imagined participation in another's experience [a *vicarious* thrill]

voluble (väl′yo͞o bəl) *adj.*   characterized by a great flow of words; talkative

fat, āpe, cär; ten, ēven; is, bīte; gō, hôrn, to͞ol, look; oil, out; up, fʉr; get; joy; yet; chin; she; thin, *then*; zh, leisure; ŋ, ring; ə for *a* in *ago, e* in *agent, i* in *sanity, o* in *comply, u* in *focus;* ′ as in *able* (ā′b'l)

Fill in each blank with the word that correctly completes the sentence. Check your answers in the back of the book.

absolve	detente	pedantic	propensity	vicarious
contiguous	licentious	precipitous	regale	voluble

1. The United States and England were once enemies but reached a _____ in the early 19th century that has lasted ever since.

2. The Venus's flytrap, a meat-eating plant, has been known to _____ itself on animals as large as a small frog.

3. Instructors should convey an excitement about important ideas rather than a _____ insistence on details.

4. You should be very careful driving on _____ mountain roads.

5. Alaska and Hawaii are not part of the 48 states in the _____ United States.

6. Stage mothers often push their children into careers in entertainment so they can get _____ pleasure from having their children do what they would have liked to do themselves.

7. A filibuster is an extremely long, irrelevant speech which some of our more _____ senators have been known to conduct in order to hinder the passage of a bill they oppose.

8. Some students have a _____ to engage in unimportant behavior such as recopying their notes rather than in meaningful behavior such as figuring out the important points to memorize for exams.

9. Most Christians believe that Jesus died to _____ man of his sins.

10. Catherine the Great of Russia is said to have engaged in a great deal of _____ behavior, including having a large variety of lovers.

The clues marked with asterisks (*) are New Words from previous chapters. Check your answers in the back of the book.

1		2		3		4	5	6		7	8	
						9				10		11
12								13				
						14				15		
16	17		18									
19					20		21					
	22											
23									24	25		
	26	27	28	29		30		31				
32		33										
34			35			36				37		
		38			39			40				

Across

*1. Prayer
9. Tint or color
10. Plant juice
12. Initials for *Daughters of the American Revolution*
13. Negative word
14. Short for *influenza*
15. Sense organ
16. Current style or fad
19. Abbr. for *electrical engineer*
21. Searched for
*22. Enjoying sensation
23. Prefix meaning "again"
24. Payment to the government
*26. Beneficial
33. The first woman
34. Root meaning "other," as in _____ter
*35. Sly
38. Abbr. of *Florence*
39. Decay
40. Distress signal

Down

*1. Dignified
*2. By or in itself
*3. Clear
*4. Irritate
5. Chemical symbol for *gold*
*6. Flimsy
*7. Showy
8. Chemical symbol for *sodium*
*11. A self-contradictory statement
17. To set again
18. Convent woman
20. Spanish-speaking Caribbean island
21. Very big
25. Alt. spelling of prefix meaning "to," as in _____cuse
27. Masculine pronoun
28. Ant. of *good*
29. City in Nevada
30. Couple
31. An undivided whole
32. Short for *laboratory*
36. Ant. of *don't*
37. Abbr. for *south*

Select ten words from your outside reading that you would like to learn and that contain roots not found in this book. After each number below, write the word, the pronunciation, and a simple definition. In the space labeled "Word Parts," write the parts of the word and their definitions.

1. _____

Word Parts _____

2. _____

Word Parts _____

3. _____

Word Parts _____

4. _____

Word Parts _____

5. _____

Word Parts _____

6. _____

Word Parts _____

7. _____

Word Parts _____

8. _____

Word Parts _____

9. _____

Word Parts _____

10. _____

Word Parts _____

chapter 10
WORD HISTORIES

Nobody knows where or when speech began, since written records occurred much later. However, the origin was probably **echoic,** as the following entries exemplify.

chat-ter (chat'ər) *vi.* [ME. *chateren*, orig. echoic] **1.** to make short, indistinct sounds in rapid succession, as birds, apes, etc. **2.** to talk fast, incessantly, and foolishly **3.** to click together rapidly, as the teeth do when the lower jaw trembles from fright or cold **4.** to rattle or vibrate [an improperly adjusted tool *chatters*] —*vt.* to utter with a chattering sound —*n.* **1.** the act or sound of chattering **2.** rapid, foolish talk —**chat'ter·er** *n.*

mur-mur (mur'mər) *n.* [ME. *murmure* < OFr. < L., a murmur, roar, muttering < IE echoic base *mormor-, *murmur-, whence Sans. *marmard-, Gr. *mormurein] **1.** a low, indistinct, continuous sound, as of a stream, far-off voices, etc. **2.** a mumbled or muttered complaint **3.** *Med.* any abnormal sound heard by auscultation of various parts of the body; esp., such a sound in the region of the heart —*vi.* **1.** to make a murmur **2.** to mumble or mutter a complaint —*vt.* to say in a murmur —**mur'mur·er** *n.* —**mur'mur·ing** *adj.*[1]

The words *chatter* and *murmur,* like many other words in our language, sound like (echo) the things they represent. So, for example, if a cave man were trying to communicate the whereabouts of a tribe of baboons, he might point in their direction and repeat the word *chatter.* Or he might say *murmur* to indicate the presence of a stream.

A later source of new words in our language is **foreign languages.** In Chapter 7 we discussed the Anglo-Saxon, Latin, and Greek roots of English. Words based on Latin and Greek are still coming into our language. Take, for example, the recently invented word *quadraphonic,* which refers to the use of four channels to record and reproduce sound. The word comes from the Latin root *quadra,* a square, and the Greek root *phōnē,* a sound. Hundreds of other languages have also contributed to English. *Alcohol* comes from Arabic, *cigar* from Spanish, *cigarette* from French, *coyote* from Nahuatl (the language of the Aztecs), *ski* from Norwegian, *tea* from Chinese, and *waltz* from German. Foreign languages are contributing new words to English even today.

Another source of new words is **names** of people, places, and events. For example, *nicotine* comes from Jean Nicot, a Frenchman who first brought tobacco seeds from America to Europe. *Cologne* comes from the name of the German city that first produced eau de cologne (which literally means "water of Cologne").

Ancient myths also contributed words. For example, in ancient Greek myth, the Titans were a race of giant gods who were overthrown by the gods of Mount Olympus. So *titanic* has come to mean "like the Titans": of great size, strength, or power. The word *erotic,* having to do with love and sex, comes from the Greek god of love, Eros. Eros was known to the Romans as Cupid.

Brand names have sometimes become words in English. For example, the trademark *Xerox* is often used to mean any type of photocopying. You might ask a secretary to xerox a letter without knowing whether the machine was made by Xerox.

Acronyms, words made from the first (or first few) letters of a series of words, have also contributed new words to our language. For example, *scuba* stands for *s*elf-*c*ontained *u*nderwater *b*reathing *a*pparatus, and *laser* stands for *l*ight *a*mplification by *s*timulated *e*mission of *r*adiation.

Finally, new words are often created to describe new inventions or discoveries. Examples are *camcorder* and *diskette.*

[1]With permission. From *Webster's New World Dictionary,* Third College Edition. Copyright © 1988 by Simon & Schuster, Inc.

Learning the etymologies of words can help you in two ways: It can help you understand the words more thoroughly and it can help you remember them better. For example, knowing the origin of the word *titanic* and the word parts of *quadraphonic* not only helps you understand why the words mean what they do but also allows you to use the etymologies as mnemonic devices.

Languages continually change. Someday people will regard the vocabulary of today as archaic, in much the same way that we think of the language of Shakespeare as belonging to the past.

REVIEW WORDS

Below are the Review Words for this chapter. We will use these words to practice the skills taught in this chapter.

annihilate (ə nī′ə lāt′) *v.*   1. to destroy completely; put out of existence; demolish [an atomic bomb can *annihilate* a city]   2. to consider or cause to be of no importance or without effect; nullify [to *annihilate* another's ambition]   3. to kill   4. to conquer decisively; crush

appall (ə pôl′) *v.*   to fill with horror or dismay; shock

clique (klēk; *also* klik) *n.*   a small, exclusive circle of people; snobbish or narrow group

eccentric (ək sen′trik, ik-) *adj.*   1. not having the same center, as two circles, one inside the other; opposed to *concentric*   2. not having the axis exactly in the center; off-center [an *eccentric* wheel]   3. not exactly circular in shape or motion   4. deviating from the norm, as in conduct; out of the ordinary; odd; unconventional

gaudy (gôd′ē) *adj.*   bright and showy, but lacking in good taste; cheaply brilliant and ornate

grotesque (grō tesk′) *adj.*   1. in or of a style of painting, sculpture, etc. in which forms of persons and animals are intermingled with foliage, flowers, or fruits in a fantastic or bizarre design   2. characterized by distortions or striking incongruities in appearance, shape, or manner; fantastic; bizarre   3. ludicrously eccentric or strange; ridiculous; absurd

guerrilla (gə ril′ə; *also* ger il′ə) *n.*   any member of a small defensive force of irregular soldiers, usually volunteers, making surprise raids, esp. behind the lines of an invading enemy army —*adj.*   of or by guerrillas

lavish (lav′ish) *adj.*   1. very generous or liberal in giving or spending, often extravagantly so   2. more than enough; very abundant; unstinted [*lavish* entertainment] —*v.*   to give or spend generously or liberally [to *lavish* time and money on pets]

lenient (lēn′yənt; lē′nē ənt) *adj.*   not harsh or severe in disciplining, punishing, judging, etc.; mild; merciful; clement

lewd (lood) *adj.*   showing, or intended to excite, lust or sexual desire, esp. in an offensive way; lascivious

---

fat, āpe, cär; ten, ēven; is, bīte; gō, hôrn, tool, look; oil, out; up, fur; get; joy; yet; chin; she; thin, *th*en; zh, leisure; ŋ, ring; ə for *a* in *ago*, *e* in *agent*, *i* in *sanity*, *o* in *comply*, *u* in *focus*; ' as in *able* (ā′b'l)

EXERCISE 1: REVIEW WORDS IN CONTEXT

Fill in each blank with the word that correctly completes the sentence. Check your answers in the back of the book.

annihilate	clique	gaudy	guerrilla	lenient
appall	eccentric	grotesque	lavish	lewd

1. Michael Jackson, the popular singer, is said to have _____ behaviors, such as extreme fear of germs.

2. Some children are afraid of clowns; instead of finding them funny, they find them _____ .

3. "Spare the rod and spoil the child" is telling parents not to be _____ .

4. The newly rich are known for buying expensive items that are _____ and in poor taste.

5. In most high schools, there is a _____ of popular students who hang out only with each other.

6. People are afraid that a modern war could _____ civilization.

7. Native Americans sometimes used _____ warfare to resist the white settlers who were taking their land.

8. You can be arrested for _____ and lascivious conduct in public places.

9. The Ancient Romans were known for their _____ feasting on such delicacies as hummingbird tongues.

10. Gwendolyn dyed her hair purple in hopes it would _____ her parents.

Paperback dictionaries usually abbreviate the etymology of a word to save space. Using the short etymologies in your dictionary as clues, match the ten Review Words in the left-hand column with the more extended etymologies in the right-hand column. Place the letter of the correct answer in the blank. Check your answers in the back of the book.

_____	1.	annihilate
_____	2.	appall
_____	3.	clique
_____	4.	eccentric
_____	5.	gaudy
_____	6.	grotesque
_____	7.	guerrilla
_____	8.	lavish
_____	9.	lenient
_____	10.	lewd

a. from an Old French word meaning "a shower of rain"

b. from a Latin word meaning "to grow pale"

c. Spanish for "a little war"

d. from an Old English word meaning "unlearned" or "not a member of the clergy"

e. from Latin word parts meaning "to reduce [our enemies] to nothing"

f. from a Latin word meaning "soft"

g. from Greek, meaning "out of center"

h. from Middle English *gaude,* meaning "a large bead in a rosary" and eventually "a trinket"

i. French, meaning "to make a noise"; originated in the practice of performers having their friends come to performances to applaud them

j. French and Italian, named for a resemblance to strange designs found in Roman caves or grottoes

abominable (ə bäm′ə nə bəl) *adj.*   nasty and disgusting; disagreeable; very bad [*abominable* taste]

crux (kruks, also krooks) *n.*   1. a basic or decisive point   2. a perplexing difficulty

decrepit (dē krep′it, di-) *adj.*   broken down or worn out by old age, illness, or long use

exonerate (eg zän′ər āt, ig-) *v.*   to free from a charge or from guilt; declare or prove blameless

idiosyncrasy (id′ē ō′ siŋ′krə sē) *n.*   1. the temperament or mental constitution peculiar to a person or group   2. any personal peculiarity, mannerism, etc.   3. an individual reaction to a food, drug, etc., that is different from the reaction of most people

jargon (jär′gən) *n.*   the specialized vocabulary and idioms of those in the same work, profession, etc., as of sportswriters or social workers

latent (lāt′′nt) *adj.*   1. present but invisible or inactive; lying hidden and undeveloped within a person or thing, as a quality or power   2. *Biol.* dormant but capable of normal development under the best conditions: said of buds, spores, cocoons, etc. 3. *Psychol.* unconsciously but not actively so [a *latent* homosexual]

laudable (lôd′ə bəl) *adj.*   worthy of praise

Platonic (plə tän′ik, plā-) *adj.*   1. of or characteristic of Plato or his philosophy   2. idealistic or impractical   3. [p] designating a relationship between a man and a woman that is purely spiritual or intellectual and without sexual activity

precocious (pri kō′shəs, prē-) *adj.*   1. developed or matured to a point beyond that which is normal for the age [a *precocious* child]   2. of or showing premature development

fat, āpe, cär; ten, ēven; is, bīte; gō, hôrn, tool, look; oil, out; up, fur; get; joy; yet; chin; she; thin, then; zh, leisure; ŋ, ring; ə for *a* in *ago, e* in *agent, i* in *sanity, o* in *comply, u* in *focus;* ′ as in *able* (ā′b′l)

Match the etymologies in the right-hand column with the New Words in the left-hand column. Use your dictionary if you need help. Check your answers in the back of the book.

_____ 1. abominable

_____ 2. crux

_____ 3. decrepit

_____ 4. exonerate

_____ 5. idiosyncrasy

_____ 6. jargon

_____ 7. latent

_____ 8. laudable

_____ 9. platonic

_____ 10. precocious

a. came into Middle English through a Middle French word meaning "a chattering of birds"

b. in Latin, meaning "to take out the onus or load"

c. Greek, meaning "a mixture of one's own"

d. Latin for "a cross or fork in the road"

e. in Latin, literally meaning "to cook before"; referred to fruits that ripened early

f. from a Latin word meaning "creaky"

g. from the name of an idealistic Greek philosopher

h. from a Latin word meaning "lurking or lying hidden"

i. from Latin, meaning "inhuman"

j. from a Latin word meaning "praise or glory"

Fill in each blank with the word that best completes the sentence. Check your answers in the back of the book.

abominable	decrepit	idiosyncrasies	latent	platonic
crux	exonerate	jargon	laudable	precocious

1. Voltaire thought Shakespeare's writing was so _____ that he referred to our greatest poet as "that drunken fool."

2. Several famous composers had _____; Mozart composed while playing billiards, Gluck wrote while seated in the middle of a field, Rossini usually composed while drunk, and Wagner would dress up in historical costumes before writing.

3. _____ philosophy describes an ideal world of which our world is only an imperfect reflection.

4. The phrase "try another tack" comes from sailing _____ and refers to a change of direction in which the sails shift from one side of the boat to the other.

5. Many psychologists believe that it is common in Western culture to develop the logical part of the brain while leaving _____ the part that could make us intuitive and creative.

6. While giving money to hungry people is _____, it may do more good to help them acquire skills they could use to earn their own money.

7. If you think there is greater chance that a jury will _____ you than a judge, you should demand a jury trial.

8. The _____ of the conservative's argument was that government interference tends to make things worse rather than better.

9. Healthy, active older people often resent the idea held by many young people that the elderly are all _____.

10. Mozart was very _____: he could play the harpsichord at the age of three and the violin at the age of five; he also wrote his first composition when he was five.

animosity (an′ə mäs′ə tē) *n.*   a feeling of strong dislike or hatred; ill will; hostility

apropos (ap′rə pō′) *adv.*   1. at the right time   2. by the way: used to introduce a remark —*adj.* fitting the occasion; relevant; apt

bourgeois (boor zhwä′, boor′ zhwä) *n.*   1. a self-employed person such as a shopkeeper or businessman   2. a member of the middle class   3. a person whose attitudes, beliefs, and practices are conventionally middle-class —*adj.*   middle-class; also used to mean conventional; smug; materialistic

candid (kan′did) *adj.*   1. very honest or frank in what one says or writes   2. unposed and informal [a *candid* photograph]

dispel (di spel′) *v.*   to scatter and drive away; cause to vanish

furtive (fur′tiv) *adj.*   done or acting in a stealthy manner, as if to avoid observation; sneaky

innuendo (in′yōō en′dō′) *n.*   an indirect remark, gesture, or reference, usually implying something negative; insinuation

lethargic (li thär′jik) *adj.*   abnormally drowsy or dull; sluggish, etc.

redundant (ri dun′dənt) *adj.*   1. more than enough; overabundant   2. using more words than are needed; wordy

trite (trīt) *adj.*   worn out by constant use; no longer having freshness, originality, or novelty; stale [a *trite* idea, remark, etc.]

fat, āpe, cär; ten, ēven; is, bīte; gō, hôrn, tōōl, look; oil, out; up, fur; get; joy; yet; chin; she; thin, *th*en; zh, leisure; ŋ, ring; ə for *a* in *ago, e* in *agent, i* in *sanity, o* in *comply, u* in *focus;* ′ as in *able* (ā′b'l)

Use your dictionary to find the etymologies of the words below. Write the appropriate word in the blank. Check your answers in the back of the book.

animosity   bourgeois   dispel   innuendo   redundant
apropos   candid   furtive   lethargic   trite

_____   1. from an Old French word meaning "a fortified town or castle"

_____   2. from a Latin word meaning "repeated surges of waves"

_____   3. from Latin, meaning "worn out by too much rubbing or use"

_____   4. from French, meaning "something that is relevant or to the purpose"

_____   5. from a Latin word meaning "thief"

_____   6. gossip passed on by nods and winks; in Latin it meant "by nodding at"

_____   7. meant "white" and came to refer to the color of toga the Romans wore when campaigning for political office; later came to mean "pure and sincere"

_____   8. originally meant "breath" in Latin; also used to symbolize life, spirit, or passion

_____   9. from the name of the river Lethe in Hades in Greek mythology; anyone who drank of its waters forgot the past; later came to mean "indifferent or listless"

_____ 10. from Latin word parts literally meaning "to drive away"

Circle the letter before the word or phrase that best defines the italicized word in each sentence.

1. The album is full of *candid* photographs of vacations and other family events.

    a. formal   b. embarrassing   c. black and white   d. unposed

2. Because sloths move so slowly they are thought to be *lethargic,* but they can strike quickly if attacked.

    a. sluggish   b. dead   c. ill   d. stupid

3. Many formerly good comparisons have become *trite;* examples are "pretty as a picture," "sharp as a tack," and "poor as a church mouse."

    a. stronger   b. stale   c. dangerous   d. insulting

4. The Tasaday tribe in the Philippine Islands has no weapons for war and no words in its language to express *animosity*.

   a. hostility   b. friendship   c. love   d. fear

5. Belief in the work ethic is a *bourgeois* value.

   a. of royalty   b. of the lower class   c. of the middle class   d. of the upper class

6. It was difficult to get used to the governor's habit of stopping in the middle of a conversation to make remarks that seemed *apropos of* nothing.

   a. relevant to   b. critical of   c. friendly toward   d. angry about

7. Recent studies of gorilla behavior have *dispelled* the belief that the animals are aggressive; they are actually very shy.

   a. gotten rid of   b. proved   c. supported   d. led to

8. If your eyes dart around and do not meet others' gaze, you will look *furtive*.

   a. open   b. sneaky   c. rude   d. violent

9. If you are innocent, it can be harder to fight *innuendo* than lies, because lies can more easily be confronted and disproven.

   a. informers   b. truth   c. falsehoods   d. suggestion

10. Calling someone a dishonest crook is *redundant*.

    a. unkind   b. repetitive   c. unwise   d. all right

EXERCISE 7: TRUE-FALSE

Write T or F in the blank. Check your answers in the back of the book.

_____   1. Louis XIV of France was bourgeois.

_____   2. Everyone has latent abilities.

_____   3. Romeo and Juliet had a platonic relationship.

_____   4. Howard Hughes was known to have many idiosyncrasies.

_____   5. The crux of a problem should be ignored.

EXERCISE 8: ANALOGIES

The analogies below are either synonyms, antonyms, classification : example, cause : effect, or part : whole. First, decide which type of comparison is used in the first pair of words. Second, find a word from the choices that will make the second pair of words have the same relationship. Check your answers in the back of the book.

1. clique : society :: jargon : _____
   a. book   b. profession   c. writer
   d. success

2. grotesque : clown :: precocious :
   _____
   a. late   b. Mickey Mouse   c. early
   d. Mozart

3. lavishness : bankruptcy :: furtiveness : _____
   a. trust   b. suspicion   c. anger   d. love

4. lenient : strict :: trite : _____
   a. old   b. tired   c. original   d. boring

5. gaudy : flashy :: lethargic : _____
   a. sleepy   b. peppy   c. excited   d. sad

EXERCISE 9: MATCHING MEANINGS

Write the letter of the word that means the opposite of the word in the first column. Check your answers in the back of the book.

_____ 1. animosity   a. youthful

_____ 2. abominable   b. friendship

_____ 3. decrepit   c. shameful

_____ 4. laudable   d. excellent

_____ 5. candid   e. deceptive

EXERCISE 10: WORD CONTRASTS

In each group below circle the word that does not mean what the others mean. Check your answers in the back of the book.

1. dispel   scatter   assemble   dissolve
2. exonerate   blame   accuse   incriminate
3. redundant   wordy   repetitious   concise
4. apropos   suitable   fitting   unrelated
5. innuendo   suggestion   statement   implication

Complete each sentence in your own words. Sample answers are provided in the back of the book.

1. As an example of Jeremy's *abominable* taste, _____
   _____.

2. To show her that he bore no *animosity*, _____
   _____.

3. *Apropos* Molly's problems in school, _____
   _____.

4. One U.S. president who was not *bourgeois* was _____
   _____.

5. Well, to be completely *candid*, _____
   _____.

6. The *crux* of the argument in favor of stricter penalties for drug users is _____
   _____.

7. In contrast with the house's *decrepit* appearance when they bought it, _____
   _____.

8. To *dispel* the rumors that she had taken bribes, the candidate _____
   _____.

9. Although he was eventually *exonerated*, _____
   _____.

10. Because of her *furtive* manner, _____
    _____.

11. One of my *idiosyncracies* is _____
    _____.

12. Candidates for office often rely on *innuendo* when _____
    _____.

13. Sports *jargon* includes terms such as _____
    _____.

14. In addition to my talents in music and art, my teacher discovered my *latent* abilities in ____

    _____.

15. Even though contributing to one's church is *laudable,* _____

    _____.

16. Danielle's *lethargic* state was caused by _____

    _____.

17. Their relationship became *platonic* after _____

    _____.

18. I was *precocious,* especially _____

    _____.

19. Two commonly used *redundant* expressions are "past history" and _____

    _____.

20. *Trite* phrases such as "clear as a bell" are _____

    _____.

accolade (ak′ə lād) *n.* anything done or given as a sign of great respect, approval, appreciation, etc.

adroit (ə droit′) *adj.* skillful in a physical or mental way; clever; expert [his *adroit* handling of an awkward situation]

chagrin (shə grin′) *n.* a feeling of embarrassment and annoyance because of failure or disappointment; mortification

erudite (er′yoo dīt′, er′oo-; er′ə-; er′yə-) *adj.* having or showing a wide knowledge gained from reading; learned; scholarly

extricate (eks′tri kāt′) *v.* to set free; release or disentangle (from a net, difficulty, embarrassment, etc.)

hackneyed (hak′nēd) *adj.* made trite and commonplace by overuse

inundate (in′ən dāt′) *v.* to engulf; flood; deluge; overwhelm with a great amount of anything

panacea (pan′ə sē′ə) *n.* a supposed remedy, cure, or medicine for all diseases or ills; cure-all

salient (sāl′yənt, sā′lē ənt) *adj.* standing out from the rest; noticeable; conspicuous; prominent

succinct (sək siŋkt′, suk-) *adj.* clearly and briefly stated

fat, āpe, cär; ten, ēven; is, bīte; gō, hôrn, tōōl, look; oil, out; up, fur; get; joy; yet; chin; she; thin, *th*en; zh, leisure; ŋ, ring; ə for *a* in *ago, e* in *agent, i* in *sanity, o* in *comply, u* in *focus;* ' as in *able* (ā′b'l)

EXERCISE 12: ADVANCED WORDS IN CONTEXT

Fill in each blank with the word that correctly completes the sentence. Check your answers in the back of the book.

accolade   chagrin   extricate   inundate   salient
adroit   erudite   hackneyed   panacea   succinct

1. The least _____ speech in the history of the U.S. Senate was that of Senator Wayne Morse of Oregon on April 24, 1953, when he spoke on the Tidelands of Oil Bill for 22 hours, 26 minutes.

2. Marriage counselors are _____ at handling interpersonal conflict.

3. The Nobel Prizes are a means of giving an _____ to great achievers in six areas: chemistry, physics, physiology, literature, economics, and the promotion of peace.

4. Jesuit priests tend to be _____ as a result of their famous academic training, which can involve more than 15 years of serious study.

5. The actress felt _____ when she saw another actress at the premiere wearing the same dress.

6. The _____ point is the main idea.

7. Harry Houdini was famous for his ability to _____ himself from bonds of every sort—locks, handcuffs, straitjackets, and submerged, sealed boxes.

8. "Don't rub the salt in the wound" is an example of an expression which sounds _____ to people raised in this culture, but which may be new and interesting to a foreigner.

9. Some people believe that vitamin C is a _____, curing everything from cancer to the common cold.

10. There have been at least 500 tidal waves (tsunamis) in recorded history, many of which have been known to _____ entire cities and cause great destruction.

Use your dictionary to find the etymologies of the ten Advanced Words for this chapter. They may be found in brackets after the part of speech or they may be listed as the first definition of the word. The first one is done for you. Check your answers in the back of the book.

1. accolades *Fr. < Pr. acolada < It. accollata, fem. pp. of accolare, to embrace < L. ad, to + collum, neck*

2. adroit _____

3. chagrin _____

4. erudite _____

5. extricate _____

6. hackneyed _____

7. inundate _____

8. panacea _____

9. salient _____

10. succinct _____

Clues marked with asterisks (*) refer to New Words from previous chapters. Check your answers in the back of the book.

Across

*1. Royal
*5. Having to do with touch
10. Smear or dim
12. Possess
*13. Beginning
15. Abbr. for *very important person*
16. Alt. spelling of prefix meaning "out," as in _____centric
17. Caffeine beverage
18. To glide on snow
20. Spanish for *my* or third note of musical scale
21. Initials of TV producer Norman Lear
22. Past tense of *tone*
23. Initials of singer Tina Turner
26. Informal greeting
28. Female sheep
29. Public disorder
31. A very long time
33. Same as 16 Across
34. Ant. of *rural*
36. Covered with lawn
37. Adam's partner
39. Past tense of *light*
41. Ant. of *outer*
*42. Evil
45. The night before
*46. Serious
49. Abbr. for *south*
50. Tool for chopping
51. Currency

Down

1. Initials of poet Robert Browning
*2. Draw forth
3. Firearm
4. Root meaning "ruler," as in hier_____
5. A legal procedure
*6. A part; component
7. Initials of ballplayer Ted Williams
*8. Unconquerable
*9. Convenient
11. Likely
*14. Length of time in office
16. Sound the letter *M* makes
19. Abbr. for *knockout*
*24. Reasonable to believe
*25. Thoughtful
26. Sound of laughter
*27. Administrations
30. Frozen water
32. Either . . . _____
35. Invisible mixture of gases
38. A climbing plant
40. Short form of *Alexander*
43. Ms. Peron
44. Door opener
46. Ant. of *don't*
47. Ant. of *out.*
48. Prefix meaning "back," as in _____trace

EXERCISE 15: OWN WORDS

List ten words from your outside reading that you would like to learn. On the first line write the word, its pronunciation, and a simple definition. On the line below list the origin of the word.

1. _____

Origin _____

2. _____

Origin _____

3. _____

Origin _____

4. _____

Origin _____

5. _____

Origin _____

6. _____

Origin _____

7. _____

Origin _____

8. _____

Origin _____

9. _____

Origin _____

10. _____

Origin _____

chapter 11

THESAURUS

This thesaurus is beneficial, serviceable, excellent, superior, advantageous, edifying, salutary, capital, exemplary.

Take exactly one minute (time yourself) and write as many synonyms as you can think of for the word *love:*

_____   _____   _____

_____   _____   _____

_____   _____   _____

_____   _____   _____

The average person thinks of about eight synonyms in a minute. Compare this number with the number of synonyms contained in the thesaurus sample on the next page. Did you think of most of them?

Because it is virtually impossible to think of all the synonyms for a word, the thesaurus is a useful tool for every college student. It is used constantly by professional writers and speakers. You can use it for writing papers and making oral reports, as well as for vocabulary improvement. For example, suppose you were writing a paper about human emotions. Instead of repeating the word *love* again and again, you could look in the thesaurus under *love* to find synonyms such as *devotion, adoration,* and *fondness.*

The purpose of a thesaurus is to suggest words you might wish to use but haven't been able to think of. A thesaurus cannot replace a dictionary. It does not give pronunciations or etymologies, and only a few give definitions and put the words in context. Some words, such as *status quo,* have no real synonyms; they do not appear in the thesaurus at all. However, a thesaurus can give you more different words to describe the same concept than you could find in any dictionary. The word *thesaurus* comes from Greek and Latin words meaning *treasury,* and a good thesaurus really is a treasury of related words.

Thesaurus Structure

Although there are several different thesauruses, the one most commonly used by college students is *The New American Roget's College Thesaurus in Dictionary Form.* The paperback edition is about the size of a pocket dictionary. Here is a sample page showing the key features.[1]

[1]Unless otherwise noted, this and the rest of the thesaurus quotations within this chapter are from *The New American Roget's College Thesaurus in Dictionary Form* by Andrew T. Morehead and Philip D. Morehead. Revised edition prepared by Philip D. Morehead. Copyright © 1958, 1962 by Albert H. Morehead. Copyright © 1978 by Andrew T. Morehead and Philip D. Morehead. © 1985 by Philip D. Morehead and Andrew T. Morehead. Reprinted by arrangement with The New American Library, Inc., New York, N.Y.

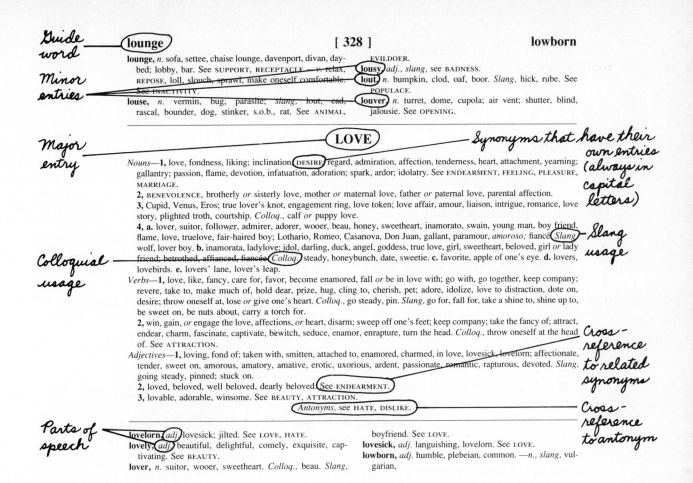

The sample thesaurus page above is annotated with the following handwritten labels:

Guide word — lounge

Minor entries

lounge, *n.* sofa, settee, chaise lounge, davenport, divan, day-bed; lobby, bar. See SUPPORT, RECEPTACLE — *v.* relax, REPOSE, loll, slouch, sprawl, make oneself comfortable. See INACTIVITY.

louse, *n.* vermin, bug, parasite; *slang*, lout, cad, rascal, bounder, dog, stinker, s.o.b., rat. See ANIMAL, EVILDOER.

lousy, *adj.*, *slang*, see BADNESS.

lout, *n.* bumpkin, clod, oaf, boor. *Slang*, hick, rube. See POPULACE.

louver, *n.* turret, dome, cupola; air vent; shutter, blind, jalousie. See OPENING.

[328]

lowborn

Major entry

LOVE — *Synonyms that have their own entries (always in capital letters)*

Nouns—**1**, love, fondness, liking; inclination DESIRE; regard, admiration, affection, tenderness, heart, attachment, yearning; gallantry; passion, flame, devotion, infatuation, adoration, spark, ardor; idolatry. See ENDEARMENT, FEELING, PLEASURE, MARRIAGE.

2, BENEVOLENCE, brotherly *or* sisterly love, mother *or* maternal love, father *or* paternal love, parental affection.

3, Cupid, Venus, Eros; true lover's knot, engagement ring, love token; love affair, amour, liaison, intrigue, romance, love story, plighted troth, courtship. *Colloq.*, calf *or* puppy love.

4, **a.** lover, suitor, follower, admirer, adorer, wooer, beau, honey, sweetheart, inamorato, swain, young man, boy friend, flame, love, truelove, fair-haired boy; Lothario, Romeo, Casanova, Don Juan, gallant, paramour, *amoroso;* fiancé. *Slang*, — *Slang usage* wolf, lover boy. **b.** inamorata, ladylove; idol, darling, duck, angel, goddess, true love, girl, sweetheart, beloved, girl *or* lady friend; betrothed, affianced, fiancée. *Colloq.*, — *Colloquial usage* steady, honeybunch, date, sweetie. **c.** favorite, apple of one's eye. **d.** lovers, lovebirds. **e.** lovers' lane, lover's leap.

Verbs—**1**, love, like, fancy, care for, favor, become enamored, fall *or* be in love with; go with, go together, keep company; revere, take to, make much of, hold dear, prize, hug, cling to, cherish, pet; adore, idolize, love to distraction, dote on, desire; throw oneself at, lose *or* give one's heart. *Colloq.*, go steady, pin. *Slang*, go for, fall for, take a shine to, shine up to, be sweet on, be nuts about, carry a torch for.

2, win, gain, *or* engage the love, affections, *or* heart, disarm; sweep off one's feet; keep company; take the fancy of; attract, endear, charm, fascinate, captivate, bewitch, seduce, enamor, enrapture, turn the head. *Colloq.*, throw oneself at the head — *Cross-reference to related synonyms* of. See ATTRACTION.

Adjectives—**1**, loving, fond of; taken with, smitten, attached to, enamored, charmed, in love, lovesick, lovelorn; affectionate, tender, sweet on, amorous, amatory, amative, erotic, uxorious, ardent, passionate, romantic, rapturous, devoted. *Slang*, going steady, pinned; stuck on.

2, loved, beloved, well beloved, dearly beloved. See ENDEARMENT.

3, lovable, adorable, winsome. See BEAUTY, ATTRACTION.

Antonyms, see HATE, DISLIKE. — *Cross-reference to antonym*

Parts of speech

lovelorn, *adj.* lovesick; jilted. See LOVE, HATE.

lovely, *adj.* beautiful, delightful, comely, exquisite, captivating. See BEAUTY.

lover, *n.* suitor, wooer, sweetheart. *Colloq.*, beau. *Slang*, boyfriend. See LOVE.

lovesick, *adj.* languishing, lovelorn. See LOVE.

lowborn, *adj.* humble, plebeian, common. —*n.*, *slang*, vulgarian,

Guide Words

Like the dictionary, the thesaurus has guide words on each page. In the sample above, the word on the left-hand page is the first entry for that page. The word on the right-hand page is the last entry on that page.

Major Entry

The New American Roget's College Thesaurus in Dictionary Form has major and minor entries. The major entries are centered on the page and are always the noun form of the word. Listed underneath are synonyms, classified by part of speech. Under each part of speech, each numbered entry is a group of synonyms for a different meaning of the word. In our sample, *love* has six different meanings as a noun. The definition for each meaning is never stated, but it can be figured out based on its synonyms. For example, the first entry for nouns under *love* has to do with *feelings for another person.*

> *Nouns*—**1**, love, fondness, liking; inclination, DESIRE; regard, admiration, affection, tenderness, heart, attachment, yearning; gallantry; passion, flame, devotion, infatuation, adoration; spark, ardor; idolatry. See ENDEARMENT, FEELING, PLEASURE, MARRIAGE.

The third entry has to do with *romance.*

> **3,** Cupid, Venus, Eros; true lover's knot, engagement ring, love token; love affair, amour, liaison, intrigue, romance, love story, plighted troth, courtship. *Colloq.,* calf *or* puppy love.

Minor Entry

Minor entries are alphabetized in two columns. They can be any part of speech.

> **lounge,** *n.* sofa, settee, chaise lounge, davenport, divan, day-bed; lobby, bar. See SUPPORT, RECEPTACLE. —*v.* relax, REPOSE, loll, slouch, sprawl, make oneself comfortable. See INACTIVITY.
>
> **louse,** *n.* vermin, bug, parasite; *slang,* lout, cad, rascal, bounder, dog, stinker, s.o.b., rat. See ANIMAL, EVILDOER.
>
> **lousy,** *adj., slang,* see BADNESS.
>
> **lout,** *n.* bumpkin, clod, oaf, boor. *Slang,* hick, rube. See POPULACE.
>
> **louver,** *n.* turret, dome, cupola; air vent; shutter, blind, jalousie. See OPENING.

Cross-references

There are four kinds of cross-references offered in the thesaurus. First, synonyms that have their own major or minor entries are printed in small capital letters. An example is *desire* in the entry for *love* on the sample thesaurus page.

> *Nouns*—**1,** love, fondness, liking; inclination, DESIRE; re-gard, admiration, affection, tenderness, heart, attachment, yearning; gallantry; passion, flame, devotion, infatuation, adoration; spark, ardor; idolatry.

— *Synonyms that have their own entries (always in capital letters)*

Another type of cross-reference is a reference to related synonyms. For example, after the entry and synonyms for *lovelorn* on the sample thesaurus page you will see a cross-reference to *love* and *hate.*

> **lovelorn,** *adj.* lovesick; jilted. See LOVE, HATE.

— *Cross-reference to related synonyms*

These are not synonyms for *lovelorn* but contain words relating to one or more of the meanings of the word. For example, the entry for *love* contains adjectives such as *taken with, smitten, enamored,* and *lovesick,* which could be used instead of *lovelorn* in a sentence.

A third type of cross-reference is related to synonyms and is used when no exact synonyms are available. For example, *low-priced* refers you to the entry for *cheapness* instead of giving a sample of synonyms.

> **low-priced,** *adj.* See CHEAPNESS.

— *Cross-reference instead of synonyms*

If you were to turn to *cheapness* you would find related words such as *cheap, under-priced, moderate, reasonable,* and *inexpensive,* all of which have slightly different meanings but could be used instead of *low-priced* in different sentences. Cross-references are used to save space and allow the thesaurus user access to as many synonyms as possible. Cross-references are worth looking up, since each of them will contain synonyms not appearing under the original entry.

The last type of cross-reference refers you to antonyms for the word, if any. These usually only follow major entries.

> *Antonyms,* see HATE, DISLIKE.

Usage

To help you use a word, the thesaurus gives you the part of speech and tells you if the word is colloquial, slang, or dialect.

lover, *n.* suitor, wooer, sweetheart. *Colloq.* beau. *Slang,* boyfriend. See LOVE.

Colloquial

Slang

Additional Material

Like a dictionary, the thesaurus has additional material at the back. Our edition of *The New American Roget's College Thesaurus in Dictionary Form* contains a list of foreign phrases with definitions and cross-references to related words in the thesaurus. It's always wise to be aware of any additional material contained in the thesaurus you own.

Using the Thesaurus in Dictionary Form

Finding the Word

Let's say you want to find synonyms for the word *ire.* The first thing you would do is look the word up in its alphabetical order. However, *The New American Roget's College Thesaurus in Dictionary Form* doesn't list this word (different thesauruses contain different words). Your next step is to try to think of another word that has the same meaning as *ire.* You might use the dictionary to provide a clue if you can't think of a synonym. The dictionary will tell you that the definition of *ire* is "anger" or "wrath." You can look up either *anger* or *wrath.* This is how the entries for *anger* and *wrath* will look in the thesaurus.

anger, *n. & v.* See RESENTMENT.
wrath, *n.* choler, anger, ire, indignation; vengeance; fury, rage. See RESENTMENT.

If you don't find the synonyms you wanted under *anger* or *wrath,* you could look up the cross-reference *resentment,* a major entry that contains many more possible synonyms.

Another possibility when you can't find a word in the thesaurus is to look for the word under another part of speech. For example, the word *compliant* (an adjective) is not listed, but *comply* (a verb) is. Synonyms listed under *comply* include *consent, conform, yield, submit,* and *obey.* You could use them as synonyms for *compliant* if you changed them to adjectives: *consenting, conforming, yielding, submissive,* and *obedient.*

Using the Word

A thesaurus should always be used in combination with a dictionary because the dictionary tells you how to use the words you find in the thesaurus. The dictionary will tell you more about the meanings of unfamiliar synonyms, such as *indignation,* a synonym for *wrath.* You know that *indignation* is supposed to have a similar meaning, but you may not know whether the two words have the same shade of meaning so that they may be used interchangeably. This is the time to go back to your dictionary and look up *indignation*. You would find that *indignation* is "righteous anger" whereas *wrath* is "intense anger." You could not always use both words in the same sentence.

indignation, *n.* RESENTMENT, ire, wrath; displeasure, vexation.

wrath, *n.* choler, anger, ire, indignation; vengeance; fury, rage. See RESENTMENT.

The dictionary will also tell you if a synonym is rarely used in modern English. For example, you will find the word *choler* as a synonym for *wrath* in the thesaurus. But as you can see in the following dictionary definition, the word is now rarely used, and you probably should not choose it as a substitute for either word when you are writing.

chol-er (käl′ər) *n.* [< L. *cholera:* see fol.] [Now Rare] anger or ill humor

The important thing to remember is that you need both books. You need the thesaurus to suggest words you haven't thought of, and you need the dictionary to tell you more about the words you're not familiar with so you can choose an appropriate synonym.

Types of Thesauruses

Another type of thesaurus, also in dictionary form, is represented by *Webster's Collegiate Thesaurus*. This type of thesaurus, unlike *The New American Roget's College Thesaurus in Dictionary Form,* provides a brief definition of all major entries and usually includes a phrase using the word in context. If the word has more than one meaning or is used in other parts of speech, this thesaurus lists a separate entry with a definition and example. The words following the entry are grouped into exact synonyms, related words, contrasted words, and antonyms. If there are any relevant idioms, they are listed after the antonyms. The more careful classification system and the use of the word in context means there is less need to use a dictionary than with *The New American Roget's College Thesaurus.* Also, this type of thesaurus has many more cross-references than *The New American Roget's College Thesaurus.* On the next page is a column from *Webster's Collegiate Thesaurus* that contains the entries for *love.* Compare it with the sample from *The New American Roget's College Thesaurus in Dictionary Form* found at the beginning of this chapter.

rel admirable, agreeable, attractive, desirable, genial, likable, pleasing, winning, winsome; alluring, appealing, bewitching, captivating, charming, enchanting, engaging, enthralling, entrancing, fetching, ravishing, seductive
con dislikable, displeasing, distasteful, unattractive, unlikable, unpleasing; odious, offensive; abhorrent, abominable, obnoxious, repellent; contemptible, despicable, detestable
ant hateful; unlovable

love *n* **1** the feeling which animates a person who is genuinely fond of someone or something ⟨a mother's *love* for her child⟩
syn affection, attachment, devotion, fondness
rel like(s), liking, regard; adoration, idolatry, piety, worship; allegiance, fealty, fidelity, loyalty; emotion, sentiment; crush, infatuation, passion, yearning; ardency, ardor, enthusiasm, fervor, zeal
con antipathy, aversion; animosity, animus, enmity, hostility, rancor; abhorrence, detestation, hatred
ant hate
2 the affection and tenderness felt by lovers ⟨the ability to distinguish between *love* and lust was the mark of her maturity⟩
syn amorousness, amour, passion
rel crush, infatuation; desire, lust, yearning; ardency, ardor, fervor
idiom (the) tender passion
3 *syn* LOVE AFFAIR, affair, amour, romance
4 *syn* SWEETHEART 1, beloved, darling, dear, honey, honeybunch, loveling, sweet, sweetling, turtledove
love *vb* **1** to like or desire actively ⟨she *loves* her material possessions all too dearly⟩
syn adore, delight (in), ‖eat up
rel appreciate, cherish, prize, treasure, value; dote (on *or* upon), fancy
idiom hold dear
con abjure, give up, reject, relinquish
2 to feel a lover's passion, devotion, or tenderness for ⟨in spite of all their misfortunes, they continued to *love* each other devotedly⟩
syn adore, affection, worship
rel deify, exalt, idolize, revere, venerate; cherish, dote (on *or* upon); admire, fancy, like
con avoid, disregard, ignore, neglect, overlook, shun, slight
3 *syn* CARESS, cosset, cuddle, dandle, fondle, pet
love affair *n* a romantic attachment or episode between lovers ⟨saddened by the end of a summer *love affair*⟩
syn affair, amour, love, romance
rel flirtation, intrigue; triangle, ménage à trois
love child *n syn* BASTARD 1, by-blow, catch colt, chance child, come-by-chance, filius nullius, illegitimate, natural child, whoreson, woods colt
loved *adj syn* FAVORITE 1, beloved, blue-eyed, darling, dear, fair-haired, pet, precious, white-haired, white-headed
love letter *n* a letter expressing a lover's affection ⟨she had never received a *love letter*⟩
syn billet-doux, mash note

---

syn synonym(s)   *rel* related word(s)
idiom idiomatic equivalent(s)   *con* contrasted word(s)
ant antonym(s)   * vulgar
‖ use limited; if in doubt, see a dictionary[2]

Another type of thesaurus commonly used is organized in the form proposed by Peter Mark Roget more than a century ago when he published the first thesaurus. Since Roget was a physician, he decided that the words should be classified by a general-to-specific system similar to that used in biology.

In this type of thesaurus each entry is given a number according to a logical category rather than appearing in alphabetical order. Therefore, to find the synonyms for a word, you must begin by turning to the alphabetized index at the back of the book. This will refer you to one of several numbered categories of synonyms. For example, under *love* you will find two categories: *desire* and *affection*.

> **LOVE** *desire* **865**
>   *affection* **897**
> **loveliness** **845**
> **lovelorn** **898**
> **lovely** *beautiful* **845**
>   *lovable* **897**
> **lover** **865, 897**
> **lovesick** **902**
> **low,** *adj. small* **32**
>   *not high* **207**

The entry number after each category refers you to the guide number printed in boldface at the top outer corner of each page in the main section of the thesaurus. The guide numbers tell you what range of entry numbers will be found on any page. Thus the synonyms for *love,* meaning *desire,* will be found under entry number 865 (*desire*), and the guide numbers at the top of that page are 863–65.

Compare the entries for *desire* and *affection* with the one for *love* found at the beginning of the chapter.

> **865. DESIRE.—**N. **desire,** wish, fancy, inclination, leaning, bent, mind, whim, partiality, predilection, propensity, liking, love, fondness, relish.
>
> longing, hankering, yearning, aspiration, ambition, eagerness, zeal, ardor, solicitude, anxiety.
>
> **need,** want, exigency, urgency, necessity.
>
> **appetite,** keenness, hunger, stomach, thirst, drought.
>
> **avidity,** greed, greediness, covetousness, ravenousness, grasping, craving, rapacity, voracity.
>
> **mania,** passion, rage, furor, frenzy, itching palm, cupidity, kleptomania, dipsomania; monomania.
>
> **Person desiring:** lover, votary, devotee, aspirant; parasite, sycophant.
>
> **attraction,** magnet, loadstone, lure, allurement, fancy, temptation, fascination; hobby.
>
> V. **desire,** wish, wish for, care for, affect, like, take to, cling to, fancy; prefer, have an eye to, have a mind to; have a fancy for, have at heart, be bent upon; set one's heart (*or* mind) upon, covet, crave, hanker after, pine for, long for; hope, etc., 858.
>
> **woo,** court, ogle, solicit; fish for.
>
> **want,** miss, need, lack, feel the want of.
>
> **attract,** allure, whet the appetite; appetize, take one's fancy, tempt, tantalize, make one's mouth water.
>
> Adj. **desirous,** desiring, appetitive, inclined, fain, wishful, longing, wistful; anxious, solicitous, sedulous.[3]

[3]From *Roget's Pocket Thesaurus* edited by C. O. Sylvester Mawson. Copyright © 1922, 1924 by Thomas Y. Crowell Company. Copyright 1946 by Simon & Schuster. Reprinted by arrangement with Pocket Books.

Synonyms for *love,* meaning "affection," will be found under entry number 897 (*love*).

> **897. LOVE.**—*N.* **love,** affection, sympathy, fellow feeling; tenderness, heart, brotherly love; charity, good will, benevolence; attachment, fondness, liking, inclination; regard, admiration, fancy.
>
> yearning, tender passion, gallantry, passion, flame, devotion, fervor, enthusiasm, rapture, enchantment, infatuation, adoration, idolatry.
>
> mother love, maternal love, natural affection.
>
> attractiveness, charm; popularity; idol, favorite, etc., 899.
>
> god of love, Cupid, Eros, Venus; myrtle.
>
> **lover,** suitor, fiancé [F.], follower [*colloq.*], admirer, adorer, wooer, beau, sweetheart, swain, young man [*colloq.*], flame [*colloq.*], love, truelove.
>
> **ladylove,** sweetheart, mistress, inamorata, darling, idol, angel, goddess; betrothed, fiancée [F.].
>
> flirt, coquette.
>
> *V.* **love,** like, fancy, care for, take an interest in, sympathize with; be in love with, regard, revere, take to, set one's affections on, adore, idolize, dote on (*or* upon), make much of, hold dear, prize; hug, cling to, cherish, caress, fondle, pet.
>
> **charm,** attract, attach, fascinate, captivate, bewitch, enrapture, turn the head.
>
> *Adj.* **loving,** affectionate, tender, sympathetic, amorous, lovesick, fond, ardent, passionate, rapturous, devoted, motherly.
>
> **loved,** beloved, well beloved, dearly beloved; dear, precious, darling, pet; favorite, popular.
>
> **lovable,** adorable, lovely, sweet, attractive, winning, winsome, charming, enchanting, captivating, fascinating, bewitching, amiable.[4]

Like the thesaurus in dictionary form, this type of thesaurus will require you to use a dictionary before choosing the most appropriate synonym.

In concluding our discussion on choosing and using a thesaurus, let us emphasize that since a variety of thesauruses are available, you should look carefully at samples of each type before choosing the one thesaurus that suits you best.

Practice

Below is a common English proverb inflated by three different students using the thesaurus.

1. Performances orate more vociferously than verbal utterances.

2. Transactions communicate more sonorously than nomenclature.

3. Behaviors verbalize more clamorously than terminology.

4. What is the proverb? _____

Check your answer in the back of the book.

[4]Ibid.

EXERCISE 1: INFLATED PROVERBS

Use your thesaurus to find substitute words for those in the proverbs below. Your answers should resemble those in the preceding exercise. Samples appear in the back of the book.

1. Variety is the spice of life.

   _____

2. A little learning is a dangerous thing.

   _____

3. Too many cooks spoil the broth.

   _____

EXERCISE 2: USING THE THESAURUS

Use the excerpt from *The New American Roget's College Thesaurus in Dictionary Form* on p. 203 to complete the following exercise. Check your answers in the back of the book.

A. Find the entry for each word below in your thesaurus.

   1. Into what three parts of speech is the entry *love* divided?

      a. _____

      b. _____

      c. _____

   2. What cross-reference is given for *lousy?*

      _____

   3. What are the two slang words for *lout?*

      a. _____

      b. _____

   4. What is a colloquial word for *lover?* _____

B. Now turn to the sample from the *Webster's Collegiate Thesaurus* on p. 207.

   1. What two synonyms are given for love letter?

      a. _____

      b. _____

2. What are the four related words for *love affair*?

   a. _____

   b. _____

   c. _____

   d. _____

3. What idiom is given for the verb form of *love*? _____

   _____

4. What part of speech is *loved*? _____

5. What example is given of usage for the first meaning of *love* as a noun? _____

   _____

REVIEW WORDS

Below are the Review Words for this chapter. We will use these words to practice the skills taught in this chapter.

affirm (ə furm′) *v.* 1. to say positively; declare firmly; assert to be true; opposed to *deny* 2. to make valid; confirm; uphold; ratify (a law, decision, or judgment) 3. *Law* to declare solemnly, but not under oath; make affirmation

aloof (ə lo͞of′) *adj.* 1. at a distance; removed 2. distant in sympathy, interest, etc.; reserved and cool [her manner was *aloof*]

antagonism (an tag′ə niz′əm) *n.* 1. the state of being opposed or hostile to another or to each other; opposition or hostility 2. an opposing force, principle, etc.; specif., a mutually opposing action that can take place between organisms, muscles, drugs, etc.

cordial (kôr′jəl) *adj.* 1. (a) warm and friendly; hearty [a *cordial* hello] (b) sincere; deeply felt [a *cordial* distaste for formality] —*n.* a syrupy alcoholic drink; liqueur

defame (dē fām′, di-) *v.* to attack or injure the reputation or honor of by false and malicious statements; malign, slander, or libel

indispensable (in′di spen′sə bəl) *adj.* that which cannot be dispensed with or neglected; absolutely necessary or required

infirmity (in fur′mə tē) *n.* 1. physical weakness or defect, frailty or ailment, as from old age 2. a moral weakness; defect

instigate (in′stə gāt′) *v.* 1. to urge on, spur on, or incite to some action [to *instigate* others to strife] 2. to cause by inciting; foment [*instigate* a rebellion]

perpetual (pər pech′o͞o əl) *adj.* 1. lasting or enduring forever or for an indefinitely long time; eternal; permanent 2. continuing indefinitely without interruption; unceasing; constant [a *perpetual* nuisance]

ravenous (rav′ən əs) *adj.* 1. greedily or wildly hungry; voracious or famished 2. very eager for gratification [*ravenous* for praise]

fat, āpe, cär; ten, ēven; is, bīte; gō, hôrn, to͞ol, look; oil, out; up, fur; get; joy; yet; chin; she; thin, *th*en; zh, leisure; ŋ, ring; ə for *a* in *ago*, *e* in *agent*, *i* in *sanity*, *o* in *comply*, *u* in *focus*; ′ as in *able* (ā′b'l)

Fill in each blank with the Review Word that correctly completes the sentence.
Check your answers in the back of the book.

| affirm | antagonism | defame | infirmity | perpetual |
| aloof | cordial | indispensable | instigated | ravenous |

1. The president should try to keep _____ from petty political squabbles.

2. To create a new product or theory, a knowledge of what others have done is _____ .

3. Although divorced, the couple maintained a _____ relationship for the sake of the children.

4. When you skip lunch, you will be _____ by dinner time.

5. The ridiculous accusations are nothing more than an attempt to _____ a rival.

6. Cave-dwelling animals that live in _____ darkness are blind.

7. People who, because of religious beliefs, cannot make sworn oaths, are allowed to _____ their statements in court.

8. Subtle forms of aggression, such as coming late for an appointment or failing to thank someone for a gift, cause _____ .

9. The CIA has _____ the overthrow of anti-American governments in other countries.

10. She had to move to a single-story house because her _____ made it impossible for her to negotiate stairs.

EXERCISE 4: REVIEW WORDS—SYNONYMS

Each italicized word below is a Review Word for this chapter. The choices are all
New Words from previous chapters. Circle the letter of the best *synonym.* Check
your answers in the back of the book.

1. The president displayed his *cordial* feelings toward the prime minister by meeting her at her car instead of waiting for a formal greeting at the door to the White House.

   a. taciturn b. congenial c. sensuous d. staunch

2. The movie star's *aloof* attitude toward her male escorts made her unpopular throughout Hollywood.

   a. sedate b. candid c. arrogant d. precocious

3. Attempting to *defame* an opponent in a political contest has become standard procedure.

   a. vilify b. depict c. repose d. flaunt

4. Despite all of the electronic modifications, strings are still an *indispensable* part of a guitar.

   a. vulnerable b. requisite c. ponderous d. enviable

5. The *antagonism* between the two men was made clear by the piercing stares they gave each other.

   a. paradox b. fatalism c. ferment d. hostility

Each italicized word below is a Review Word for this chapter. The choices are all New Words from previous chapters. Circle the letter of the best antonym. Check your answers in the back of the book.

1. The phrase "I do" in a marriage ceremony serves to *affirm* the bride and groom's commitment to each other.

    a. negate b. placate c. sedate d. dispel

2. Far from being just a disease of old age, arthritis can cause *infirmity* in a child as well as in an adult.

    a. credibility b. multiplicity c. soundness d. supplication

3. Orson Welles's "War of the Worlds" radio broadcast was meant to be entertaining, but it *instigated* a panic in New York, where people thought it was a real newscast reporting that the earth was being invaded from outer space.

    a. thwarted b. expedited c. fermented d. alienated

4. Many pests are becoming a *perpetual* problem because they have developed an immunity to the chemicals that are used to destroy them.

    a. malevolent b. susceptible c. tenable d. transitory

5. "Eating like a bird" means that you don't eat much, but in reality birds have *ravenous* appetites, eating more than 90 times their weight in food each year.

    a. insidious b. ostentatious c. satiated d. obnoxious

augment (ôg ment′) *v.*   to make or become greater

benign (bi nīn′) *adj.*   1. good-natured; kindly   2. favorable; beneficial   3. *Med.* not malignant

elite (i lēt′, ā lēt′) *n.*   the group or part of a group regarded as the best, most powerful, etc.

impetuous (im pech′ o͞o əs) *adj.*   acting or done suddenly with little thought; rash

impregnable (im preg′nə bəl) *adj.*   1. that cannot be overcome or entered by force [an *impregnable* fortress]   2. unyielding

indiscreet (in′di skrēt′) *adj.*   careless about what one does or says; not prudent; esp. revealing information that should remain private, such as other people's confidences

insipid (in sip′id) *adj.*   1. without flavor; tasteless   2. not exciting or interesting; dull; lifeless

nebulous (neb′yə ləs) *adj.*   unclear; vague; cloudy

reproach (ri prōch′) *v.*   1. to accuse of a fault   2. to scold in a sharp way —*n.*   1. shame, disgrace, etc.   2. a scolding or censure

retribution (ret′rə byo͞o′shən) *n.*   punishment given in return for some wrong committed

fat, āpe, cär; ten, ēven; is, bīte; gō, hôrn, to͞ol, look; oil, out; up, fʉr; get; joy; yet; chin; she; thin, *th*en; zh, leisure; ŋ, ring; ə for *a* in *ago, e* in *agent, i* in *sanity, o* in *comply, u* in *focus;* ′ as in *able* (ā′b'l)

Fill in each blank with the word that best completes the sentence. Check your answers in the back of the book.

| augment | elite | impregnable | insipid | reproach |
| benign | impetuous | indiscreet | nebulous | retribution |

1. Every country wants to have an _____ defense system.

2. A koala bear never needs to _____ its diet with water; it gets liquid it needs from the vegetation it eats.

    KOALA
    (27-35 in. long)

3. So many people thought that Secretary of State Seward's purchase of Alaska from Russia in 1867 was _____ and irresponsible that they labeled this oil-and-mineral rich region Seward's Folly.

4. St. Nicholas is said to have been a real person whose _____ personality made him loved by everyone, especially the children of the small Belgian town where he lived.

5. Most police forces now have an _____ group of riflemen, called a S.W.A.T. team, to assist them in situations where criminals are holding hostages.

6. If you are _____ enough to betray someone's confidence, you will be distrusted both by the one you betrayed and by the ones you betrayed him to.

7. Many people dislike cooked vegetables because, unless they are prepared properly, they taste _____.

8. The Incas considered bridges so sacred that anyone found tampering with one was not given a _____, but was immediately put to death.

9. The essay was so bad that the professor couldn't tell whether it was the writing that was _____, or the thinking.

10. According to scholars, the Old Testament of the Bible seems more concerned with _____, the New Testament with mercy.

blatant (blāt′nt) *adj.*   1. disagreeably loud; noisy   2. glaringly obvious [*blatant* ignorance]

condone (kən dōn′) *v.*   to forgive, pardon, or overlook (an offense)

deter (dē tur′, di-) *v.*   to keep or discourage (a person), through fear, doubt, etc., from doing something

fastidious (fas tid′ē əs, fə stid′-) *adj.*   1. not easy to please   2. daintily refined; oversensitive   3. overly critical or discriminating

fervor (fur′vər) *n.*   great warmth of emotion; zeal

inherent (in hir′ənt *also,* -her′-) *adj.*   existing in someone or something as a natural and inseparable quality

lithe (līth) *adj.*   bending easily; flexible; supple; limber

raucous (rô′kəs) *adj.*   1. hoarse; rough-sounding [a *raucous* shout]   2. loud and rowdy [a *raucous* party]

rigorous (rig′ər əs) *adj.*   1. characterized by inflexibility; very strict or harsh [a *rigorous* rule, master, etc.]   2. very severe or sharp [a *rigorous* climate]   3. rigidly precise; thoroughly accurate or exact [*rigorous* scholarship]

wrath (rath) *n.*   1. intense anger; rage; fury   2. vengeance motivated by anger

fat, āpe, cär; ten, ēven; is, bīte; gō, hôrn, tool, look; oil, out; up, fur; get; joy; yet; chin; she; thin, *th*en; zh, leisure; ŋ, ring; ə for *a* in *ago, e* in *agent, i* in *sanity, o* in *comply, u* in *focus;* ′ as in *able* (ā′b'l)

Circle the letter before the word that best defines the italicized word in each sentence. Check your answers in the back of the book.

1. In *blatant* defiance of the rules, the dog chewed up the shoe right in front of his master.

   a. minor   b. common   c. subtle   d. obvious

2. Some parents punish their children for hitting each other regardless of who started it, to show that they don't *condone* violence as a way of solving problems.

   a. pardon   b. praise   c. deny   d. believe

3. According to the postal workers' motto, neither rain nor snow will *deter* mail carriers from the delivery of the mail.

   a. encourage   b. please   c. discourage   d. defend

4. People in the public eye have to eat with *fastidious* table manners.

   a. careless   b. ridiculous   c. new   d. careful

5. Young people usually display more *fervor* for social causes than middle-aged people do.

   a. indifference   b. threatening   c. silence   d. passion

6. Although it seems that some stress is *inherent* in living, excessive stress has become the number-one health problem in our country, leading to heart attacks, ulcers, migraine headaches, and even arthritis.

   a. discovered   b. reduced   c. natural   d. accepted

7. The *lithe* movements of the Russian ballerina Anna Pavlova made her one of the most famous dancers of all time.

   a. supple   b. clumsy   c. inventive   d. energetic

8. As people get older, their parties tend to get less and less *raucous*.

   a. timid   b. rowdy   c. silent   d. big

9. *Rigorous* geographers have calculated that the exact center of the United States is latitude 39°50′ north and longitude 98°35′ west, a point located in Kansas.

   a. sloppy   b. young   c. exacting   d. inexperienced

10. In 1397, during the Black Plague, the citizens of Lubeck, Germany, in attempting to quiet the *wrath* of God, threw large amounts of money and jewelry into a monastery courtyard, but the priests, fearing contamination, threw the valuables back over the walls.

    a. love   b. anger   c. sight   d. existence

EXERCISE 8: TRUE-FALSE

Write T or F in the blank. Check your answers in the back of the book.

_____ 1. Members of an elite group are special.

_____ 2. Evangelists are filled with religious fervor.

_____ 3. In the United States every citizen has the inherent right to liberty unless he or she violates the law.

_____ 4. A bank clerk who is indiscreet with secret information can expect to be praised by his employers.

_____ 5. You reward somebody by seeking retribution.

EXERCISE 9: ANALOGIES

The analogies below are either synonyms, antonyms, classification : example, cause : effect, or part : whole. First, decide which type of comparison is used in the first pair of words. Second, find the word from the choices that will make the second pair of words have the same relationship. Check your answers in the back of the book.

1. affirm : support :: fastidious : _____
   a. sloppy   b. neat   c. dangerous
   d. useless

2. cordial behavior : being a good host :: rigorous methods : _____
   a. carelessness   b. random ideas
   c. scientific research   d. opinions

3. antagonism : love :: impregnable : _____
   a. safe   b. strong   c. kind
   d. susceptible

4. old age : infirmity :: nebulous statement : _____
   a. confusion   b. honesty   c. books
   d. creativity

5. indispensable activity : breathing :: lithe animal : _____
   a. all animals   b. graceful animal
   c. gazelle   d. quick movement

EXERCISE 10: MATCHING MEANINGS

Write the letter of the word that means the *opposite* of the word in the first column. Check your answers in the back of the book.

_____	1. raucous		a.	exciting
_____	2. reproach		b.	encourage
_____	3. insipid		c.	menacing
_____	4. deter		d.	quiet
_____	5. benign		e.	congratulation

EXERCISE 11: WORD CONTRASTS

In each group below circle the word that does not mean what the others mean. Check your answers in the back of the book.

1. augment   supplement   deplete   increase
2. blatant   obvious   loud   modest
3. condone   disapprove   blame   reproach
4. impetuous   deliberate   hasty   abrupt
5. wrath   anger   pleasure   rage

EXERCISE 12: SYNONYMS

Each word in the left-hand column is a New Word from this chapter. Match each with a synonym in the right-hand column. Write the letter of the synonym in the space provided. Check your answers in the back of the book.

_____	1. wrath		a.	trite
_____	2. reproach		b.	overt
_____	3. insipid		c.	ire
_____	4. blatant		d.	retaliation
_____	5. retribution		e.	reprimand
_____	6. rigorous		f.	countenance
_____	7. fastidious		g.	intrinsic
_____	8. impregnable		h.	meticulous
_____	9. inherent		i.	stringent
_____	10. condone		j.	invincible

EXERCISE 13: ANTONYMS

Each word in the left-hand column is a New Word from this chapter. Match each with an antonym in the right-hand column. Write the letter of the antonym in the space provided. Check your answers in the back of the book.

_____	1. augment	a.	extrinsic
_____	2. nebulous	b.	menial
_____	3. inherent	c.	vulnerable
_____	4. benign	d.	deplete
_____	5. raucous	e.	ponderous
_____	6. elite	f.	lucid
_____	7. lithe	g.	lethargy
_____	8. indiscreet	h.	taciturn
_____	9. fervor	i.	prudent
_____	10. impregnable	j.	malign

EXERCISE 14: SENTENCE COMPLETION

Complete each sentence in your own words. Sample answers are provided in the back of the book.

1. To *augment* your income, you might _____
_____ .

2. A man with a *benign* personality is _____
_____ .

3. An example of a *blatant* act of cheating is _____
_____ .

4. A teacher should not *condone* students talking in class unless _____
_____ .

5. You can *deter* burglars by _____
_____ .

6. An example of an *elite* group might be the movie stars who get to _____
_____ .

7. You might find it difficult to live with a *fastidious* person because _____
_____ .

8. If you support a position with *fervor,* _____
_____ .

9. An *impetuous* act might be necessary when _____
_____ .

10. A fortress should be *impregnable;* otherwise, _____
_____ .

11. *Indiscreet* people can get into trouble at work if they _____
_____ .

12. You should look at the problems *inherent* in buying a house before you purchase one, or
else _____
_____ .

13. When hospital food is *insipid,* _____
_____ .

14. A ballerina must be *lithe* so that _____
_____ .

15. If an idea is *nebulous,* _____
_____ .

16. A *raucous* party might disturb your neighbors; therefore, _____
_____ .

17. A teacher will *reproach* you when _____
_____ .

18. You seek *retribution* after _____
_____ .

19. You must be *rigorous* when measuring the chemicals for a chemistry experiment; otherwise,
_____
_____ .

20. The last time I was filled with *wrath* _____
_____ .

austere (ô stir′) *adj.* 1. having a severe or stern look, manner, etc.; forbidding 2. showing strict self-discipline and self-denial 3. very plain; lacking ornament or luxury [*austere* surroundings]

clandestine (klan des′tin) *adj.* kept secret or hidden, esp. for some improper purpose

delineate (di lin′ē āt′) *v.* 1. to trace the outline of; sketch out 2. to draw; depict 3. depict in words; describe

esoteric (es′ə ter′ik) *adj.* 1. intended for or understood by only a chosen few, as an inner group of disciples 2. confidential; private; withheld [an *esoteric* plan]

exacerbate (ig zas′ər bāt′, eg-) *v.* 1. to make more intense or sharp; aggravate (disease, pain, annoyance, etc.) 2. to exasperate; annoy; irritate; embitter

innocuous (in näk′yoo əs) *adj.* 1. that which does not injure or harm; harmless [an *innocuous* insect] 2. not controversial, offensive, or stimulating; dull and uninspiring [an *innocuous* speech]

loquacious (lō kwā′shəs) *adj.* very talkative; fond of talking

mollify (mäl′ə fī′) *v.* 1. to soothe the temper of; pacify; appease 2. to make less intense, severe, or violent

stratagem (strat′ə jəm) *n.* 1. a trick, scheme, or plan for deceiving an enemy in war 2. any trick or scheme for achieving some purpose

vacillate (vas′ə lāt′) *v.* to waver in motion, opinion, etc.

fat, āpe, cär; ten, ēven; is, bīte; gō, hôrn, too̅l, look; oil, out; up, fʉr; get; joy; yet; chin; she; thin, *th*en; zh, leisure; ŋ, ring; ə for *a* in *ago, e* in *agent, i* in *sanity, o* in *comply, u* in *focus;* ′ as in *able* (ā′b'l)

EXERCISE 15: ADVANCED WORDS IN CONTEXT

Fill in each blank with the word that best completes the sentence. Check your answers in the back of the book.

austere   delineate   exacerbate   loquacious   stratagem
clandestine   esoteric   innocuous   mollify   vacillate

1. The Rosicrucians are members of an _____ society who claim that their order has existed since the days of ancient Egypt.

2. Because people like to talk about themselves, even a very shy person can become _____ if the listener shows enough interest, understanding, and acceptance.

3. Because the gopher snake in California cannot be distinguished from a rattlesnake except at a very close range, it is best to avoid it even though it is _____.

4. George Clemenceau thought he could _____ Hitler and avoid a world war by giving him Belgium and Poland.

5. To avoid misunderstandings, it is important that business partners _____ their responsibilities in advance.

6. Early monasteries were designed to be _____ places where monks would not be distracted from their duties to God.

7. When someone is angry at you, making excuses and blaming others will only _____ the problem.

8. A _____ involving a purposeful leak of "top-secret information"—that the Allies planned to invade beaches on the central and south coast of France—allowed the American and British navies to sail 4066 landing craft undetected across the English Channel to invade Northern France on D-Day, 1945.

9. _____ meetings between representatives of heads of governments often precede official negotiation of peace treaties.

10. If you _____ between majors, you could accumulate a lot of credits without graduating.

In the left-hand column are the ten Advanced Words from this chapter. In the right-hand column are ten words that are either synonyms or antonyms for them. First, find the synonym or antonym for each word in the left-hand column. Write its letter in the column marked "Match." In the column marked "Relationship" write *A* if the two words are antonyms and *S* if the words are synonyms.

Match   **Relationship**

Match	Relationship				
_____	_____	1.	clandestine	a.	staunch
_____	_____	2.	austere	b.	depict
_____	_____	3.	innocuous	c.	ruse
_____	_____	4.	delineate	d.	mitigate
_____	_____	5.	stratagem	e.	placate
_____	_____	6.	esoteric	f.	covert
_____	_____	7.	loquacious	g.	mundane
_____	_____	8.	mollify	h.	malevolent
_____	_____	9.	vacillating	i.	ostentatious
_____	_____	10.	exacerbate	j.	voluble

Clues marked with asterisks (*) refer to New Words from previous chapters. Check your answers in the back of the book.

Across

*1. Personal peculiarity
8. Prefix meaning "not," as in
   _____sense
9. Ant. of *fro*
*10. Trickery
12. Abbr. of *unidentified flying object*
13. Gull-like seabird
14. Man's name
*15. Emptiness
17. Abbr. for *November*
18. Ant. of *crazy*
19. A metal
20. To possess
21. A standard, basic measure
23. Ant. of *in*
24. Computer word
26. Alt. spelling of prefix meaning "to," as in
   _____tract
29. Sightseeing trip
30. Alt. spelling of prefix meaning "against," as in
   _____pose, _____press
*31. Side or aspect
33. Prefix meaning "against," as in _____social
35. Abbr. for *tuberculosis*
*36. Able to float

Down

*1. Hint
2. Ant. of *don't*
*3. Bankrupt
*4. Things as they are
5. Long ago (days of _____)
6. Metal currency
*7. Hostility
*11. Impermanent

*16. Falling apart
22. Almond, pecan, etc.
24. The husks of grain
25. Small child
26. Abbr. for *American Federation of Teachers*
27. Diet cola
28. Abbr. for *debutante*
32. Abbr. for *Tuesday*
34. Abbr. for *New Testament*

EXERCISE 18: OWN WORDS

List ten words from your outside reading that have at least one synonym and one antonym and that you would like to learn. On the line below the word, write a synonym and an antonym.

1. _____

   _____

2. _____

   _____

3. _____

   _____

4. _____

   _____

5. _____

   _____

6. _____

   _____

7. _____

   _____

8. _____

   _____

9. _____

   _____

10. _____

    _____

chapter 12

USING WORDS CORRECTLY

© 1981 King Features Syndicate, Inc.

Since you started this book you have learned about 400 words. You have also gained the tools for locating additional new words and finding their definitions, their pronunciations, their etymologies, their word parts, and their synonyms and antonyms. But you haven't completely mastered a word until you are able to use it correctly and comfortably in speech and writing.

Shades of Meaning

Look at the thesaurus entry below:

INSANITY

Nouns—**1,** insanity, lunacy, derangement, craziness, feeble-mindedness; psychosis, psychopathy, schizophrenia, split personality, paranoia, *dementia praecox*, neurosis; madness, mental illness, abnormality, aberration; dementia, frenzy, raving, delirium, hallucination; lycanthropy; rabies, hydrophobia; disordered reason *or* intellect; diseased, unsound, *or* abnormal mind; idiocy, imbecility, anility, senility, dotage (see AGE). See UNCONFORMITY, FOLLY.

2, vertigo, dizziness, swimming; sunstroke, moon-madness; [nervous] breakdown, collapse.

3, mania; monomania, megalomania, nymphomania, bibliomania, pyromania, logomania, theomania, kleptomania, dipsomania, Anglomania; delirium tremens; hypochondriasis, melancholia, hysteria (see DEJECTION); obsession, fixation; shell shock; phobia (see FEAR). *Slang,* hangup.

4, madman, madwoman, maniac, bedlamite, lunatic; demoniac, dipsomaniac, megalomaniac; neurotic, psychotic, psychopath, schizophrenic, catatonic, paranoiac; idiot, imbecile, cretin, moron, lunatic. *Colloq.,* couch case. *Slang,* nut, crank, loon[y], bat, bug, screwball, oddball, case, crackpot.

5, insane asylum, sanitarium, sanatorium, mental hospital *or* institution, bedlam, madhouse, booby hatch; straight jacket, padded cell. *Slang,* nuthouse, bughouse, loony bin.

6, psychiatrist, alienist (see INTELLECT).

Verbs—**1,** be insane, be out of one's mind; lose one's senses *or* reason; lose one's faculties *or* wits; go mad, run mad *or* amuck, rave, rant, dote, ramble, wander; drivel; take leave of one's senses, go into a tailspin *or* nosedive, break *or* crack up, go to pieces; lose one's head. *Colloq.,* come apart at the seams. *Slang,* have a screw loose, have bats in the belfry, not have all one's marbles *or* buttons; go off one's nut *or* rocker, see things, flip [one's lid], flip *or* freak out.

2, drive mad *or* crazy, craze, distract, shatter, unhinge, madden, dement, addle the wits of, derange; infatuate, obsess, turn the brain, turn one's head, go to one's head.

3, commit, put away, institutionalize, lock up (see RESTRAINT); certify.

Adjectives—**1,** insane, mad, lunatic; crazy, crazed, *non compos mentis,* unhinged, unbalanced, disturbed; paranoid, manic, psychopathic, psychotic, psychoneurotic, manic-depressive; not right, touched; bereft of reason; unhinged, unsettled in one's mind; insensate, reasonless, beside oneself, demented, daft; frenzied, frenetic; possessed [of a devil]; far gone, maddened, moonstruck; scatterbrained, crackbrained, off one's head; maniacal; delirious, irrational, lightheaded, incoherent, rambling, doting, wandering; amuck, frantic, raving, stark mad, staring mad. *Slang,* crazy as a bedbug, loco, psycho, nutty [as a fruitcake], screwy, wacky, bananas, off the wall, off one's trolley *or* rocker, freaky, bonkers; tetched, pixilated, bughouse; mental (*Brit.*).

2, rabid, giddy, dizzy, cuckoo, daft, vertiginous, wild, slap-happy; mazed, flighty; distracted, distraught; mad as a hatter *or* March hare; of unsound mind; touched [in one's head], not in one's right mind; in a fog *or* haze; out of one's mind, head, senses, *or* wits; on the ragged edge. *Colloq.,* daffy. *Slang,* off one's nut, haywire, barmy, balmy.

3, fanatical, obsessed, infatuated; odd, eccentric (see UN-CONFORMITY); hipped; hypochondriac; idiot, imbecile, silly.

4, monomaniacal, kleptomaniacal, *etc.* (see *Nouns, 3*).

Adverbs—insanely; like one possessed; maniacally, etc.

Antonyms, see SANITY.[1]

All the words given in the entry are supposed to be synonyms for insanity in its various parts of speech. But does it really mean the same thing to say a person is *scatterbrained* as to say he is *demented* or *stark raving mad?* Is there a difference between a *psychopath* and an *imbecile?* The thesaurus does not deal with these differences.

In Chapter 11 you were directed to check words in the dictionary to learn more about usage. Most pocket dictionary entries don't go into usage in much detail, but larger dictionaries often do. Below is a dictionary entry for *insanity*. Note the discussion of shades of meaning under *SYN*.

> **in·san·i·ty** (in san′ə tē) *n., pl.* -**ties** [L. *insanitas* < *insanus*] **1** the state of being insane; mental illness or derangement, usually excluding amentia: not a technical term **2** *Law* any form or degree of mental derangement or unsoundness of mind, permanent or temporary, that makes a person incapable of what is regarded legally as normal, rational conduct or judgment: it usually implies a need for hospitalization **3** great folly; extreme senselessness
>
> **SYN.—insanity,** current in popular and legal language but not used technically in medicine (see definition above), implies mental derangement in one who formerly had mental health; **lunacy** specifically suggests periodic spells of insanity, but is now most commonly used in its extended sense of extreme folly; **dementia** is the general term for an acquired mental disorder, now generally one of organic origin, as distinguished from *amentia* (congenital mental deficiency); **psychosis** is the psychiatric term for any of various specialized mental disorders, functional or organic, in which the personality is seriously disorganized —**ANT.** sanity

You can see, for example, that a different word would be used in a legal setting than in a medical one.

The discussion of shades of meaning just shown is not repeated under each synonym for *insanity*. Instead, the entries for these synonyms contain cross-references to the main synonym, *insanity*. See, for example, the entry for *lunacy*.

> **lu·na·cy** (loo′nə sē) *n.* [LUNA(TIC) + -CY] **1** a) orig., intermittent insanity, formerly supposed to change in intensity with the phases of the moon b) mental unsoundness; insanity **2** *pl.* -**cies** great folly or a foolish act —
> **SYN.** INSANITY

Synonyms can differ in **intensity.** For example, a person who is *giddy* is only slightly out of his mind, whereas a *psychotic* is much farther gone. In addition to intensity, a word may have various other connotations. **Connotations** are ideas or associations suggested by a word or phrase in addition to its official meaning, or **denotation.** For example, the word *flag* denotes a piece of cloth symbolizing a country or state. However, it can connote everything from good citizenship to patriotism to extreme nationalism. Because of its connotations, one person may be

---

[1] *The New American Roget's College Thesaurus in Dictionary Form* by Andrew T. Morehead and Philip D. Morehead. Revised edition prepared by Philip D. Morehead. Copyright © 1958, 1962 by Albert H. Morehead. Copyright © 1978 by Andrew T. Morehead and Philip D. Morehead. Copyright © 1985 by Philip D. Morehead and Andrew T. Morehead.

arrested for burning it whereas another may be willing to die to defend it. *To lose one's head* connotes temporary insanity, but *not to have all one's marbles* connotes a more permanent problem.

It can be difficult to use an unfamiliar word correctly, since you may be unaware of its connotations. If usage is not discussed in your dictionary, try to note the context in which you saw the word and use it in a similar way. If you need to memorize the word, include a sentence showing the usage on the back of your flash card. The only way you can be positive that you are using the word correctly is to see or hear it many times in context.

Idiomatic Usage

Idiomatic usage refers to the usual way in which words of a language are joined together to express thought. Idiomatic usage is generally part of a dictionary entry.

> **a-gree** (ə grē′) *vi.* **-greed′, -gree′ing** [ME. *agreen* < OFr. *agreer*, to receive kindly < OFr. *a gre*, favorably < *a* (L. *ad*), to + *gre*, good will < L. *gratus*, pleasing] **1.** to consent or accede (*to*); say "yes" **2.** to be in harmony or accord [their versions *agree*] **3.** to be of the same opinion; concur (*with*) **4.** to arrive at a satisfactory understanding (*about* prices, terms, etc.) **5.** to be suitable, healthful, etc. (followed by *with*) [this climate does not *agree* with him] **6.** *Gram.* to be inflected so as to correspond in number, person, case, or gender —*vt.* to grant or acknowledge: followed by a noun clause [we *agreed* that it was true]

The entry above distinguishes among *agree to, agree with, agree about,* and *agree that.* Idiomatic usage is one of the hardest things to learn when trying to master a foreign language. For example, how would you explain to a foreigner why we say *think about* rather than *think on* or why *in the right* has a different meaning from *on the right?*

The dictionary provides some help, but sometimes paperback dictionary entries are too brief to explain idiomatic usage fully. That's why you sometimes hear unidiomatic sentences such as "I'm going to conform my skirt to the fashionable length" or "The mountain is eminent." In the end, you must rely mainly on context to learn usage.

Words That Look or Sound Alike

Some pairs of words are confused in writing because they look very similar (*altar* and *alter*) or because they sound alike (*access* and *excess*). These problems are much easier to solve than confusions caused by shades of meaning or idiomatic usage, for you can simply use word parts or word histories and mnemonic devices. For example, the spellings of *access* and *excess* can be memorized based on their word parts. *Access* comes from *ad*(to) and *cedere* (to go). The word's meaning, "act of approaching, entering, or using" (going *to*), comes directly from these parts. On the other hand, *excess* comes from *ex* (out, beyond) and *cedere* (to go). *Excess* means "action, conduct, or amount that is greater than necessary or usual" (go *beyond*). To distinguish *cereal,* a grain used as food, from *serial,* something arranged or appearing in a series, you could memorize the words' etymologies: *cereal* comes from *Ceres,* the Roman goddess of agriculture; *serial* comes from the same root as *series.* To differentiate *altar,* a raised platform, and *alter,* change, you could remember that *altar* comes from *altus,* "high" (use the vowel sound in *tall* as a mnemonic), whereas *alter* is still spelled the same way as its Latin root, *alter,* meaning "other."

The following Review Words are often confused with words similar to them in meaning. Read each definition, then read the dictionary excerpts describing their usage.

cumbersome (kum′bər səm) *adj.*   hard to handle or deal with because of size, weight, or many parts; burdensome; unwieldy; clumsy

> *SYN.*—**cumbersome** implies a heaviness and bulkiness that makes for awkward handling and, in extended use, connotes unwieldiness [*cumbersome* formalities]; **heavy** implies relatively great density, quantity, intensity, etc. and figuratively connotes a pressing down on the mind, spirits, or senses [*heavy* water, *heavy*-hearted]; **weighty** suggests heaviness as an absolute rather than a relative quality and figuratively connotes great importance or influence [a *weighty* problem]; **ponderous** applies to something that is very heavy because of size or bulk and figuratively connotes a labored or dull quality [a *ponderous* dissertation]; **massive** stresses largeness and solidity rather than heaviness and connotes an impressiveness due to great magnitude [*massive* structures]

devastate (dev′əs tāt′) *v.*   1. to lay waste; make desolate; ravage; destroy   2. to make helpless; overwhelm [the teacher's criticism *devastated* him]

> *SYN.*—**devastate** implies near total destruction [the drought *devastated* the crops]; **destroy** implies a tearing down or bringing to an end by wrecking, ruining, killing, eradicating, etc. and is the term of broadest application here [to *destroy* a city, one's influence, etc.]; **demolish** implies such destructive force as to completely smash to pieces [the bombs *demolished* the factories]; **raze** means to level to the ground, either destructively or by systematic wrecking with a salvaging of useful parts; to **annihilate** is to destroy so completely as to blot out of existence [rights that cannot be *annihilated*]

insurrection (in′sə rek′shən) *n.*   a rising up against established authority; rebellion; revolt

> *SYN.*—**insurrection** suggests a less extensive or less organized outbreak than rebellion [the Philippine *Insurrection*]; **rebellion** implies organized, armed, open resistance to the authority or government in power, and, when applied historically, connotes failure [Shays' *Rebellion*]; **revolution** applies to a rebellion that succeeds in overthrowing an old government and establishing a new one [the American *Revolution*] or to any movement that brings about a drastic change in society [the Industrial *Revolution*]; **revolt** stresses a casting off of allegiance or a refusal to submit to established authority [the *revolt* of the angels led by Lucifer]; **mutiny** applies to a forcible revolt of soldiers, or especially sailors, against their officers [*mutiny* on the Bounty]; **uprising** is a simple, direct term for any outbreak against a government and applies to small, limited actions or to initial indications of a general rebellion [local *uprisings* against the Stamp Act]

remorse (ri môrs′) *n.*   a deep, torturing sense of guilt felt over a wrong that one has done; self-reproach

> *SYN.*—**remorse** implies a deep and torturing sense of guilt; **penitence** implies sorrow over having sinned or done wrong; **repentance** implies full realization of one's sins or wrongs and a will to change one's ways; **contrition** implies a deep, crushing sorrow for one's sins, with a true purpose of amendment; **compunction** implies a pricking of the conscience and therefore suggests a sharp but passing feeling of uneasiness about wrong-doing; **regret** may refer to sorrow over any unfortunate occurrence as well as over a fault or act of one's own

fat, āpe, cär; ten, ēven; is, bīte; gō, hôrn, tōōl, look; oil, out; up, fʉr; get; joy; yet; chin; she; thin, *th*en; zh, leisure; ŋ, ring; ə for *a* in *ago*, *e* in *agent*, *i* in *sanity*, *o* in *comply*, *u* in *focus*; ′ as in *able* (ā′b'l)

virtuous (vur′choo əs) *adj.*   having, or characterized by, moral virtue; righteous

> *SYN.*—**virtuous** implies a morally excellent character, connoting justice, integrity, and often, specif., chastity; **moral** implies conformity with the generally accepted standards of goodness or rightness in conduct or character, sometimes, specif., in sexual conduct [a *moral* woman]; **ethical** implies conformity with an elaborated, ideal code of moral principles, sometimes, specif., with the code of a particular profession [an *ethical* lawyer]; **righteous** implies a being morally blameless or justifiable [*righteous* anger]

The following Review Words are often confused with words similar to them in sound. Read each definition; then read the word or words with which the Review Word is often confused.

hordes (hôrdz) *n.*   1. wandering tribes or groups   2. large moving crowds or throngs; swarms

Confused with: hoards

libel (lī′bəl) *n.*   1. any false and malicious written or printed statement, or any sign, picture, or effigy, tending to expose a person to public ridicule, hatred, or contempt or to injure a person's reputation in any way   2. the act of publishing or displaying publicly such a thing   3. anything that gives an unflattering or damaging picture of the subject with which it is dealing —*v.*   1. to publish or make libel against   2. to give an unflattering or damaging picture of   3. to bring suit against by presenting a libel

Confused with: liable

lien (lēn, lē′ən) *n.*   *Law* a claim on the property of another as security for the payment of a just debt

Confused with: lean

populace (päp′yoo lis, -yə-) *n.*   1. the common people; the masses   2. the population of country, region, etc.

Confused with: populous

urbane (ur bān′) *adj.*   polite and courteous in a smooth, polished way; refined

Confused with: urban

fat, āpe, cär; ten, ēven; is, bīte; gō, hôrn, tool, look; oil, out; up, fur; get; joy; yet; chin; she; thin, *th*en; zh, leisure; ŋ, ring; ə for *a* in *ago, e* in *agent, i* in *sanity, o* in *comply, u* in *focus;* ' as in *able* (ā′b'l)

EXERCISE 1: REVIEW WORDS—USING WORDS CORRECTLY

The italicized word in each group is a Review Word for this chapter. The other two words are often confused with it. Each of the sentences can be best completed by only one of the three words. Choose the best word and write it in the space provided. Use each word only once. Check your answers in the back of the book. Use a dictionary if you need help.

A. *devastated*   razed   annihilated

1. She was _____ when her boyfriend did not invite her out on New Year's Eve.

2. In the 17th century in Europe, smallpox _____ about 60 million people.

3. At the end of the Third Punic War (149–146 B.C.), the Romans destroyed the power of Carthage and _____ the city.

B. *cumbersome*   ponderous   massive

1. People who have cancer are sometimes given _____ doses of radiation.

2. The best way to handle a _____ task such as writing a term paper is to break it into manageable parts.

3. Although the moose's antlers, which can measure seven feet across and weigh 60 pounds, seem _____ to us, the moose seems to carry them with no problem.

C. *virtuous*   moral   ethical

1. Guinevere's _____ behavior came to an end when she fell in love with Sir Lancelot.

2. Some people believe that it's hard to find a(n) _____ lawyer.

3. A parable is a story with a(n) _____ lesson.

D. *remorse*   penitence   regret

1. An executioner could not perform his job well if he felt deep _____ each time he had to kill someone.

2. True _____ implies not only guilt for having done wrong but also an intention to change one's behavior.

3. I felt _____ about not being able to attend the party.

E. *insurrection*   revolution   mutiny

1. The success of the Cuban _____, led by Fidel Castro and aided by Che Guevara, caused many anti-Castro Cubans to flee to the United States.

2. According to military law, _____ is punishable by court-martial.

3. John Brown (1800–1859) was an American abolitionist who led a(n) _____ that he thought would help to liberate the slaves.

EXERCISE 2: REVIEW WORDS—FREQUENTLY CONFUSED WORDS

Each word in italics is a Review Word for this chapter, and the other word is one that is often confused with it. Write the word that correctly completes the sentence. Use a dictionary if you need assistance. Check your answers in the back of the book.

1. _____ of little mouselike animals called lemmings have been known to drown trying to walk across wide bodies of water. (Hoards, *Hordes*)

2. A $640 million _____ suit was brought by the California resort La Costa against *Penthouse* magazine in March 1975. (*libel*, liable)

3. In 1974 a _____ was imposed upon cotton mills belonging to Vittorio and Ida Riva in Milan for $64.8 million in back taxes. (lean, *lien*)

4. _____ problems increased after the Industrial Revolution. (*Urbane*, Urban)

5. The most _____ city in the world is Tokyo, with 26,950,000 people in 1991. (populous, *populace*)

EXERCISE 3: REVIEW WORDS—MNEMONICS

Take any five words from the ten Review Words for this chapter, and, using mnemonic devices or word parts, create a method of remembering the correct definition of each. Write the mnemonic next to the word. Answers will differ, so they are not given in the back of the book.

1. _____   _____

                  Word   Memory Technique

2. _____   _____

                  Word   Memory Technique

3. _____   _____

                  Word   Memory Technique

4. _____   _____

                  Word   Memory Technique

5. _____   _____

                  Word   Memory Technique

NEW WORDS I

The following ten New Words are often confused with words similar to them in meaning. Read each definition, then read the dictionary excerpt describing its usage.

amenable (ə mē′nə bəl, -men′ə-) *adj.*   1. responsible or answerable   2. able to be controlled or influenced; responsive; submissive [a person *amenable* to suggestion; an illness *amenable* to treatment]   3. that which can be tested by (with *to*) [*amenable* to the laws of physics]

> *SYN.*—**amenable** suggests such amiability or desire to be agreeable as would lead one to submit readily [he is *amenable* to discipline]; **obedient** suggests a giving in to the orders or instructions of one in authority or control [an *obedient* child]; **docile** implies a temperament that submits easily to control or that fails to resist domination [a *docile* wife]; **tractable** implies ease of management or control but does not connote the submissiveness of **docile** and applies to things as well as people [silver is a *tractable*, i.e., malleable, metal]; **compliant** suggests a weakness of character that allows one to yield meekly to another's request or demand [army life had made him *compliant*]

constrain (kən strān′) *v.*   1. to force into, or hold in, close bounds; confine   2. to hold back (*from* an action) *by* force or strain; restrain   3. to force; compel; oblige [he was *constrained* to agree]

> *SYN.*—**constrain** implies the operation of a restricting force and therefore suggests a strained, repressed, or unnatural quality in that which results [a *constrained* laugh]; **force** implies the exertion of power in causing a person or thing to act, move, or comply against his or its resistance and may refer to physical strength or to any impelling motive [circumstances *forced* him to lie]; **compel** implies a driving irresistibly to some action, condition, etc.; to **coerce** is to compel submission or obedience by the use of superior power, intimidation, threats, etc.

cryptic (krip′tik) *adj.*   having a hidden or ambiguous meaning; mysterious or baffling [a *cryptic* comment]; obscure and curt in expression

> *SYN.*—**enigmatic** and **cryptic** are used of that which baffles or perplexes, the latter word implying deliberate intention to puzzle [his *enigmatic* behavior, a *cryptic* warning]; **obscure** applies to that which is perceived with difficulty either because it is concealed or veiled or because of obtuseness in the perceiver [his reasons remain *obscure*]; **vague** implies such a lack of precision or exactness as to be indistinct or unclear [a *vague* idea]; **ambiguous** applies to that which puzzles because it allows of more than one interpretation [an *ambiguous* title]; **equivocal** is used of something ambiguous that is deliberately used to mislead or confuse [an *equivocal* answer]

discern (di surn′, -zurn′) *v.*   1. to separate (a thing) mentally from another or others; recognize as separate or different   2. to perceive or recognize; make out clearly

> *SYN.*—**discern** implies a making out or recognizing of something visually or mentally [to *discern* one's motives]; **perceive** implies recognition by means of any of the senses, and, with reference to mental apprehension, often implies keen understanding or insight [to *perceive* a change in attitude]; **distinguish**, in this connection, implies a perceiving clearly or distinctly by sight, hearing, etc. [he *distinguished* the voices of men down the hall]; **observe** and **notice** both connote some measure of attentiveness, and usually suggest use of the sense of sight [to *observe* an eclipse, to *notice* a sign]

fat, āpe, cär; ten, ēven; is, bīte; gō, hôrn, tōōl, look; oil, out; up, fʉr; get; joy; yet; chin; she; thin, *th*en; zh, leisure; ŋ, ring; ə for *a* in *ago, e* in *agent, i* in *sanity, o* in *comply, u* in *focus;* ′ as in *able* (ā′b'l)

discreet (di skrēt′) *adj.*   careful about what one says or does; prudent, esp. keeping silent or preserving confidences when necessary

> *SYN.*—**discreet** implies the exercise of discernment and judgment in the guidance of one's speech and action and suggests careful restraint; **careful** implies close attention to or great concern for whatever is one's work or responsibility, and usually connotes thoroughness, a guarding against error or injury, etc.; **meticulous** implies extreme, sometimes finicky, carefulness about details; **scrupulous** implies a conscientious adherence to what is considered right, true, accurate, etc.; **circumspect** implies a careful consideration of all circumstances to avoid error or unfavorable consequences; **cautious** implies a careful guarding against possible dangers or risks; **prudent** implies the exercise of both caution and circumspection, suggesting careful management in economic and practical matters

divulge (də vulj′) *v.*   to make known; disclose; reveal

> *SYN.*—**divulge** suggests that what has been disclosed should properly have been kept secret or private [do not *divulge* the contents of this letter]; **reveal** implies a making known of something hidden or secret, as if by drawing back a veil [to *reveal* one's identity]; **disclose** suggests a laying open, as to inspection, of what has previously been concealed [he refuses to *disclose* his intentions]; **tell** may also imply a breach of confidence [kiss and *tell*] but more commonly suggests the making known of necessary or requested information [*tell* me what to do]; **betray** implies either faithlessness in divulging something [*betrayed* by an informer] or inadvertence in revealing something [her blush *betrayed* embarrassment]

frugal (frōō′gəl) *adj.*   1. not wasteful; not spending freely or unnecessarily; thrifty; economical   2. not costly or luxurious; inexpensive or meager [a *frugal* meal]

> *SYN.*—**frugal** stresses the idea of saving and suggests spending which excludes any luxury or lavishness and provides only the simplest fare, dress, etc. [the Amish are a *frugal* people]; **thrifty** implies industry and clever management of one's money or resources, usually so as to result in some savings [the *thrifty* housewife watched for sales]; **sparing** implies such restraint in spending as restricts itself to the bare minimum or involves deprivation [*sparing* to the point of niggardliness]; **economical** implies prudent management of one's money or resources so as to avoid any waste in expenditure or use [it is often *economical* to buy in large quantities]; **provident** implies management with the foresight to provide for future needs [never *provident*, he quickly spent his inheritance]

indignation (in′dig nā′shən) *n.*   anger or scorn resulting from injustice, ingratitude, or meanness; righteous anger

> *SYN.*—**indignation** implies righteous anger aroused by what seems unjust, mean, or insulting; **anger** is broadly applicable to feelings of resentful or revengeful displeasure; **rage** suggests a violent outburst of anger in which self-control is lost; **fury** implies a frenzied rage that borders on madness; violence; **ire,** chiefly a literary word, suggests a show of great anger in acts, words, looks, etc.; **wrath** implies deep indignation expressing itself in a desire to punish or get revenge

obliterate (ə blit′ə rāt′, ō-) *v.*   1. to blot out or wear away, leaving no traces; erase; efface   2. to do away with as if by effacing; destroy

> *SYN.*—**obliterate** implies a thorough blotting out of something so that all visible traces of it are removed; **erase** implies a scraping or rubbing out of something written or drawn, or figuratively, the removal of an impression; to **expunge** is to remove or wipe out completely; **efface** implies a rubbing out from a surface and, in extended use, suggests a destroying of the distinguishing marks, or even of the very existence, of something; **delete** implies the marking of written or printed matter for removal, or the removal of the matter itself

reiterate (rē it′ə rāt′) *v.*   to repeat (something done or said); say or do again or repeatedly

> *SYN.*—**iterate** and **reiterate** both suggest a repeating, either once or several times, but **reiterate** strongly implies insistent repetition over and over again [he keeps *reiterating* his innocence]; **repeat** is the common, general word meaning to say, do, make, present, etc. over again [will you *repeat* that question, please?]; **recapitulate** suggests a repeating briefly of the main points in a discourse in summarizing [he will *recapitulate* his account of the ball game at 8:00 o'clock]; **quote** means to repeat word for word.

fat, āpe, cär; ten, ēven; is, bīte; gō, hôrn, tōōl, look; oil, out; up, fur; get; joy; yet; chin; she; thin, *th*en; zh, leisure; ŋ, ring; ə for *a* in *ago*, *e* in *agent*, *i* in *sanity*, *o* in *comply*, *u* in *focus*; ' as in *able* (ā′b'l)

Use the dictionary usage excerpts in the New Words list to complete the following exercise. In each sentence, circle the word that best completes the thought. Check your answers in the back of the book.

1. Most companies prefer to hire people who are confident yet (obedient, tractable, compliant, amenable) to suggestions for improvement.

2. Because they want to appeal to everybody and offend nobody, politicians will often give (enigmatic, equivocal, cryptic, ambiguous) answers when put on the spot.

3. Some people hang containers of sugar water in their yards so they can (discern, perceive, distinguish, observe) hummingbirds at close range.

4. Friends won't tell you anything if you (reveal, disclose, divulge, betray) their confidences.

5. The squirrel's behavior in storing nuts for the winter can be called (thrifty, frugal, economical, provident).

6. In tornado country, cellars offer people refuge from the (indignation, fury, ire, wrath) of a storm.

7. He was (forced, compelled, coerced, constrained) by his upbringing from being rude to a guest.

8. Part of an editor's job is (erasing, effacing, obliterating, deleting) passages that are repetitious or off the subject.

9. Because it helps their audiences remember, good speakers will (repeat, reiterate, recapitulate, quote) their main points at the end of a speech.

10. It is wise to be (meticulous, prudent, discreet, wary) of strangers.

Fill in each blank with the word that best completes the sentence. Check your answers in the back of the book.

amenable	cryptic	discreet	frugal	obliterated
constrain	discern	divulge	indignation	reiterating

1. The Rosetta Stone, inscribed by ancient Egyptian priests with the same message in two ancient Egyptian writing systems and in ancient Greek, provided the key to our understanding of the _____ hieroglyphics.

2. Christ's face in Leonardo da Vinci's *Last Supper* is nearly _____ because Napoleon's soldiers used Christ's head in the painting for target practice when they occupied Milan.

3. A security clearance means that you will have access to information that you must not _____.

4. In order to be _____ with energy, it is recommended that people wear sweaters indoors instead of turning up the heat.

5. The finest chefs are supposed to be able to _____ all the ingredients in a dish from a single taste.

6. The strict discipline of the Army forces young recruits to _____ their natural rebelliousness.

7. A former president of du Pont kept pet iguanas that proved so _____ to training that he succeeded in teaching them to stand at attention and to come when called.

8. When engaging in conduct that is socially disapproved, it is best to be _____.

9. A method of getting your way that is taught in assertiveness-training classes is to keep _____ your request until someone does what you want.

10. In their _____ at all things German during World War I, some Americans made a practice of kicking dachshund dogs.

The following New Words are often confused with other words that have similar spellings.

adept (ə dept′) *adj.*   highly skilled; expert

    Confused with: adapt

allusion (ə lōō′zhən, a-) *n.*   an indirect reference; casual mention

    Confused with: illusion

amicable (am′ik ə bəl) *adj.*   friendly in feeling; showing good will; peaceable [an *amicable* discussion]

    Confused with: amiable

assent (ə sent′) *v.*   to express acceptance of; agree (*to*) —*n.*   consent or agreement

    Confused with: ascent

censure (sen′shər) *n.*   1. strong disapproval   2. a judgment or resolution condemning a person for misconduct, specif. an official expression of disapproval passed by a legislature —*v.*   to express strong disapproval of

    Confused with: censor

dissent (di sent′) *v.*   1. to differ in belief or opinion; disagree (often with *from*)   2. to reject the doctrines and forms of an established church —*n.*   the act of dissenting, specif. (*a*) the rendering of a minority opinion in the decision of a law case (*b*) religious nonconformity

    Confused with: descent

illicit (i lis′it) *adj.*   not allowed by law, custom, rule, etc.; unlawful; improper; prohibited; unauthorized

    Confused with: elicit

parameter (pə ram′ət ər) *n.*   1. a characteristic element; a factor   2. a fixed limit or guideline   3. *Math.* a quantity or constant whose value varies with the circumstances of its application, as the radius line of a group of concentric circles, which varies with the circle under consideration   4. any constant, with variable values, used as a point of reference for determining other variables

    Confused with: perimeter

fat, āpe, cär; ten, ēven; is, bīte; gō, hôrn, tōōl, look; oil, out; up, fur; get; joy; yet; chin; she; thin, then; zh, leisure; ŋ, ring; ə for *a* in *ago, e* in *agent, i* in *sanity, o* in *comply, u* in *focus;* ′ as in *able* (ā′b'l)

précis (prā sē′, prā′sē) *n.,   pl.,* **pré-cis′** (-sēz′, -sēz) a concise abridgment; summary; abstract —*v.*   to make a précis of

Confused with: precise

sensual (sen′shōō əl) *adj.*   1. of the body and the senses as distinguished from the intellect or spirit; bodily [*sensual* pleasures]   2. (*a*) connected or preoccupied with bodily or sexual pleasures (*b*) full of lust; lewd   3. resulting from, or showing preoccupation with, bodily or sexual pleasure [a *sensual* expression]

Confused with: sensuous

---

fat, āpe, cär; ten, ēven; is, bīte; gō, hôrn, tōōl, look; oil, out; up, fʉr; get; joy; yet; chin; she; thin, *th*en; zh, leisure; ŋ, ring; ə for *a* in *ago, e* in *agent, i* in *sanity, o* in *comply, u* in *focus;* ′ as in *able* (ā′b′l)

EXERCISE 6: FREQUENTLY CONFUSED WORDS

Write the correct word in the blank. Check your answers in the back of the book.

1. Potters are _____ at working with clay. (adept, adapt)

2. Throughout the interview the star made _____ to his upcoming Las Vegas appearance. (allusions, illusions)

3. Some divorcing couples fight bitterly, whereas others easily reach an

    _____ settlement. (amicable, amiable)

4. When asked for permission to borrow the car, she nodded her

    _____. (assent, ascent)

5. Remarks by guests of Arsenio Hall are often _____ by a train whistle. (censured, censored)

6. Jacques Cousteau has made many _____ beneath the surface of the ocean. (dissents, descents)

7. _____ activities attract the attention of the police. (Illicit, Elicit)

8. The sentry patrolled the _____ of the camp. (parameter, perimeter)

9. The author made a _____ of her new book that could be used for advertising purposes. (précis, precise)

10. The feel of the mink coat against his skin was extremely _____. (sensual, sensuous)

EXERCISE 7: MULTIPLE CHOICE

Circle the letter before the word or phrase that best defines the italicized word in each sentence. Check your answers in the back of the book.

1. Annie Oakley, known as "Little Sure-shot," was an *adept* markswoman who once broke 4,772 balls out of 5,000 thrown from traps 15 yards away.

    a. poor   b. skilled   c. lucky   d. famous

2. Shakespeare's plays contain many *allusions* to scenes from the Bible.

    a. quotations   b. frightening passages   c. puzzling scenes   d. references

3. The mongoose, a bright, *amicable* little mammal that makes an excellent pet, is the only creature who will attack a deadly cobra, an animal four times larger than itself.

   a. friendly b. hostile c. furry d. cute

4. In some cultures, young people cannot marry without the *assent* of their families.

   a. loan b. financial help c. agreement d. refusal

5. If parental approval means a lot to a child, the threat of *censure* will often be enough to keep him in line.

   a. disapproval b. support c. praise d. beating

6. The freedom to *dissent* is guaranteed by the U.S. Constitution, but armed rebellion is illegal.

   a. voice minority opinions b. vote by secret ballot c. overthrow the government
   d. bribe government officials

7. Some people believe that former FBI director J. Edgar Hoover had ties to organized crime and protected many of their *illicit* activities.

   a. illegal b. corporate c. legal d. charitable

8. To avoid punishment by society, people must behave within the *parameters* established by law.

   a. religion b. location c. business d. rules

9. The students were required to watch the documentary and write a *précis* of it.

   a. finished copy b. first draft c. summary d. outline

10. Most parents object to having *sensual* TV programs air before the time that most children go to bed.

    a. artistic b. intellectual c. sexy d. illegal

EXERCISE 8: TRUE-FALSE

Write T or F in the blank. Check your answers in the back of the book.

_____ 1. You are free to act when you are constrained.

_____ 2. Insults cause indignation.

_____ 3. A mirage is an optical illusion.

_____ 4. You can best cope with a situation if you are aware of all its parameters.

_____ 5. You can't hit a target that you can't discern.

EXERCISE 9: ANALOGIES

The analogies below are either synonyms, antonyms, classification : example,
cause : effect, or part : whole. First, decide which type of comparison is used in
the first pair of words. Second, find a word from the choices that will make the
second pair of words have the same relationship. Check your answers in the back
of the book.

1. cumbersome : large box :: frugal :   a. extravagant   b. cheap   c. spendthrift
     _____   d. miser

2. populace : nation :: dissent :   a. rebellion   b. agreement   c. silence
     _____   d. obedience

3. libel : lawsuit :: censure : _____   a. pride   b. editing   c. shame
                                                 d. approval

4. urbane : sophisticated :: précis :   a. summary   b. thesis   c. outline
     _____   d. expansion

5. virtuous : evil :: divulge : _____   a. tell   b. sell   c. conceal   d. buy

EXERCISE 10: MATCHING MEANINGS

Write the letter of the word that means the opposite of the word in the first column.
Check your answers in the back of the book.

_____ 1. obliterate   a. careless

_____ 2. discreet   b. plain

_____ 3. adept   c. create

_____ 4. cryptic   d. disagree

_____ 5. assent   e. clumsy

EXERCISE 11: WORD CONTRASTS

In each group below circle the word that does not mean what the others mean.
Check your answers in the back of the book.

1. amicable   rude   hostile   unfriendly

2. reiterate   repeat   restate   request

3. amenable   stubborn   pliant   obedient

4. sensual   arousing   spiritual   passionate

5. illicit   illegal   unauthorized   honest

Complete each sentence in your own words. Sample answers are provided in the back of the book.

1. In addition to being *adept* at algebra, _____

_____.

2. His work was full of *allusions* to _____

_____.

3. Although he was sure of his opinion, he was *amenable* to _____

_____.

4. Elvis and Priscilla Presley had an *amicable* _____

_____.

5. Unless your parents *assent*, _____

_____.

6. As a result of being *censured* by her colleagues, _____

_____.

7. We are *constrained* by law to _____

_____.

8. Because his answers were so *cryptic*, _____

_____.

9. Fog makes it difficult to *discern* _____

_____.

10. John was *discreet* when _____

_____.

11. The party's method of dealing with *dissent* was _____

_____.

12. Unless you *divulge* your sources, _____

_____.

13. As a result of Tommy's *frugal* habits, _____

_____.

14. People sometimes offer *illicit* gifts to _____

_____.

15. Josh felt *indignation* when _____

_____.

16. If a memory is *obliterated,* _____

_____.

17. The teacher established certain *parameters* for classroom behavior; these included _____

_____.

18. Reading a *précis* instead of the whole article will _____

_____.

19. When I am asked to *reiterate* the main points of a lecture, _____

_____.

20. An example of a *sensual* delight is _____

_____.

ADVANCED WORDS

ardor (är′dər) *n.*   1. emotional warmth; passion   2. eagerness; enthusiasm; zeal   3. intense heat; fire

> *SYN.*—**fervor** and **ardor** both imply emotion of burning intensity, **fervor** suggesting a constant glow of feeling [religious *fervor*], and **ardor,** a restless, flamelike emotion [the *ardors* of youth]; **passion** usually implies a strong emotion that has an overpowering or compelling effect [his *passions* overcame his reason]; **enthusiasm** implies strongly favorable feelings for an object or cause and usually suggests eagerness in the pursuit of something [his *enthusiasm* for golf]; **zeal** implies intense enthusiasm for an object or cause, usually as displayed in vigorous and untiring activity in its support [a *zeal* for reform]

deft (deft) *adj.*   skillful in a quick, sure, and easy way; dexterous

> *SYN.*—**deft** suggests a nimbleness and sureness of touch [a *deft* seamstress]; **dexterous** implies an expertness, natural or acquired, demonstrated in the ability to do things with skill and precision [a *dexterous* mechanic]; **adroit** adds to this a connotation of cleverness and resourcefulness and is now generally used of mental facility [an *adroit* evasion]; **handy** suggests skill, usually without training, at a variety of small tasks [a *handy* man around the house]

exorbitant (eg zôr′bi tənt, ig-) *adj.*   going beyond what is reasonable, just, proper, usual, etc.; excessive; extravagant; immoderate: said esp. of charges, prices, etc.

> *SYN.*—**exorbitant** is applied to that which is unreasonably excessive and often connotes a greedy desire for more than is just or due [*exorbitant* prices]; **excessive** applies to that which goes beyond what is proper, right, or usual [*excessive* demands]; **extravagant** and **immoderate** both imply excessiveness resulting from a lack of restraint or of prudence [*extravagant* praise, *immoderate* laughter]; **inordinate** implies a going beyond the orderly limits of convention or the bounds of good taste [his *inordinate* pride]

intrepid (in trep′id) *adj.*   not afraid; bold; fearless; dauntless; very brave

> *SYN.*—**intrepid** implies absolute fearlessness and esp. suggests dauntlessness in facing the new or unknown; **brave** implies fearlessness in meeting danger or difficulty and has the broadest application of the words considered here; **courageous** suggests constant readiness to deal with things fearlessly by reason of a stout-hearted temperament or a resolute spirit; **bold** stresses a daring temperament, whether displayed courageously, presumptuously, or defiantly; **audacious** suggests an imprudent or reckless boldness; **valiant** emphasizes a heroic quality in the courage or fortitude shown; **plucky** emphasizes gameness in fighting against something when one is at a decided disadvantage —*ANT.* **craven, cowardly**

surreptitious (sʉr′əp tish′əs) *adj.*   secret, stealthy, clandestine

> *SYN.*—**surreptitious** connotes a feeling of guilt in the one who is acting in a furtive or stealthy manner [she stole a *surreptitious* glance at him]; **secret,** the general term, implies a concealing or keeping from the knowledge of others, for whatever reason [my *secret* opinion of him]; **covert** implies a concealing as by disguising or veiling [a *covert* threat]; **clandestine** suggests that what is being kept secret is of an illicit, immoral, or proscribed nature [their *clandestine* meetings in the park]; **stealthy** implies a slow, quiet secrecy of action in an attempt to elude notice and often connotes deceit [the *stealthy* advance of the panther]; **furtive** adds to this connotations of slyness or watchfulness and suggests a reprehensible objective [the *furtive* movement of his hand toward my pocket]; **underhanded** implies a stealthiness characterized by fraudulence or deceit [*underhanded* business dealings] —*ANT,* **open, obvious**

fat, āpe, cär; ten, ēven; is, bīte; gō, hôrn, tōol, look; oil, out; up, fʉr; get; joy; yet; chin; she; thin, *th*en; zh, leisure; ŋ, ring; ə for *a* in *ago, e* in *agent, i* in *sanity, o* in *comply, u* in *focus;* ' as in *able* (ā′b'l)

ascetic (ə set′ik) *adj.* self-denying; austere —*n.* 1. a person who leads a life of contemplation and self-denial for religious purposes 2. anyone who lives with strict self-discipline and abstinence

Confused with: aesthetic

flout (flout) *v.* to be scornful; show contempt; jeer; scoff

Confused with: flaunt

imminent (im′ə nənt) *adj.* likely to happen without delay; impending; threatening: said of danger, evil, misfortune, etc.

Confused with: eminent

iniquity (i nik′wi tē) *n.* wickedness; injustice

Confused with: inequity

proscribe (prō skrīb′) *v.* 1. to denounce or forbid the practice, use, etc., of 2. to banish; exile

Confused with: prescribe

fat, āpe, cär; ten, ēven; is, bīte; gō, hôrn, tōol, look; oil, out; up, fʉr; get; joy; yet; chin; she; thin, *th*en; zh, leisure; ŋ, ring; ə for *a* in *ago, e* in *agent, i* in *sanity, o* in *comply, u* in *focus;* ′ as in *able* (ā′b′l)

EXERCISE 13: ADVANCED WORDS IN CONTEXT

Fill in each blank with the word that correctly completes the sentence. Check your answers in the back of the book.

| ardor | deft | flout | iniquity | proscribe |
| ascetic | exorbitant | imminent | intrepid | surreptitious |

1. The Chinese bandit Hsien-Chung, a model of _____ , is said to have killed 40 million people between 1643 and 1648.

2. The male Indian tailorbird sews his nest; using his bill as a needle, he pushes holes along the edges of leaves and then, using vegetable fibers as thread, sews them together with _____ strokes.

3. The _____ Robert Peary faced certain hardship and possible death to be the first to reach the North Pole.

4. If you shop at exclusive stores with excellent service, you are likely to pay _____ prices.

5. Dimming the lights in a theater signals that the start of the performance is _____ .

6. The authorities in 14th-century Spain had to _____ the wearing of false beards because no one knew who was who; creditors could not recognize debtors, police could not recognize criminals, and wives often slept with the wrong husbands.

7. In 16th-century China one obtained revenge by arranging the _____ addition of chopped tiger's whiskers to an enemy's food; the whisker barbs would cause sores and infections in the victim's digestive tract.

8. The phrase "Latin lover" implies that Latinos show more _____ than other men do.

9. According to legend, Siddhartha Gautama, who became a Buddha at 35, was born a prince and lived in great luxury until the age of 29, when he left his wife and son to become a wandering _____ .

10. Beatniks in the 1950s and hippies in the 1960s liked to _____ convention to shock the middle class.

EXERCISE 14: USING ADVANCED WORDS I

After the definition of each of the first five Advanced Words for this chapter is a dictionary excerpt that compares the word with its synonyms. Below are sentences that use those words. Cross out any word in the parentheses that cannot properly be used in the sentence. Check your answers in the back of the book.

1. Whirling dervishes work themselves up into a religious (fervor, ardor, enthusiasm, zeal).

2. Tax evaders become (dexterous, adroit, deft, handy) at manipulating tax law to their own advantage.

3. Although one dollar a gallon for gasoline seems cheap now, it was not so long ago that such a price was considered (excessive, exorbitant, extravagant, immoderate).

4. The gambler was notorious for taking (courageous, audacious, valiant, intrepid) risks.

5. She claimed that her financial contributions were motivated by generosity, but her (covert, stealthy, furtive, surreptitious) motive was the tax deduction.

EXERCISE 15: USING ADVANCED WORDS II

Choose the right word in each sentence and cross out the other. Check your answers in the back of the book.

1. One receives (ascetic, aesthetic) satisfaction from looking at great art.

2. Some people are modest; others believe that if you have it you should (flout, flaunt) it.

3. Advertisers try to get (imminent, eminent) personalities to plug their products.

4. The Equal Rights Amendment is an attempt to resolve (iniquities, inequities) in opportunity for women.

5. Incest is (proscribed, prescribed) by nearly all cultures.

Fill in the puzzle using a pencil. The clues with asterisks (*) refer to New Words from this and previous chapters. Check your answers in the back of the book.

Across

- *1. Unyielding
- *12. Vague
- 13. Ant. of *out*
- 14. Suffix meaning "one who," as in *profess____*
- 16. Prefix meaning "not," as in *____equity*
- *17. To forgive or pardon
- *20. From birth
- 22. First woman
- 23. Slice
- 24. Abbr. for *south*
- 25. A single unit
- 27. Theodore Roosevelt's initials
- *28. The basic point, gist
- *30. Stale
- 33. A suffix added to a drink made from a fruit, as in *lemon____*
- 34. Oak or maple
- *35. To rub out
- 40. Chemical symbol for *gold*
- 41. A man's name common in Sweden and Norway
- *42. To make greater
- *44. Free of charge
- 48. Suffix meaning "one who," as in *bank____*
- *49. Sober and settled
- 53. Prefix meaning "with," as in *____pilot*
- *54. Agree
- *55. Harmless

Down

- *1. Lacking sound judgment
- 2. First-person pronoun
- 3. Initials for singer Pat Boone
- 4. Chemical symbol for *ruthenium*
- *5. Most powerful group
- 6. Past participle of *go*
- 7. 13th letter of the Greek alphabet
- *8. The act of climbing
- 9. A long, thin mark
- 10. Ant. of *begin*
- 11. A pastry with a hole
- *15. Punishment for a wrong committed
- *18. Open
- 19. Prefix meaning "against," as in *____casion*
- 21. Neither . . . ____
- 26. Heated water mist
- *29. Skillful
- 31. Prefix meaning "not," as in *____regular*
- 32. Abbr. for *electrical engineer*
- 33. Prefix meaning "to," as in *____cept*
- 36. Dictionary abbr. for *French*
- 37. A pear-shaped fruit
- 38. Units of measure for land
- 39. Ant. of *slow*
- 40. Prefix meaning "to," as in *____nounce*
- 43. Prefix meaning "out," as in *____pedite*
- 45. I am, he is, we ____
- 46. Suffix meaning "one who," as in *scient____*
- 47. Abbr. for *Louisiana*
- 50. Prefix meaning "away," as in *____ominable*
- 51. Latin abbr. meaning "that is"
- 52. Initials for actor David Niven
- 53. Abbr. for *Coast Guard*

EXERCISE 17: OWN WORDS

List ten words from your outside reading that you would like to learn. Check the usage of each word in the dictionary, then write a sentence containing the word, being careful to use the word properly.

Word   **Sentence**

_____   _____

_____   _____

_____   _____

_____   _____

_____   _____

_____   _____

_____   _____

_____   _____

_____   _____

_____   _____

FINAL REVIEW

Review Words: Chapters 2–12

A. True-False

If the sentence is true write T in the blank. If the sentence is false write F.

_____ 1. Arrogant people are egocentric.

_____ 2. Rulers try to suppress insurrections.

_____ 3. King Lear was a patriarch who had two daughters who were ingrates.

_____ 4. An appalling number of people were annihilated in the Civil War.

_____ 5. A lenient boss will forgive some lapses in your performance.

_____ 6. A city with hordes of people is populous.

_____ 7. The per annum income of some families is so low that they could not survive without being subsidized.

_____ 8. We feel antagonism toward our benefactors.

_____ 9. The government decapitates all aliens.

_____ 10. Guerrillas have lavish lifestyles.

_____ 11. If you don't pay your debts, a lien may be imposed against your assets.

_____ 12. A delectable buffet can make you feel ravenous.

_____ 13. If they trace their genealogy back far enough, most people will find that they are remotely related to someone famous.

_____ 14. The fence around the perimeter of a prison encompasses the yard and all the cell blocks.

_____ 15. When you are resolute about holding on to your rights, you relinquish them.

_____ 16. Some people are so perceptive that their understanding seems almost uncanny.

_____ 17. An urbane person can appreciate aesthetic masterpieces.

_____ 18. Homicide is ethical.

_____ 19. Resourceful people expend the effort to get what they want.

_____ 20. Social agencies provided interim food and shelter for Florida citizens in the area devastated by Hurricane Andrew.

B. Synonyms and Antonyms

If the pairs are synonyms, mark S in the blank. If the pairs are antonyms, mark A.

_____	1.	penitence	remorse		_____	6.	placid	perturbed
_____	2.	homogeneous	differentiated		_____	7.	defame	libel
_____	3.	requisite	indispensable		_____	8.	virtuous	lewd
_____	4.	discredit	substantiate		_____	9.	gaudy	ornate
_____	5.	eccentric	unorthodox		_____	10.	cordial	aloof

C. Sentence Completions

Circle the word that best completes the sentence.

1. She campaigned for the candidate with great _____. (zeal, velocity)

2. Better methods of solving problems _____ over time. (conform, evolve)

3. _____ remarks in class are resented by instructors. (superlative, impertinent)

4. The overthrow of the government was _____ by the military. (elapsed, instigated)

5. Compared to the small personal computers we have today, the old-style mainframe computers were very _____. (cumbersome, pretentious)

6. His _____ caused him to limp. (domestic, infirmity)

7. The _____ elected him president by a huge majority. (populace, affiliate)

8. "_____ motion" machines keep moving because of the rotation of the earth. (Perpetual, Remedial)

9. His excellent job performance _____ the confidence we placed in him. (inclines, affirms)

10. Landlords will _____ tenants for nonpayment of rent. (reconcile, evict)

11. A ball and chain will _____ your progress. (impede, solidify)

12. Some children are afraid of clowns because they consider their appearance _____ rather than amusing. (intact, grotesque)

13. In order for people to forgive you, you must generally not only apologize but also _____ the wrong that you did. (rectify, paraphrase)

14. A(n) _____ helps in committing a crime. (clique, accomplice)

15. A _____ is inexperienced. (novice, pitfall)

16. When you _____, you see or hear things that other people don't. (hallucinate, idealize)

17. Many people have a(n) _____ to spiders. (aversion, premonition)

18. _____ gossip hurts people. (Judicious, Malicious)

19. Mammals sit on their _____ end. (posterior, distinctive)

20. Although he made a _____ effort, he was so badly outnumbered that he couldn't win. (valiant, reserved)

21. Some textbooks are written so poorly that it is difficult to _____ their meaning. (apprehend, motivate)

22. _____ is usually a white-collar crime. (Acknowledgment, Graft)

23. The priest gave a _____ to the newly married couple. (benediction, commune)

24. I am trying to _____ you to do what I want. (induce, extract)

25. It is important to _____ our natural resources in a responsible manner, without waste. (enunciate, exploit)

New Words: Chapters 2–12

A. Multiple Choice

Circle the letter of the word that is closest in meaning to the numbered word.

1. fortitude   a. memory   b. courage   c. outlook   d. weight
2. negate   a. change   b. place   c. propose   d. cancel
3. ascent   a. fall   b. rise   c. goal   d. road
4. inception   a. reduction   b. discovery   c. start   d. option
5. presumptuous   a. forward   b. harsh   c. quiet   d. talkative
6. chafe   a. question   b. irritate   c. ignore   d. surpass
7. deviate   a. follow   b. overlook   c. commit   d. differ
8. discrepancy   a. disagreement   b. agreement   c. sameness   d. hugeness
9. soundness   a. health   b. life   c. length   d. wisdom
10. technicality   a. idea   b. detail   c. gesture   d. mistake
11. semblance   a. appearance   b. difference   c. intelligence   d. beauty

12. equilibrium   a. disagreement   b. weakness   c. flow   d. balance

13. intrinsic   a. inborn   b. created   c. external   d. unimportant

14. credence   a. thought   b. belief   c. question   d. time

15. adversity   a. misfortune   b. uncertainty   c. reward   d. support

16. tenuous   a. firm   b. flimsy   c. sincere   d. destroyed

17. dissolute   a. godlike   b. forceful   c. friendly   d. immoral

18. vanquish   a. defeat   b. fight   c. protect   d. enlist

19. abominable   a. great   b. cautious   c. nasty   d. unnecessary

20. redundant   a. copied   b. useless   c. original   d. wordy

21. impregnable   a. weak   b. unyielding   c. old   d. new

22. lithe   a. flexible   b. awkward   c. disciplined   d. warm

23. adept   a. educated   b. expert   c. curious   d. accurate

24. amenable   a. submissive   b. rude   c. grumpy   d. interesting

25. parameter   a. goal   b. record   c. limit   d. description

B. Sentence Completion

Choose the word that best completes the sentence.

1. A government official using taxpayers' money to rent a plane for private use can cause a _____ if discovered. (furor, prerogative)

2. A secretary in Texas invented liquid correction fluid to _____ mistakes made when typing. (rationalize, obliterate)

3. The front of a building is called the _____. (façade, lineage)

4. It is _____ that Hawaii, which grows more sugar cane than any other state in the United States, must import most of its sugar. (holistic, ironic)

5. An elephant is _____. (rigorous, ponderous)

6. A treatment that promotes healing is _____. (therapeutic, cohesive)

7. A clear idea is _____. (lucid, congenital)

8. Some overweight people never feel _____, even after a large meal. (satiated, ingratiated)

9. Someone who anticipates the worst is a(n) _____. (facet, alarmist)

10. Every college professor wishes to have _____ because it offers job security. (inequity, tenure)

11. When something _____, it takes place. (transpires, assents)

12. When you are _____, you feel free to express yourself. (translucent, uninhibited)

13. Most people think owning a lot of land is _____. (enviable, conscientious)

14. Government is based on a(n) _____ of officials. (predecessor, hierarchy)

15. _____ jobs are generally poorly paid. (Menial, Compensatory)

16. The lecturer made frequent _____ to the works of Shakespeare. (fixations, allusions)

17. Because crime is caused by a(n) _____ of factors, you cannot prove that violence on television has caused an increase in violent crimes. (multiplicity, extremity)

18. The _____ income in the United States is only the fifth highest in the world. (transitory, per capita)

19. It's your _____ to choose a major you like. (fatalism, prerogative)

20. Because you failed to perform, I have the right to _____ the contract. (constrain, void)

C. Synonyms and Antonyms

If the words in each pair are synonyms, write S in the blank. If they are antonyms, write A in the blank.

_____	1.	recapitulate	reiterate
_____	2.	wrath	indignation
_____	3.	gist	crux
_____	4.	compliant	tractable
_____	5.	insidious	candid
_____	6.	reprimand	condone
_____	7.	vulnerable	invincible
_____	8.	amiable	congenial
_____	9.	meticulous	fastidious
_____	10.	placate	alienate
_____	11.	benign	malevolent
_____	12.	terminology	jargon
_____	13.	innate	inherent
_____	14.	susceptible	prone

	15.	raucous	discreet
_____	16.	furtive	stealthy
_____	17.	regal	bourgeois
_____	18.	sedate	staid
_____	19.	digression	tangent
_____	20.	insipid	trite
_____	21.	laud	vilify

D. True-False

If the sentence is true, write T in the blank. If the sentence is false, write F.

_____ 1. Anarchists enjoy a dictatorial regime.

_____ 2. The most expedient solutions are not always the most prudent.

_____ 3. A derogatory remark could cause an altercation.

_____ 4. Complacent people accept the status quo without complaint.

_____ 5. Eminent people are renowned.

_____ 6. Lethargic people often repose.

_____ 7. One should certainly flaunt an illicit affair.

_____ 8. Frugal people usually drive ostentatious cars.

_____ 9. Sensuous individuals enjoy tactile contact.

_____ 10. Derelicts are generally insolvent.

_____ 11. A nation will retaliate when it feels the need for retribution.

_____ 12. Platonic relationships are filled with romantic fervor.

_____ 13. Precocious children can easily appear insolent.

_____ 14. Staunch believers are sometimes militants.

_____ 15. Amicable encounters are filled with animosity.

_____ 16. A message written in cipher is cryptic.

_____ 17. Idiosyncrasies can be discerned in nearly everyone.

_____ 18. Subservient people are usually audacious.

_____ 19. When charges against a prisoner are proved erroneous the judge should exonerate the person.

_____ 20. It is difficult to elicit a response from a taciturn person.

_____ 21. Resplendent surroundings are decrepit.

_____ 22. A hindrance usually thwarts your progress.

_____ 23. Wary people constantly do impetuous things.

_____ 24. Your arguments prevail when someone else refutes them.

_____ 25. Incumbents need the votes of their constituents to be reelected.

_____ 26. Many children like to patronize fast-food franchises.

_____ 27. Nearly every religion has methods for indoctrinating new members into its ideology.

_____ 28. An indiscreet person is apt to divulge secrets about his or her friends.

_____ 29. The more nebulous the charges are, the more difficult it is to categorically deny them.

_____ 30. People who are equivocal will intersperse positive and negative statements about a topic.

_____ 31. Dissent does not have to be inflammatory.

_____ 32. People who deal in contraband often use artifice to avoid detection.

_____ 33. Pensive people are generally obnoxious and loud.

_____ 34. Oppressed people are allowed to act according to their own volition.

_____ 35. When you censure someone you reproach him.

E. Matching

Match the word in the first column with the definition in the second. Write the letter of the correct definition in the space provided.

_____	1. sensual	a. free
_____	2. lament	b. self-contradictory statement
_____	3. malign	c. summary
_____	4. oblique	d. cheerful
_____	5. facility	e. approve
_____	6. enormity	f. upcoming
_____	7. blatant	g. casual
_____	8. coerce	h. erase
_____	9. impending	i. hint
_____	10. supplication	j. fury
_____	11. countenance	k. stick to
_____	12. adhere	l. glaring
_____	13. paradox	m. external
_____	14. innuendo	n. appropriate
_____	15. buoyant	o. mourn
_____	16. extrinsic	p. force
_____	17. ire	q. painful
_____	18. gratis	r. slanting
_____	19. efface	s. prayer
_____	20. cavalier	t. skill
_____	21. précis	u. sexy
_____	22. prolific	v. slander
_____	23. apropos	w. plentiful
_____	24. excruciating	x. hugeness

F. Fill-in

Using the words below, fill in the blanks in the story.

augment   deter   exhaustive   latent   renaissance
credibility   dire   expedite   misgivings   stringent
depicted   dispel   exponents   overt   tenable
depleted   elite   ferment   per se   utilitarian

Solar Power

The dream of harnessing the power of the sun has been man's goal since the first cave man realized that a fire could be created by the sun reflecting off some quartz crystals. Originally _____ of sun power were
1
_____ as impractical dreamers. But they have gained
2
_____ as technological advances have increased the use of solar
3
power for _____ purposes. At one time the government and private
4
industry seemed to wish to _____ scientists from pursuing the nec-
5
essary _____ research, favoring instead coal, oil, and eventually
6
nuclear power. But with our _____ need for new sources of energy
7
because of our _____ natural supplies and the high cost of foreign
8
oil, there has been a _____ of interest in solar power. Nuclear
9
power, once thought to be the ultimate answer to the energy problem, has proven somewhat dangerous. Even with a _____ regulatory system, many
10
people are expressing _____ about its safety.
11

In an attempt to motivate private individuals to begin using solar power in homes and industry, the government has offered tax incentives. This
_____ support has led to more private industry involvement and
12
drastic reductions in the cost of power units. But the cost _____ has
13
not been the only problem. The usefulness of solar power as the sole source of energy has always seemed uncertain.

To _____ any confusion about this type of power and its safety
14
we must look at the sun itself. The sun is an ordinary, medium-sized star. As such, its
_____ and active power almost defy description. This mass of glow-
15
ing matter is a trillion times the volume of the earth. To the naked eye it appears to be calm, but, in fact, it is in a constant state of _____. Every second,
16
four million tons of hydrogen are destroyed in explosions that start somewhere near its core. The core temperature is about 25 million degrees Fahrenheit. The sun gives off more energy in a second than all of the energy used in the history of mankind.

Today, the use of this power source is becoming more _____
17
as scientists are finding ways to store the energy gathered during the day for later use.
This new phase of research will _____ utilization of solar power
18
in residences for heating and cooking. Solar power is being seen as a method to
_____ conventional sources. Persons using this source consider
19
themselves an _____ group of modern-day pioneers. Despite such
20
encouraging signs, the future of solar power will remain uncertain until questions of
cost and practicality can be satisfactorily resolved.

Advanced Words: Chapters 2–12

A. True-False

Mark T if the sentence is true and F if it is false.

_____ 1. A vacillating person will always be indefatigable in getting what he or she wants.

_____ 2. A lawyer who makes a speech filled with non sequiturs can be said to have spoken incisively.

_____ 3. Rapacious people are altruistic.

_____ 4. Solicitous hosts will never regale their guests with food and drink.

_____ 5. A lawyer who charges exorbitant fees is quite likely to create enmity in her clients.

_____ 6. Iniquity is innocuous.

_____ 7. Paragons of virtue should be emulated.

_____ 8. A docile child will seek to mollify an annoyed parent.

_____ 9. The salient points in a speech should be stated succinctly.

_____ 10. An erudite scientific article may go into pedantic detail.

_____ 11. An edifice that has been razed will bring in especially good rents.

_____ 12. Sedentary jobs require inordinate amounts of sitting.

_____ 13. A state of detente between two nations means that they desist from unfriendly behavior toward one another.

_____ 14. Good athletes will always feel chagrin when their performance is abysmal.

_____ 15. A town that is inundated by enemy troops will quickly capitulate.

_____ 16. If a person can get someone to corroborate his alibi, a court will usually absolve him of blame.

_____ 17. Complicity in a crime means that two or more people consorted to bring it about.

_____ 18. Pastoral paintings always delineate city surroundings.

_____ 19. When you peruse a contract, you give it only a cursory examination.

_____ 20. An intrepid person is the antithesis of a coward.

B. Synonyms and Antonyms

If the pairs are synonyms, mark S in the blank. If the pairs are antonyms, mark A.

_____	1.	mundane	esoteric	_____	6.	stricture	proscription
_____	2.	surreptitious	clandestine	_____	7.	licentious	monastic
_____	3.	admonishment	accolade	_____	8.	hackneyed	innovative
_____	4.	austere	ascetic	_____	9.	mitigate	exacerbate
_____	5.	deft	adroit	_____	10.	voluble	loquacious

C. Sentence Completions

Circle the word that best completes the sentence.

1. _____ evidence is based on experiments, not on theory. (Sporadic, Empirical)

2. When something is _____, it is scattered over a wide area. (dissipated, eclectic)

3. A _____ project is workable. (viable, provident)

4. _____ rooms are adjacent. (Contiguous, Gratuitous)

5. A _____ meal is a joy to have. (formidable, succulent)

6. _____ people are insane. (Demented, Enigmatic)

7. When you are fired from a job, you frequently are given _____ pay or two weeks' notice. (fabricated, severance)

8. Romeo courted Juliet with great _____. (eclecticism, ardor)

9. If laws were not _____ in books it would be impossible to remember them all. (codified, covert)

10. A(n) _____ person cannot be appeased. (precipitous, implacable)

11. Some people see problems as a(n) _____ between black and white solutions, while others see many alternatives. (dichotomy, oligarchy)

12. The lecturer gave examples to _____ his point. (elucidate, superimpose)

13. _____ circumstances can cause a judge to reduce a guilty person's sentence. (Aggrandizing, Extenuating)

14. The melodrama made the audience shed _____ tears. (ubiquitous, copious)

15. _____ are cure-alls for a variety of problems. (Panaceas, Logistics)

16. The spy used a _____ to cover her true purpose. (ruse, propensity)

17. Simple Simon was _____. (obtuse, extraneous)

18. Houdini could _____ himself from any type of handcuffs. (flout, extricate)

19. A(n) _____ liar can make anybody believe him. (imminent, consummate)

20. Scrooge MacDuck's motives are often _____. (vicarious, mercenary)

21. _____ is forbidden in the Bible. (Idolatry, Dissonance)

22. The thief _____ with the funds. (absconded, rescinded)

23. _____ people are easy prey for con artists. (Repressive, Credulous)

24. The Old Woman Who Lived in a Shoe had many _____. (progeny, surrogates)

25. Music was Beethoven's _____. (forte, strategem)

Check your answers in the back of the book. Circle the words you missed on the lists inside the front and back covers. Use either the lists or flash cards to memorize the words before you take the posttest.

Circle the letter of the word that is closest in meaning to the numbered word.

1. menial   a. important   b. lowly   c. new   d. boring

2. dire   a. exhausted   b. temporary   c. questionable   d. dreadful

3. amiable   a. secretive   b. good-natured   c. corrupt   d. perfect

4. audacious   a. bold   b. sympathetic   c. thoughtful   d. sober

5. coerce   a. seize   b. accept   c. force   d. advise

6. cipher   a. zero   b. factor   c. nonsense   d. action

7. ferment   a. help   b. seethe   c. join   d. steal

8. void   a. invalid   b. healthy   c. illegal   d. reduced

9. meticulous   a. acceptable   b. careless   c. precise   d. direct

10. erroneous   a. cheap   b. mistaken   c. brief   d. sloppy

11. prolific   a. thankful   b. successful   c. plentiful   d. peaceful

12. transpire   a. intrude   b. occur   c. expect   d. expose

13. alienate   a. befriend   b. unite   c. suggest   d. estrange

14. placate   a. surround   b. calm   c. seize   d. separate

15. repose   a. request   b. pray   c. decline   d. rest

16. sedate   a. brutal   b. smart   c. quiet   d. inflexible

17. insolvent   a. bankrupt   b. isolated   c. undetected   d. controversial

18. malevolent   a. masculine   b. evil   c. wishful   d. cooperate

19. exonerate   a. blame   b. reveal   c. acquit   d. refuse

20. latent   a. common   b. serious   c. doubtful   d. inactive

21. benign   a. burning   b. harmless   c. restricted   d. specific

22. impetuous   a. deceptive   b. talkative   c. rash   d. moody

23. raucous   a. courteous   b. embarrassing   c. critical   d. loud

24. frugal   a. exciting   b. effective   c. economical   d. hesitant

25. précis   a. summary   b. table   c. story   d. outline

26. depict   a. show   b. exchange   c. relay   d. return

27. excruciating   a. exciting   b. secret   c. loud   d. painful

28. utilitarian   a. powerful   b. ordinary   c. useful   d. strict

29. eminent   a. kind   b. rich   c. strong   d. remarkable

30. staid   a. conservative   b. weak   c. strict   d. trained

31. semblance   a. appearance   b. result   c. characteristic   d. thought

32. prevail   a. increase   b. avoid   c. succeed   d. irritate

33. equivocal   a. vague   b. clear   c. equal   d. thoughtless

34. discrepancy   a. disagreement   b. excellence   c. quickness   d. frequency

35. inequity   a. envy   b. injustice   c. equality   d. alarm

36. adept   a. new   b. awkward   c. slick   d. expert

37. credence   a. politeness   b. criticism   c. wisdom   d. belief

38. reprimand   a. scold   b. teach   c. tell   d. reward

39. exponent   a. opponent   b. offspring   c. student   d. supporter

40. insidious   a. apparent   b. peculiar   c. treacherous   d. distant

41. expedient   a. slow   b. convenient   c. new   d. dangerous

42. volition   a. will   b. strength   c. trick   d. duty

43. animosity   a. openness   b. jealousy   c. assistance   d. hatred

44. lethargic   a. sluggish   b. educated   c. superior   d. thin

45. condone   a. threaten   b. punish   c. discover   d. overlook

46. fastidious   a. careless   b. husky   c. inclined   d. picky

47. nebulous   a. insincere   b. responsible   c. unclear   d. uneven

48. amicable   a. peaceable   b. suspicious   c. fierce   d. honest

49. divulge   a. desire   b. reveal   c. summarize   d. forgive

50. indignation   a. anger   b. hesitation   c. modesty   d. fitness

Check your answers in the back of the book. Record your score on the Progress Chart and memorize any words you missed before you take the Final Exam.

Fill in your score here _____

PROGRESS CHART

Mark each space on the graph below with your percentile score for each test and then connect your marks to show your progress.

You calculate your percentage as follows: Divide the number of correct answers by the total number of items on the test and multiply by 100.

Example: 30 correct answers on the Pretest out of a possible 50 items.

$$30 \div 50 = .60 \times 100 = 60\%$$

		10	20	30	40	50	60	70	80	90	100
Pretest	New Words										
Chapter 2	Review										
	New Words										
	Advanced										
Chapter 3	Review										
	New Words										
	Advanced										
Chapter 4	Review										
	New Words										
	Advanced										
Chapter 5	Review										
	New Words										
	Advanced										
Chapter 6	Review										
	New Words										
	Advanced										
Midterm	Review										
	New Words										
	Advanced										
Chapter 7	Review										
	New Words										
	Advanced										
Chapter 8	Review										
	New Words										
	Advanced										
Chapter 9	Review										
	New Words										
	Advanced										
Chapter 10	Review										
	New Words										
	Advanced										
Chapter 11	Review										
	New Words										
	Advanced										
Chapter 12	Review										
	New Words										
	Advanced										
Posttest	New Words										
Final	Review										
	New Words										
	Advanced										

ANSWERS

CHAPTER 1

Pretest (p. 5)

1. a	11. c	21. d	31. a	41. b
2. b	12. a	22. a	32. c	42. a
3. c	13. b	23. b	33. c	43. c
4. a	14. c	24. b	34. c	44. b
5. b	15. c	25. d	35. c	45. c
6. a	16. a	26. c	36. b	46. a
7. d	17. d	27. b	37. a	47. a
8. b	18. c	28. a	38. a	48. b
9. c	19. d	29. c	39. c	49. b
10. b	20. b	30. b	40. d	50. b

CHAPTER 2

Proverb Pronunciation (p. 10)

a. Birds of a feather flock together.
b. Too many cooks spoil the broth.
c. A stitch in time saves nine.

Exercise 1 (p. 13)

1. egocentric	6. penitence
2. conform	7. ornate
3. pitfall	8. Judicious
4. delectable	9. enunciate
5. requisite	10. valiant

Exercise 2 (p. 14)

A. 1. a. being sorry
   b. Sinners must feel penitence to be forgiven.
   2. a. required
   b. A cake is requisite for a birthday party.
   3. a. delicious
   b. Most people will overeat when the food is delectable.
   4. a. pronounce clearly
   b. Shakespearean actors are taught to enunciate clearly.
   5. a. to accept the rules of others
   b. It takes a while to conform to military life.

B. Here are some sample mnemonic devices. Check yours with your instructor.
   1. brave Prince Valiant   4. good judgment
   2. ornamented   5. ego trip
   3. fall in a pit

New Words (p. 15)

These are some possible mnemonic devices:
   depict: draw a picture
   deplete: completely empty
   excruciating: being crucified
   furor: being furious
   negate: When you feel negative about a law you will vote to negate it.
   renown: well known
   satiate: satisfy
   semblance: to resemble
   utilitarian: useful
   vilify: call vile names or make a villain

Exercise 3 (p. 16)

1. satiate	6. utilitarian
2. excruciating	7. furor
3. depicting	8. negated
4. depleted	9. semblance
5. renown	10. vilified

New Words II (p. 17)

Check your sentences with your instructor.

Exercise 4 (p. 18)

1. b	6. b
2. a	7. d
3. c	8. b
4. a	9. c
5. a	10. a

Exercise 5 (p. 19)

1. F
2. F
3. T
4. F
5. F

Exercise 6 (p. 19)

1. d
2. a
3. c
4. b
5. a

Exercise 7 (p. 20)

1. c
2. a
3. b
4. e
5. d

Exercise 8 (p. 20)

1. straightforward
2. wary
3. dull
4. useless
5. unimportant

Exercise 9 (p. 20): Sample answers:

1. Everyone wants *conscientious* employees because *they work harder.*
2. Some groups object to TV shows that *depict* acts of violence; others *enjoy violence.*
3. When you *deplete* your savings, *you'd better not need emergency funds.*
4. Telling lies can have *dire* consequences, such as *preventing people from trusting you when you really need their trust.*
5. Politicians will make *equivocal* statements as long as *doing so wins votes.*
6. Besides *excruciating* pain, arthritis can cause *immobility in the joints.*
7. Not everyone has the *fortitude* to *go backpacking in the mountains.*
8. Even though he knew the decision would cause a *furor, he did what he thought was right.*
9. Before you make an *insolent* remark, *think about the consequences.*
10. He didn't know whether to *lament* the decision or *to celebrate it.*
11. A *militant* approach is sometimes best; however, *in other situations a peaceful approach works better.*
12. Unless you want to *negate* all our work, *you'd better sign the contract now.*
13. If we don't *refute* Jim's argument, *people will lose confidence in us.*
14. His *renown* grew as a result of *his successful performance in his first major film.*
15. Her gown was *resplendent,* except that *it had a grease stain on the bodice.*
16. Alison's urge to shop was impossible to *satiate;* consequently, *she spent money faster than her husband could earn it.*
17. He had the *semblance* of a kindly old uncle, but *he was really a nasty old man.*
18. It has *utilitarian* purposes, too—for example, *you can use it to peel potatoes.*
19. Jason likes to *vilify* Jane, especially *since she started dating other men.*
20. Although we must be *wary* around Christine, *she can also be a powerful ally.*

Exercise 10 (p. 23)

1. razed
2. emulate
3. copious
4. eclectic
5. incisive
6. enmity
7. pastoral
8. indefatigable
9. rapacious
10. aggrandize

Exercise 11 (p. 24)

No answers provided.

CHAPTER 3

Exercise 1 (p. 29)

1. homicide
2. elapsed
3. aesthetic
4. perimeter
5. uncanny
6. apprehension
7. velocity
8. perturb
9. ethical
10. zeal

Exercise 2 (p. 30)

1. aesthetic
2. perimeter
3. elapsed
4. zeal
5. homicide
6. velocity
7. perturbed
8. ethical
9. uncanny
10. apprehend

Exercise 3 (p. 33)

1. flaunt
2. stringent
3. eminent
4. irony
5. Prudent
6. audacious
7. staid
8. coerce
9. thwart
10. tractable

Exercise 4 (p. 35)

1. b
2. d
3. a
4. b
5. d
6. c
7. d
8. d
9. a
10. c

Exercise 5 (p. 36)

1. T
2. T
3. F
4. F
5. T

Exercise 6 (p. 36)

1. d
2. b
3. b
4. b
5. b

Exercise 7 (p. 36)

1. d
2. e
3. a
4. b
5. c

Exercise 8 (p. 37)

1. calmness
2. light
3. amiable
4. respectful
5. headstrong

Exercise 9 (p. 37): Sample answers:

1. If you are an *amiable* person, *you probably get along well with people.*
2. An *ascent* of Mt. Everest would be exciting, although *it could be very tiring.*
3. Talking back to a policeman is not only *audacious but also unwise.*
4. You might feel *coerced if your boss told you that you didn't have to work overtime but the company was depending on you.*
5. When an *eminent* American dies, *the president usually orders all flags to be flown at half-mast.*
6. A rich man might *flaunt* his wealth by *driving an expensive sports car.*
7. If you cannot understand the *gist* of an argument, *you will not be able to argue the other point of view intelligently.*
8. I would react with *ire if someone betrayed my trust repeatedly.*
9. It is a form of *irony* when *a tow truck breaks down and has to be towed.*
10. A bank teller must be *meticulous* when counting out money; otherwise, *his or her balance sheet will be wrong at the end of the day.*
11. An example of a *ponderous* task is *writing a term paper.*
12. Bill was so *presumptuous* that just after he met Cathy *he asked if he could use her washing machine to wash his dirty clothes.*
13. Before *prudent* people go out to buy a car, *they read a good consumer report about the subject.*
14. Dating a *staid* person might be boring because *he or she would never want to go to a new restaurant.*
15. One thing a *stealthy* robber might do is *dress in dark clothes.*
16. Some bosses have very *stringent* standards; consequently, *the workers feel restricted.*
17. A *taciturn* woman would probably not be comfortable if *she had to give a speech.*
18. While it might be heroic to try to *thwart* a bank robbery, *it would be dangerous.*
19. Many private schools accept only *tractable* youngsters because *they do not want discipline problems in classes.*
20. I am most *vulnerable* to a cold when *I am taking my final exams.*

Exercise 10 (p. 40)

1. empirical
2. inordinate
3. detriment
4. sporadic
5. peruse
6. ruse
7. ubiquitous
8. admonish
9. mitigate
10. cursory

Exercise 11 (p. 41)

¹C	²O	³N	S	⁴C	⁵I	E	⁶N	⁷T	⁸I	⁰O	U	S
¹⁰O	N	E	■	¹¹B	S	■	¹²B	I	T	■	T	¹³R
N	¹⁴A	¹⁵N	■	N	■	R	■	¹⁶D	I	R	E	F
¹⁷F	¹⁸O	R	T	¹⁹I	T	U	²⁰D	E	■	L		F
²¹O	R	■	T	■	I	■	²²P	²³I	O	U		T
R	²⁴T	²⁵V	■	²⁶D	E	P	I	C	T	■		T
²⁷M	²⁸I	L	²⁹I	T	A	N	T	■	³⁰A	³¹B	E	
R	L	N	■	³²A	F	I	R	E				
³⁴S	A	T	³⁵I	A	T	E	³⁷A	U	■	I	³⁸B	
A	■	³⁹F	T	⁴⁰A	⁴¹B	R	■	⁴²A	T	E		
⁴³W	⁴⁴A	R	Y	⁴⁵R	E	N	O	W	N	E		
	V	⁴⁶C	A	S	T	R	■	⁴⁷J	R			

Exercise 12 (p. 42)

No answers provided.

CHAPTER 4

Finding the Main Entry (p. 50)

1. pursue
2. petty
3. across
4. omit
5. liberate
6. fundamental
7. protrude
8. describe
9. appreciate
10. superstition

Using the Pronunciation Guide (p. 51)

1. a. plan; scheme
   b. to propose; to throw forward
2. a. trans'pôrts
   b. trans pôrts'
3. a. *v.*
   b. *n.*

Choosing the Correct Definition (p. 52)

a. 5
b. 1
c. 4
d. 5
e. 1
f. 3

Types of Dictionaries (p. 55)

1. two
2. *Host* suggests order.
3. Old English; Indo-European
4. seven
5. Crowd¹ has to do with numbers of people; crowd² is a musical instrument.

Exercise 1 (p. 58)

1. induce
2. lapse
3. reserved
4. inclines
5. affiliate
6. commune
7. graft
8. domestic
9. exploit
10. extract

Exercise 2 (p. 59)

1. eks′ploit
2. in′klīnz
3. eks′trakt
4. ə fil′ē it
5. kə myōōn′

6. ik sploit′
7. in klīnz′
8. ik strakt′
9. ə fil′ē āt′
10. käm′yōōn

Exercise 3 (p. 60)

graft: 1. 1*a*
    2. 3*a*
reserved: 3. 2
    4. 1
induce: 5. 1
    6. 3

lapse: 7. 4
    8. 1

domestic: 9. 2
    10. 3

Exercise 4 (p. 61)

B.
  1. *et cetera*—and so forth
  2. *id est*—that is (to say)
  3. *exempli gratia*—for example
  4. *et alii*—and others
  5. *répondez s'il vous plâit*—please reply
  6. *confer*—compare
  7. a. folios
    b. following (pages, lines, etc.)
    c. fortissimo

C.
  1. a. a
  2. see the following entry (*instant*) for the etymology
  3. skate¹ 2. (a similar frame or shoe with two pairs of small wheels) should be circled
  4. Persian
  5. singular
  6. see the preceding entry (*vindicate*) for the etymology
  7. etymology unknown
  8. dialect usage
  9. poetic usage
  10. irregular plural

Exercise 5 (p. 64)

1. 1, menial
2. 2, prone
3. 5, extremities
4. 2, patronizes
5. 2, franchise

6. 2, facility
7. 1, façade
8. 2, countenances
9. 1, buoyant
10. 2, facet

Exercise 6 (p. 66)

1. c
2. b
3. c
4. d
5. b

6. b
7. c
8. b
9. a
10. c

Exercise 7 (p. 67)

1. F
2. T
3. T
4. T
5. F

Exercise 8 (p. 67)

1. d
2. b
3. a
4. d
5. d

Exercise 9 (p. 68)

1. d
2. a
3. c
4. e
5. b

Exercise 10 (p. 68)

1. incumbent
2. punish
3. totality
4. safety
5. quiet

Exercise 11 (p. 68): Sample answers:

1. Danielle had a very *buoyant* personality until *the death of her mother.*
2. Jesse has a *cavalier* attitude toward studying; consequently, *his grades have suffered.*
3. People who *chafe* under the authority of others *should work for themselves.*
4. Timothy was such a complete *cipher* that *nobody who met him could remember his name.*
5. Although I cannot *countenance* Natalie's behavior, *I can understand her anger.*
6. Children who *deviate* from classroom rules *must be brought into line.*
7. An example of a bodily *extremity* is *the toes.*
8. Due to his very clever *façade, nobody knew his real personality.*
9. People who have many *facets* to their personality are *usually very interesting.*
10. If you have a *facility* for math, *you can be an engineer.*
11. When grape juice *ferments it can make wine.*
12. One of the most famous *franchise* operations is *McDonald's.*
13. One of the duties *incumbent* upon citizens is to *pay taxes.*
14. *Menial* tasks are often *boring.*
15. Some subjects are so sensitive that an *oblique* approach is best; an example is *religious beliefs.*
16. Instead of *patronizing* discount stores, *I shop at Saks Fifth Avenue.*
17. Most people expect right to *prevail;* however, *crime sometimes does pay.*
18. Seth is *prone* to accept most conservative beliefs, provided that *they don't conflict with his religion.*
19. After giving his *staunch* support to the project, *he suddenly changed his mind.*
20. If a contract is *void it cannot be enforced.*

Exercise 12 (p. 71)

1. dissipate
2. consummate
3. viable
4. forte
5. consort

6. mercenary
7. formidable
8. succulent
9. mundane
10. obtuse

Exercise 13 (p. 72)

P	R	E	S	U	M	P	T	U	O	U	S	
O		G		O		S	P		N	O		
N	E	G	A	T	E		P		W	I	N	
D		I				S		O				
E	X	C	R	U	C	I	A	T	I	N	G	
R	O			O	R		E					
O		V	U	L	N	E	R	A	B	L	E	
U	S	E		O			A	L	E		M	
S	T	R	I	N	G	E	N	T		P	I	
	A	R	E		N		H	O	R	N		
F	I	D	O			T	R	Y		Y	E	
	D	O	N	E		E			H		N	
	N	Y		P	R	U	D	E	N	T		

Exercise 14 (p. 73)

No answers provided.

CHAPTER 5

The Case of the Missing Blow Gun (p. 76)

1. or
2. ous
3. ist
4. al
5. ure
6. ly
7. ish
8. ible
9. ly
10. en
11. ity
12. er
13. ant
14. ment
15. ly
16. ious
17. ar
18. ist
19. ary
20. ion
21. less
22. ant
23. ive
24. ent
25. ity
26. ful
27. age
28. ence
29. y
30. ence
31. able
32. ify
33. ious
34. ent
35. al
36. ate
37. ize
38. al
39. ness
40. ent
41. er
42. ly
43. ude
44. ish
45. ery
46. ion
47. ory

Spelling Changes (p. 80)

1. a. conformity
   b. repellent
   c. summary
   d. allotment
   e. transferral
2. a. communion
   b. obliquely
   c. extremity
   d. survival
   e. depletion
3. a. librarian
   b. surveyor
   c. defiance
   d. deployment
   e. warily

4. a. lamentable
   b. feasible
   c. audible
   d. excusable
   e. eligible
5. a. E for excellent
   b. Adam Ant
   c. Some cemetery markers are made of cement.
   d. A dictionary is in the library.
   e. You can't make a dent in his self-confidence.

Exercise 1 (p. 82)

1. conscience
2. ethic
3. stealth
4. tacit
5. enigma
6. extreme
7. lament
8. patron
9. require
10. negate

Exercise 2 (p. 84)

1. Remedial
2. remotely
3. distinctive
4. motivate
5. solidify
6. idealize
7. populous
8. acknowledgment
9. resourceful
10. differentiate

Exercise 3 (p. 85)

1. populate
2. different
3. remedy
4. ideally
5. remote
6. acknowledge
7. resource
8. distinctively
9. solid
10. motive, motivation

Exercise 4 (p. 85)

1. stealthiness
2. obtusely
3. abhorrent
4. chafing
5. admirable
6. conformist
7. zealous
8. admittance
9. equivocally
10. adversary

Exercise 5 (p. 86)

1. (correct as is)
2. fashionable
3. usable
4. replacement
5. prevailing
6. variance
7. completeness
8. (correct as is)
9. finalize
10. (correct as is)

Exercise 6 (p. 88)

1. fatalism
2. alarmist
3. compliant
4. fixation
5. compensatory
6. rationalize
7. Holistic
8. lineage
9. exhaustive
10. categorical

Exercise 7 (p. 90)

1. c
2. d
3. b
4. b
5. a
6. c
7. a
8. c
9. c
10. d

Exercise 8 (p. 91)

1. F
2. F
3. T
4. T
5. F

Exercise 9 (p. 91)

1. d
2. c
3. b
4. c
5. c

Exercise 10 (p. 92)

1. rebelling
2. help
3. transitory
4. instability
5. soothing

Exercise 11 (p. 92)

1. d
2. c
3. e
4. a
5. b

Exercise 12 (p. 92): Sample answers:

1. You should not act like an *alarmist* when your children have minor accidents because *it will make them cry more easily.*
2. You may *categorically* deny you caused an accident; however, *if there is physical proof, you will be held responsible.*
3. A *compensatory* payment is needed when *you cause damage to another car.*
4. One should always be *compliant* with a police officer because *it could be dangerous to disobey.*
5. Assessing the *enormity* of a problem is important before *you decide on a course of action.*
6. Beauty is an *enviable* attribute; nevertheless, *it is not the most important one in choosing someone to marry.*
7. *Erroneous* information can lead to *serious errors in judgment.*
8. Scientists are doing *exhaustive* research to find a cure for AIDS because *it is killing more people every year.*
9. Believers in *fatalism* think that *they cannot change their future.*
10. If you have a food *fixation*, baseball will make you think of *peanuts and hot dogs.*
11. Having young children wash dishes is often more of a *hindrance* than a help since *they do not always get the dishes clean.*
12. *Holistic* doctors treat the whole body because *they believe that every body part affects every other body part.*
13. It is unwise to make an *inflammatory* remark to a professor during class because *the professor can expel you from the class.*
14. Proof of a show dog's *lineage* is essential in order to *enter the dog in AKC competition.*
15. A person can *rationalize* cheating on his or her income tax forms, but *the IRS will not be sympathetic.*
16. An example of a *sensuous* experience would be *eating a beautifully prepared meal in a romantic setting.*
17. The *soundness* of your school's English program depends on many things, including *the background of the professors and the variety of courses offered.*
18. Courts sometimes make decisions based on a *technicality* of the law, and so *criminals sometimes go free.*
19. Hot water can have a *therapeutic* effect on swollen joints; thus, *it is good to take hot baths when you are sore.*
20. A *transitory* condition changes quickly whereas *a permanent one does not.*

Exercise 13 (p. 95)

1. provident
2. abysmal
3. solicitous
4. codify
5. monastic
6. enigmatic
7. fabricated
8. strictures
9. Idolatry
10. severance

Exercise 14 (p. 96)

Exercise 15 (p. 97)

No answers provided.

CHAPTER 6

Exercise 1 (p. 102)

No answers provided.

Exercise 2 (p. 103)

1. en
2. inter
3. per
4. super
5. post
6. pre
7. re
8. para
9. mal
10. bene

Exercise 3 (p. 105)

1. malicious
2. encompass
3. premonition
4. per annum
5. reconcile
6. paraphrase
7. benediction
8. posterior
9. superlative
10. interim

Exercise 4 (p. 107)

1. digress
2. subservient
3. per se
4. intrinsic
5. misgivings
6. prolific
7. adhere
8. predecessor
9. contraband
10. discrepancy

Exercise 5 (p. 109)

1. a
2. b
3. b
4. d
5. b
6. c
7. b
8. d
9. a
10. a

Exercise 6 (p. 110)

1. T
2. F
3. T
4. T
5. F

Exercise 7 (p. 110)

1. d
2. c
3. a
4. c
5. d

Exercise 8 (p. 111)

1. c
2. d
3. b
4. e
5. a

Exercise 9 (p. 111)

1. restricted
2. subservient
3. separate
4. obnoxious
5. extrinsic

Exercise 10 (p. 111): Sample answers:

1. When you do not *adhere* to the rules of the game, *people won't play with you.*
2. *Cohesion* among members of a group can be increased by *giving them a common enemy.*
3. Each year customs officials seize *contraband* such as *foreign machine guns.*
4. Speakers will *digress* from their main points when *they lose their train of thought.*
5. If there is a *discrepancy* between the figures on your tax return and the IRS's figures, *it's up to you to prove your figures are right.*
6. What caused me to lose my *equilibrium* was *my high-heeled shoes.*
7. *Extrinsic* rewards given by teachers include *grades, honors, awards, and privileges.*
8. Women complain of *inequities* in their salaries compared with those of men; in fact, *they make only 60 percent of what men make in comparable jobs.*
9. *Interspersed* with the roses were *ferns.*
10. Learning has *intrinsic* rewards, such as *inner satisfaction.*

11. Although candidates commonly *malign* their opponents, *they avoid crossing the line into actual libel.*
12. I had *misgivings* about my appointment with Darryl; consequently, *I canceled it.*
13. One of the most *obnoxious* things I have ever seen was *the loud group of people talking and laughing during the concert.*
14. It isn't amount of money *per se* that determines one's lifestyle, it's also *education and background.*
15. George Bush was the *predecessor* of *Bill Clinton.*
16. Chelsea was such a *prolific* songwriter that *she wrote 50 songs in the past year.*
17. Three historical figures who were opposed to *retaliation* were *Mahatma Gandhi, Martin Luther King, and Jesus Christ.*
18. Some jobs require *subservience;* for instance, *nurses have to take orders from doctors.*
19. The events in the story actually *transpired* in *Czechoslovakia.*
20. *Uninhibited* behavior is usually increased by *drinking.*

Exercise 11 (p. 114)

1. antithesis
2. corroborate
3. abscond
4. dichotomy
5. demented
6. paragon
7. rescinded
8. extraneous
9. non sequitur
10. dissonance

Exercise 12 (p. 115)

C	A	T	E	G	O	R	I	C	A	L			R
O	R		D	I	R	E		S	T	I	R		R
M	M		S		D			N				E	E
P	S		A	T		F	A	R	E				H
E		F	M		V	O	I	D		A			H
N	A		C		E	X			G	O	A	T	
S	I	T		O	S		A		S	E		U	S
A	L	A	R	M	I	S	T		T		E	S	P
T		L	P	S		I		A	T			T	
O		I	L	L		H	O	L	I	S	T	I	C
R	R	S		I		E	N	D		I	V	E	
Y	A	M		A	B	A		H		O	P	E	N
	E	N	O	R	M	I	T	Y		T			
F	A	C	E	T		S	I	T		Y	E	S	

Exercise 13 (p. 116)

No answers provided.

MIDTERM REVIEW

REVIEW WORDS: CHAPTERS 2–6 (p. 117)

A.

1. enunciates
2. penitence
3. domestic
4. resourceful
5. differentiate
6. motivate
7. solidifies
8. remedial
9. lapse
10. extract

B.

1. T
2. T
3. F
4. T
5. T
6. F
7. T
8. T
9. T
10. F

C.

1. a
2. d
3. c
4. b
5. b
6. a
7. d
8. c
9. a
10. d

NEW WORDS: CHAPTERS 2–6 (p. 118)

A.

1. Stealthy
2. renown
3. cipher
4. Utilitarian
5. satiate
6. equilibrium
7. discrepancy
8. Sensuous
9. equivocal
10. extremities
11. therapeutic
12. staunch
13. retaliate
14. fermented
15. transitory
16. enormity

B.

1. S
2. S
3. A
4. A
5. A
6. A
7. A
8. A
9. S
10. S

C.

1. T
2. T
3. T
4. T
5. F
6. F
7. T
8. F
9. T
10. T
11. T
12. T
13. T
14. T

D.

1. thwarted
2. militant
3. wary
4. alarmists
5. furor
6. dire
7. prone
8. prudent
9. ponderous
10. meticulously
11. eminent
12. facet
13. misgivings
14. soundness
15. depleted
16. excruciating
17. deviate
18. erroneous
19. transpired
20. adhere

ADVANCED WORDS: CHAPTERS 2–6 (p. 121)

A.

1. copious
2. enigmatic
3. cursory
4. extraneous
5. razed
6. forte
7. viable
8. provident
9. Severance
10. rescind

B.

1. F
2. T
3. T
4. F
5. T
6. T
7. T
8. T
9. T
10. F

C.

1. b
2. a
3. c
4. b
5. b
6. a
7. c
8. c
9. a
10. b

CHAPTER 7

Exercise 1 (p. 129)

No answers provided.

Exercise 2 (p. 129)

1. al
2. gen
3. logy
4. press
5. plac
6. cred
7. rog
8. dox
9. grat
10. arch

Exercise 3 (p. 131)

1. patriarch
2. alien
3. suppress
4. genealogy
5. discredit
6. placid
7. homogeneous
8. arrogant
9. ingrate
10. unorthodox

Exercise 4 (p. 133)

1. hierarchy
2. congenital
3. indoctrinate
4. ingratiated
5. terminology
6. paradox
7. prerogative
8. alienated
9. ideology
10. anarchy

Exercise 5 (p. 135)

1. b
2. d
3. c
4. a
5. a
6. c
7. d
8. a
9. d
10. b

Exercise 6 (p. 136)

1. T
2. T
3. T
4. F
5. T

Exercise 7 (p. 136)

1. c
2. a
3. a
4. b
5. a

Exercise 8 (p. 137)

1. d
2. a
3. e
4. b
5. c

Exercise 9 (p. 137)

1. incompatible
2. unite
3. credence
4. praising
5. obligation

Exercise 10 (p. 137): Sample answers:

1. You are likely to *alienate* someone if *you lie to her.*
2. An *altercation* may not be avoidable, yet *you should try to avoid a fight.*
3. It is frightening to be in a country where there is *anarchy* because *there is no effective police force or laws.*
4. As long as a person is *complacent,* he will accomplish very little.
5. You should try to be *congenial* at a party; otherwise *people will not talk to you.*
6. A *congenital* defect can cause the death of a newborn unless *it is corrected by surgery.*
7. If you give *credence* to politicians, *you believe what they say.*
8. Our political leaders need to have high *credibility,* since *they control a great deal of power and money.*
9. Besides making *derogatory* remarks, an obnoxious person might *do crude things.*
10. When something is *gratis* you *don't have to pay for it.*
11. Unless you understand the *hierarchy* of command at your job, *you will likely make your boss angry with you.*
12. Even if you disagree with a person's religious *ideology, you can be friends.*
13. The army *indoctrinates* new recruits by various methods, including *making them drill for hours.*
14. It is wise to *ingratiate* yourself to a new boss because *you will be unhappy at work if she dislikes you.*
15. Because in a democracy people do not *oppress* others, *there is often public debate on major issues.*
16. It sounds like a *paradox* when someone tells you that *the faster you try to finish a task, the longer it will take you to do it correctly.*
17. You can *placate* angry parents by *swearing you will never do what made them angry again.*
18. Because in professional football the winner of the coin toss has the *prerogative* to choose which goal his team will defend, *both teams hope their captain is lucky.*
19. A parent is likely to *reprimand* a child who *paints on the walls.*
20. If you don't know the *terminology* being used in an article you are reading, *look the words up in the dictionary.*

Exercise 11 (p. 140)

1. repressive
2. altruism
3. credulous
4. progeny
5. docile
6. oligarchy
7. surrogate
8. gratuitous
9. implacable
10. logistics

Exercise 12 (p. 141)

■	¹C	²O	³N	⁴T	⁵R	⁶A	⁷B	⁸A	⁹N	D
¹⁰P	R	O	L	I	F	I	C	¹¹T	O	O
R	¹²H	D	■	¹³M	T	S	■	¹⁴T	¹⁵A	¹⁶R
¹⁷O	¹⁸N	E	■	¹⁹C	■	²⁰K	■	²¹S	S	E
²²N	A	S	■	²³M	²⁴A	²⁵L	²⁶I	G	N	T
E	²⁷I	²⁸N	T	R	I	N	S	I	C	²⁹D A
³⁰M	O	O	■	M	■	T	■	³¹M	I	L
³²O	B	N	O	X	I	³³O	³⁴U	³⁵S	³⁶A	³⁷G I
A	N	N	■	³⁸S	A	I	D	■	³⁹R	A
⁴⁰F	■	⁴¹S	■	⁴²P	W	H	■	H	■	⁴³E T
⁴⁴A	⁴⁵B	⁴⁶I	N	T	E	⁴⁷R	S	⁴⁸P	E	⁴⁹R S E
⁵⁰C	O	A	⁵¹T	■	⁵²I	R	A	■	⁵³O	R ⁵⁴S S
⁵⁵E	X	T	R	I	N	S	⁵⁶I	C	⁵⁷C	⁵⁸E ⁵⁹M
T	■	⁶⁰T	B	S	■	⁶¹E	L	K	■	⁶²D I R E

Exercise 13 (p. 142)

No answers provided.

CHAPTER 8

Exercise 1 (p. 147)

No answers provided.

Exercise 2 (p. 147)

1. fac
2. ten
3. sta
4. nov
5. pose
6. vers
7. plic
8. sid
9. luc
10. capit

Exercise 3 (p. 149)

1. pretentious
2. decapitate
3. hallucinate
4. novice
5. subsidize
6. impose
7. accomplice
8. benefactor
9. substantiate
10. aversion

Exercise 4 (p. 151)

1. supplication
2. constituents
3. multiplicity
4. repose
5. status quo
6. innate
7. insidious
8. translucent
9. effacing
10. recapitulate

Exercise 5 (p. 153)

1. a	6. c
2. a	7. b
3. d	8. a
4. d	9. c
5. d	10. b

Exercise 6 (p. 154)

1. F
2. T
3. T
4. T
5. F

Exercise 7 (p. 154)

1. a
2. b
3. d
4. c
5. a

Exercise 8 (p. 155)

1. d
2. e
3. b
4. c
5. a

Exercise 9 (p. 155)

1. acquired
2. refusal
3. introduce
4. insidious
5. decay

Exercise 10 (p. 155): Sample answers:

1. Most of our grandparents can remember times of great *adversity,* such as *the Great Depression.*
2. Feminists reject the use of "feminine *artifice*" because *it is dishonest.*
3. Representatives elected by their *constituents* include *senators and members of Congress.*
4. Because of air pollution, monuments are being *effaced at a faster rate then previously.*
5. Political conservatives are usually *exponents* of *capital punishment.*
6. He showed his *innate* honesty by *returning the extra change the cashier gave him.*
7. Lead poisoning is so *insidious* that *the effects aren't recognizable for a long time.*
8. During *lucid* moments, victims of Alzheimer's disease *understand what is happening to them.*
9. Because the trade deficit has a *multiplicity* of causes, *it will not be easy to correct.*
10. Some examples of *ostentatious* cars are *Rolls-Royces and Ferraris.*
11. The sergeant engaged in such *overt* acts of cruelty as *making his soldiers stand at attention for two hours at a time.*
12. Residents of Westchester County, N.Y., have a higher *per-capita* income than *residents of New Orleans.*
13. The summary *recapitulates the main points.*
14. In the 1980s there was a *renaissance* of *interest in making a lot of money.*
15. Jeffrey's *repose* was interrupted by *the alarm clock.*
16. Sedate people usually wear *navy, brown, and charcoal gray.*
17. If you are happy with the *status quo, you will vote for another term for the current administration.*
18. The actress's repeated *supplications* to the casting director finally led to *a role.*
19. His argument contained only the most *tenuous* reasons; in fact, *it didn't make any sense.*
20. Architects use *translucent* materials such as glass block walls to *allow light to enter without people outside being able to see in.*

Exercise 11 (p. 158)

1. desist	6. edifice
2. sedentary	7. superimposed
3. capitulate	8. innovation
4. covert	9. elucidate
5. complicity	10. extenuating

Exercise 12 (p. 159)

Exercise 13 (p. 160)

No answers provided.

CHAPTER 9

Exercise 1 (p. 167)

No answers provided.

Exercise 2 (p. 167)

1. vict	6. tact
2. volv	7. cept
3. pend	8. rect
4. ped	9. linqu
5. tin	10. solu

Exercise 3 (p. 169)

1. impertinent	6. intact
2. relinquish	7. expend
3. impede	8. evolve
4. resolute	9. perceptive
5. evict	10. rectify

Exercise 4 (p. 171)

1. regime
2. tenure
3. tenable
4. tangent
5. elicit
6. susceptible
7. dissolute
8. expedient
9. insolvent
10. pensive

Exercise 5 (p. 173)

1. b
2. c
3. d
4. a
5. b
6. b
7. a
8. b
9. b
10. c

Exercise 6 (p. 174)

1. T
2. F
3. F
4. F
5. T

Exercise 7 (p. 174)

1. a
2. c
3. d
4. c
5. a

Exercise 8 (p. 175)

1. d
2. e
3. b
4. a
5. c

Exercise 9 (p. 175)

1. retard
2. distant
3. malevolent
4. completion
5. yield

Exercise 10 (p. 175): Sample answers:

1. Many people avoid a *derelict* because *they fear someone who looks dirty.*
2. *Dissolute* people often *die young.*
3. A new baby usually *elicits* great joy in the parents; nevertheless, *most new parents also worry about their new offspring.*
4. It might be *expedient* to buy frozen food; on the other hand, *it can be expensive.*
5. If you can *expedite* the renewal of your driver's license by mailing in a form, *it is wise to do so.*
6. When there is an *impending* hurricane, you should *board up the windows and stay inside.*
7. During the *inception* of a new project at work, *you might have to work more hours than usual.*
8. A person might become *insolvent* if *he or she loses a lot of money on the stock market.*
9. Some drunks think they are *invincible;* therefore, *they will pick a fight with anyone.*
10. An example of a mother-in-law being *malevolent* is *spreading rumors she knows are untrue.*
11. If you feel *pensive, you may not want people around you.*
12. Princess Diana of England looks *regal* because *she walks like a queen.*
13. Before you go on a strict dietary *regime,* you should check *with your doctor to be sure you are healthy.*
14. You might be *susceptible* to a cold even if *you take a lot of vitamin C.*
15. The *tactile* sense is especially important when *you are knitting.*
16. A teacher who goes off on a *tangent* during a lecture *can confuse the class.*
17. An idea is *tenable* unless *it is inconsistent with facts we know.*
18. If you have job *tenure, you usually cannot be fired without serious reasons.*
19. After an army has been *vanquished, its leaders formally surrender.*
20. When you are arrested, if you don't submit of your own *volition, the police will use force.*

Exercise 11 (p. 178)

1. detente
2. regale
3. pedantic
4. precipitous
5. contiguous
6. vicarious
7. voluble
8. propensity
9. absolve
10. licentious

Exercise 12 (p. 179)

Exercise 13 (p. 180)

No answers provided.

CHAPTER 10

Exercise 1 (p. 185)

1. eccentric
2. grotesque
3. lenient
4. gaudy
5. clique
6. annihilate
7. guerrilla
8. lewd
9. lavish
10. appall

Exercise 2 (p. 186)

1. e	6. j
2. b	7. c
3. i	8. a
4. g	9. f
5. h	10. d

Exercise 3 (p. 188)

1. i	6. a
2. d	7. h
3. f	8. j
4. b	9. g
5. c	10. e

Exercise 4 (p. 189)

1. abominable	6. laudable
2. idiosyncrasies	7. exonerate
3. platonic	8. crux
4. jargon	9. decrepit
5. latent	10. precocious

Exercise 5 (p. 191)

1. bourgeois	6. innuendo
2. redundant	7. candid
3. trite	8. animosity
4. apropos	9. lethargic
5. furtive	10. dispel

Exercise 6 (p. 191)

1. d	6. a
2. a	7. a
3. b	8. b
4. a	9. d
5. c	10. b

Exercise 7 (p. 192)

1. F
2. T
3. F
4. T
5. F

Exercise 8 (p. 193)

1. b
2. d
3. b
4. c
5. a

Exercise 9 (p. 193)

1. b
2. d
3. a
4. c
5. e

Exercise 10 (p. 193)

1. assemble
2. exonerate
3. concise
4. unrelated
5. statement

Exercise 11 (p. 194): Sample answers:

1. As an example of Jeremy's *abominable* taste, *look at the purple plaid suit he is wearing today.*
2. To show her that he bore no *animosity, he split the savings account with her when they broke up.*
3. *Apropos* Molly's problems in school, *I think it would be a good idea for her to see a counselor.*
4. One U.S. president who was not *bourgeois* was *Franklin Delano Roosevelt, who inherited enormous wealth.*
5. Well, to be completely *candid, yellow is not your best color.*
6. The *crux* of the argument in favor of stricter penalties for drug users is *that they will make people think twice before using drugs.*
7. In contrast with the house's *decrepit* appearance when they bought it, *it was positively glamorous when they listed it for sale.*
8. To *dispel* the rumors that she had taken bribes, the candidate *published a list of all the gifts she had received in the previous five years.*
9. Although he was eventually *exonerated, his reputation in the industry was ruined.*
10. Because of her *furtive* manner, *everyone thought Bianca was guilty.*
11. One of my *idiosyncrasies* is *eating pizza for breakfast.*
12. Candidates for office often rely on *innuendo* when *they can't dig up a genuine scandal involving their opponent.*
13. Sports *jargon* includes terms such as *"TKO"* in boxing, *"end run"* in football, and *"slam dunk"* in basketball.
14. In addition to my talents in music and art, my teacher discovered my *latent* abilities in *creative writing.*
15. Even though contributing to one's church is *laudable, there are many other worthy causes.*
16. Danielle's *lethargic* state was caused by *an infection.*
17. Their relationship became *platonic* after *he became involved with someone else.*
18. I was *precocious,* especially *in music.*
19. Two commonly used *redundant* expressions are "past history" and *"future plans."*
20. *Trite* phrases such as "clear as a bell" are *boring.*

Exercise 12 (p. 197)

1. succinct	6. salient
2. adroit	7. extricate
3. accolade	8. hackneyed
4. erudite	9. panacea
5. chagrin	10. inundate

Exercise 13 (p. 198)

1. Fr. < Pr. *acolada* < It. *accollata,* fem. pp. of *accolare,* to embrace < L. *ad,* to + *collum,* neck
2. Fr. *à,* to + *droit,* right < L. *directus,* pp. of *dirigere,* direct
3. Fr., grief, sorrow, vexation, prob. < Norm. *chagreiner,* to become gloomy < *graim,* sorrowful < Gmc. *gram,* sorrow, trouble
4. M.E. *erudit* < L. *eruditus,* pp. of *erudire,* to instruct < *e-,* out + *rudis,* rude
5. < L. *extricatus,* pp. of *extricare,* to disentangle < *ex-,* out + *tricae,* hindrances, vexations
6. M.E. *hakene, hakenei* < *Hakeney* (now *Hackney*), an English village
7. < L. *inundatus,* pp. of *inundare,* to overflow < *in-,* in, on + *undare,* to move in waves, flood < *unda,* a wave

8. L. < Gr. *panakeia* < *pan,* all + *akeisthai,* to cure < ? I.E. base* *yēk-,* to cure, whence prob. W. *iach,* healthy, OIr. *hicc,* cure

9. L. *saliens,* prp. of *salire,* to leap < I.E. base* *sel-,* to jump, whence Gr. *halma,* a leap

10. M.E., girdled, girded < L. *succinctus,* prepared, short, contracted, pp. of *succingere,* to grid, tuck up, prepare < *sub-,* under + *cingere,* to gird

Exercise 14 (199)

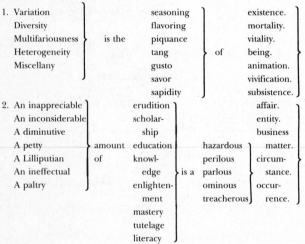

Exercise 15 (p. 200)

No answers provided.

CHAPTER 11

Proverb (p. 209)

Actions speak louder than words.

Exercise 1 (p. 210)

Here are a few possible answers:

1. Variation / Diversity / Multifariousness / Heterogeneity / Miscellany — is the — seasoning / flavoring / piquance / tang / gusto / savor / sapidity — of — existence. / mortality. / vitality. / being. / animation. / vivification. / subsistence.

2. An inappreciable / An inconsiderable / A diminutive / A petty / A Lilliputian / An ineffectual / A paltry — amount of — erudition / scholarship / education / knowledge / enlightenment / mastery / tutelage / literacy — is a — hazardous / perilous / parlous / ominous / treacherous — affair. / entity. / business / matter. / circumstance. / occurrence.

3. Multitudinous / Myriad / Pullulating / Profuse / Superfluous / Excess / A disproportionate number of / A plethora of / A surplusage of — chefs / gastronomists — taint / putrefy / curdle / ruin / impair — the — bouillon. / stock. / consommé. / soup du jour. / borscht.

Exercise 2 (p. 210)

A. 1. a. noun
      b. verb
      c. adjective
   2. badness
   3. a. hick
      b. rube
   4. beau

B. 1. a. billet-doux
      b. mash note
   2. a. flirtation
      b. intrigue
      c. triangle
      d. ménage à trois
   3. hold dear
   4. adjective
   5. (A mother's love of her child.)

Exercise 3 (p. 213)

1. aloof
2. indispensable
3. cordial
4. ravenous
5. defame
6. perpetual
7. affirm
8. antagonism
9. instigated
10. infirmity

Exercise 4 (p. 214)

1. b
2. c
3. a
4. b
5. d

Exercise 5 (p. 215)

1. a
2. c
3. a
4. d
5. c

Exercise 6 (p. 217)

1. impregnable
2. augment
3. impetuous
4. benign
5. elite
6. indiscreet
7. insipid
8. reproach
9. nebulous
10. retribution

Exercise 7 (p. 219)

1. d	6. c
2. a	7. a
3. c	8. b
4. d	9. c
5. d	10. b

Exercise 8 (p. 220)

1. T
2. T
3. T
4. F
5. F

Exercise 9 (p. 220)

1. b
2. c
3. d
4. a
5. c

Exercise 10 (p. 221)

1. d
2. b
3. a
4. e
5. c

Exercise 11 (p. 221)

1. deplete
2. modest
3. condone
4. deliberate
5. pleasure

Exercise 12 (p. 221)

1. c	6. i
2. e	7. h
3. a	8. j
4. b	9. g
5. d	10. f

Exercise 13 (p. 222)

1. d	6. b
2. f	7. e
3. a	8. i
4. j	9. g
5. h	10. c

Exercise 14 (p. 222): Sample answers:

1. To *augment* your income, you might *get a part-time job.*
2. A man with a *benign* personality is *not likely to say mean things about you.*
3. An example of a *blatant* act of cheating is *a student stealing a copy of a test.*
4. A teacher should not *condone* students talking in class unless *they are doing so as part of an assignment.*
5. You can *deter* burglars by *having dead-bolt locks on all of the doors.*
6. An example of an *elite* group might be the movie stars who get to *go to movie premiers.*
7. You might find it difficult to live with a *fastidious* person because *he or she will complain that you are sloppy.*
8. If you support a position with *fervor*, you are not likely to *be swayed from your point of view.*
9. An *impetuous* act might be necessary when *a building is on fire and small children are inside.*
10. A fortress should be *impregnable*, otherwise *it can be overrun by the enemy.*
11. *Indiscreet* people can get into trouble at work if they *gossip about other workers.*
12. You should look at the problems *inherent* in a house before you purchase one, or else *you might find you have made a poor decision.*
13. When hospital food is *insipid, patients eat poorly.*
14. A ballerina must be *lithe* so that *she can jump high.*
15. If an idea is *nebulous, it is difficult to understand.*
16. A *raucous* party might disturb your neighbors; therefore, *you should try to keep your guests reasonably quiet.*
17. A teacher will *reproach* you when *you don't have your assignments done on time.*
18. You might seek *retribution* after *your neighbor cut down your prize maple for firewood.*
19. You must be *rigorous* when measuring the chemicals for a chemistry experiment, otherwise *you might end up with a dangerous chemical reaction.*
20. The last time I was filled with *wrath was when my roommate wrecked my new car.*

Exercise 15 (p. 225)

1. esoteric	6. austere
2. loquacious	7. exacerbate
3. innocuous	8. stratagem
4. mollify	9. Clandestine
5. delineate	10. vacillate

Exercise 16 (p. 226)

1. f S	6. g A
2. i A	7. j S
3. h A	8. e S
4. b S	9. a A
5. c S	10. d A

Exercise 17 (p. 227)

Exercise 18 (p. 228)

No answers provided.

CHAPTER 12

Exercise 1 (p. 235)

A. 1. devastated
2. annihilated
3. razed
B. 1. massive
2. ponderous
3. cumbersome
C. 1. virtuous
2. ethical
3. moral

D. 1. remorse
2. penitence
3. regret
E. 1. revolution
2. mutiny
3. insurrection

Exercise 2 (p. 236)

1. Hordes
2. libel
3. lien
4. Urban
5. populous

Exercise 3 (p. 237)

No answers provided.

Exercise 4 (p. 240)

1. amenable
2. equivocal
3. observe
4. betray
5. provident
6. fury
7. constrained
8. deleting
9. recapitulate
10. wary

Exercise 5 (p. 241)

1. cryptic
2. obliterated
3. divulge
4. frugal
5. discern
6. constrain
7. amenable
8. discreet
9. reiterating
10. indignation

Exercise 6 (p. 244)

1. adept
2. allusions
3. amicable
4. assent
5. censored
6. descents
7. Illicit
8. perimeter
9. précis
10. sensuous

Exercise 7 (p. 244)

1. b
2. d
3. a
4. c
5. a
6. a
7. a
8. d
9. c
10. c

Exercise 8 (p. 245)

1. F
2. T
3. T
4. T
5. T

Exercise 9 (p. 246)

1. d
2. a
3. c
4. a
5. c

Exercise 10 (p. 246)

1. c
2. a
3. e
4. b
5. d

Exercise 11 (p. 246)

1. amicable
2. request
3. stubborn
4. spiritual
5. honest

Exercise 12 (p. 247): Sample answers:

1. In addition to being *adept* at algebra, *he was also a good writer.*
2. His work was full of *allusions* to *Shakespeare.*
3. Although he was sure of his opinion, he was *amenable* to *suggestions.*
4. Elvis and Priscilla Presley had an *amicable divorce.*
5. Unless your parents *assent, you may not use their car.*
6. As a result of being *censured* by her colleagues, *she apologized publicly.*
7. We are *constrained* by law to *obey the speed limit.*
8. Because his answers were so *cryptic, nobody knew what he really thought.*
9. Fog makes it difficult to *discern other cars on the road.*
10. John was *discreet* when *dating three women at the same time.*
11. The party's method of dealing with *dissent* was *to shoot suspected dissenters.*
12. Unless you *divulge* your sources, *nobody will believe your story.*
13. As a result of Tommy's *frugal* habits, *he was able to save half his salary each month.*
14. People sometimes offer *illicit* gifts to *judges.*
15. Josh felt *indignation* when *Molly broke their date.*
16. If a memory is *obliterated, it can no longer be recalled.*
17. The teacher established certain *parameters* for classroom behavior; these included *raising hands before speaking.*
18. Reading a *précis* instead of the whole article will *give you an overview.*
19. When I am asked to *reiterate* the main points of a lecture, *I get annoyed.*
20. An example of a *sensual* delight is *a massage.*

Exercise 13 (p. 251)

1. iniquity
2. deft
3. intrepid
4. exorbitant
5. imminent
6. proscribe
7. surreptitious
8. ardor
9. ascetic
10. flout

Exercise 14 (p. 252)

The following words should not be crossed out:
1. fervor
2. adroit
3. exorbitant
4. audacious
5. covert

Exercise 15 (p. 252)

1. aesthetic
2. flaunt
3. eminent
4. inequities
5. proscribed

Exercise 16 (p. 253)

Exercise 17 (p. 254)

No answers provided.

FINAL REVIEW

REVIEW WORDS: CHAPTERS 2–12 (p. 255)

A.

1. T	8. F	15. F
2. T	9. F	16. T
3. T	10. F	17. T
4. T	11. T	18. F
5. T	12. T	19. T
6. T	13. T	20. T
7. T	14. T	

B.

1. S	6. A
2. A	7. S
3. S	8. A
4. A	9. S
5. S	10. A

C.

1. zeal	10. evict	19. posterior
2. evolve	11. impede	20. valiant
3. Impertinent	12. grotesque	21. apprehend
4. instigated	13. rectify	22. Graft
5. cumbersome	14. accomplice	23. benediction
6. infirmity	15. novice	24. induce
7. populace	16. hallucinate	25. exploit
8. Perpetual	17. aversion	
9. affirms	18. Malicious	

NEW WORDS: CHAPTERS 2–12 (p. 257)

A.

1. b	10. b	19. c
2. d	11. a	20. d
3. b	12. d	21. b
4. c	13. a	22. a
5. a	14. b	23. b
6. b	15. a	24. a
7. d	16. b	25. c
8. a	17. d	
9. a	18. a	

B.

1. furor	8. satiated	15. Menial
2. obliterate	9. alarmist	16. allusions
3. façade	10. tenure	17. multiplicity
4. ironic	11. transpires	18. per capita
5. ponderous	12. uninhibited	19. prerogative
6. therapeutic	13. enviable	20. void
7. lucid	14. hierarchy	

C.

1. S	8. S	15. A
2. S	9. S	16. S
3. S	10. A	17. A
4. S	11. A	18. S
5. A	12. S	19. S
6. A	13. S	20. S
7. A	14. S	21. A

D.

1. F	13. T	25. T
2. T	14. T	26. T
3. T	15. F	27. T
4. T	16. T	28. T
5. T	17. T	29. T
6. T	18. F	30. T
7. F	19. T	31. T
8. F	20. T	32. T
9. T	21. F	33. F
10. T	22. T	34. F
11. T	23. F	35. T
12. F	24. F	

E.

1. u	9. f	17. j
2. o	10. s	18. a
3. v	11. e	19. h
4. r	12. k	20. g
5. t	13. b	21. c
6. x	14. i	22. w
7. l	15. d	23. n
8. p	16. m	24. q

F.

1. exponents	8. depleted	15. latent
2. depicted	9. renaissance	16. ferment
3. credibility	10. stringent	17. tenable
4. utilitarian	11. misgivings	18. expedite
5. deter	12. overt	19. augment
6. exhaustive	13. per se	20. elite
7. dire	14. dispel	

ADVANCED WORDS: CHAPTERS 2–12 (p. 264)

A.

1. F	8. T	15. T
2. F	9. T	16. T
3. F	10. T	17. T
4. F	11. F	18. F
5. T	12. T	19. F
6. F	13. T	20. T
7. T	14. T	

B.

1. A	6. S
2. S	7. A
3. A	8. A
4. S	9. A
5. S	10. S

C.

1. Empirical	10. implacable	19. consummate
2. dissipated	11. dichotomy	20. mercenary
3. viable	12. elucidate	21. Idolatry
4. Contiguous	13. Extenuating	22. absconded
5. succulent	14. copious	23. Credulous
6. Demented	15. Panaceas	24. progeny
7. severance	16. ruse	25. forte
8. ardor	17. obtuse	
9. codified	18. extricate	

POSTTEST (p. 267)

1. b	11. c	21. b	31. a	41. b
2. d	12. b	22. c	32. c	42. a
3. b	13. d	23. d	33. a	43. d
4. a	14. b	24. c	34. a	44. a
5. c	15. d	25. a	35. b	45. d
6. a	16. c	26. a	36. d	46. d
7. b	17. a	27. d	37. d	47. c
8. a	18. b	28. c	38. a	48. a
9. c	19. c	29. d	39. d	49. b
10. b	20. d	30. a	40. c	50. a

INDEX OF WORDS